Kierkegaard: The Aesthetic and the Religious

Also by George Pattison

AGNOSIS: THEOLOGY AND THE VOID

ANXIOUS ANGELS

ART MODERNITY AND FAITH

KIERKEGAARD: THE AESTHETIC AND THE RELIGIOUS

KIERKEGAARD AND THE CRISIS OF FAITH

KIERKEGAARD ON ART AND COMMUNICATION (editor)

PAINS OF GLASS (with Wendy Beckett)

'POOR PARIS!' KIERKEGAARD'S CRITIQUE OF THE
SPECTACULAR CITY

SPIRIT AND TRADITION: AN ESSAY ON CHANGE
(with Stephen Platten)

Kierkegaard: The Aesthetic and the Religious

From the Magic Theatre to the Crucifixion of the Image

George Pattison

Second Edition

SCM PRESS

0 334 02762 4

First published 1992 by Macmillan Academic and
Professional Ltd, Houndsmill, Basingstoke,
Hampshire RG21 2XS and London

Second edition published 1999 by
SCM Press
9–17 St Albans Place London N1 0NX

SCM Press is a division of
SCM–Canterbury Press Ltd.

Printed in Great Britain by
Biddles Ltd, Guildford and King's Lynn

ROMEO: Peace, peace! Mercutio, peace!
   Thou talk'st of nothing.

MERCUTIO: True, I talk of dreams,
   Which are the children of an idle brain,
   Begot of nothing but vain fantasy;
   Which is as thin of substance as the air,
   And more inconstant than the wind . . .

                         Shakespeare, *Romeo and Juliet*, I.4.96–9.

THESEUS:
   And, as imagination bodies forth
   The forms of things unknown, the poet's pen
   Turns them to shapes, and gives to airy nothing
   A local habitation and a name.
   Such tricks hath strong imagination . . .

                  Shakespeare, *A Midsummer-Night's Dream*, V.1.14–18

Il n'y a pas moins d'éloquence dans le ton de la voix, dans les yeux, et dans l'air de la personne, que dans le choix des paroles.

                                   La Rochefoucauld

Contents

Preface   ix

Acknowledgements   xii

Introduction: On Reading Kierkegaard Religiously   xiv

1 Idealism and the Justification of the Image   1

2 The Genealogy of Art   35

3 The Dialectics of Communication   63

4 Life in the Magic Theatre   95

5 Nihilism and the Novel   125

6 Reading, Repentance and the Crucifixion of the Image   155

Notes   189

Bibliography   201

Index   205

Preface

This book has developed out of my PhD thesis, *Kierkegaard's Theory and Critique of Art: Its Theological Significance* (Durham University, 1983), and Chapters 1 and 2 in particular are very closely related to that earlier work. The discussion of Kierkegaard's genealogical reduction of art and the significance of *angst* as a defining boundary for aesthetic experience (in Chapter 2) represents more or less the position I had reached at that point. Where I have moved on has to do with having recognised the crucial role of indirect communication (and of strategies of communication in general) in Kierkegaard's authorship. No one can read very far in Kierkegaard without becoming aware that there is an issue to be addressed here, but that is a very different thing from realising its full significance. I partly owe my awakening to this to Birgit Bertung's analysis of the role of indirect communication in Kierkegaard's writings on women (B. Bertung, *Om Kierkegaard, Kvinder og Kaerlighed*, København: Reitzel, 1987), although I do not discuss this here, since my own concerns are primarily religious (not, of course, that women's issues and theology are in any way mutually exclusive – nor do I mean to imply that I *agree* with every detail of Ms Bertung's argument).

It is important to my argument that Kierkegaard's theory and practice of religious communication took the form it did because of culturally specific factors, and I have therefore taken considerable pains to see Kierkegaard's work in its contemporary context, thus acknowledging the debt which all interpretation owes to history. This also helps to set off all the more sharply the distinctiveness of Kierkegaard's own approach. Idealism, Romantic and Hegelian alike, tended to see 'the image' in terms of its function as a form or means of knowledge; that is, as a problem for epistemology. Kierkegaard's inversion of this, whereby the image comes instead to be seen as a masking or a mystification of the inner conflicts of the self, is original enough, but if we go on from there and try to see his work as an experiment in the direction of a full-scale Christian Rhetoric, it will become clear that he has travelled an even greater distance beyond the idealists' epistemological interests than we might at first have judged. Yet, it might be said, we cannot

miss the cognitive charge in his later Christological writings, where
the image, specifically the image of the crucified One, serves as a
revelation of the horrific violence of which human beings are
capable. Nonetheless this should not be taken as implying that
Kierkegaard replaced his rhetorical concerns with a well-disguised
piece of knowledge-communication in a last-minute substitution.
It is rather that his need to cast theology in the mould of rhetoric
(rather than of metaphysical or historical knowledge) has much to
do with the evaluation of human life as being constitutionally
vulnerable to eruptions of violence: physical, verbal and spiritual.
My reading of Kierkegaard at this point owes a great deal to the
theory of religion and culture of René Girard, developed in his
Violence and the Sacred (Baltimore and London: Johns Hopkins
University Press, 1977) and other works. I believe, and hope to
develop on another occasion, that there is a profound congruence
between the views of Girard and Kierkegaard on many points: the
understanding of society, philosophy, Christianity and the task of
the individual – although Girard has systematic ambitions that
Kierkegaard could scarcely endorse.

Issues of aesthetics and communication are increasingly at the
centre of Kierkegaard studies, not merely because these issues
reflect the intellectual bias of the age but also because they are
recognised to be major themes in his own writing. There are many
commentators who want to find in Kierkegaard a high evaluation
of poetry, art and the life of the imagination. A good example of
this tendency is David Gouwens, *Kierkegaard's Dialectic of the Imagination* (New York: Peter Lang, 1989), a well-researched and clearly
argued book which overlaps with my own work at many points.
Nonetheless, whereas I stress the negative implications of Kierkegaard's work for aesthetics, Gouwens seeks to accentuate the
abiding role of the imagination even in Kierkegaard's account of
the religious life. Crucial to his account is Kierkegaard's own
dictum that imagination is the 'capacity *instar omnium'*, but
although Gouwens disavows the programme of the old faculty
psychology in which such an expression would seem naturally to
belong, insisting that we must (with Kierkegaard) be attentive to
the differing contexts in which imagination is deployed (the *how*
rather than the *what* of imagination), the term itself (imagination,
that is) does seem to draw associations of such notions as 'capacity'
or 'faculty' along with it. This reinforces the impression that
Kierkegaard's understanding of faith is as an intra-individual pro-

cess. By choosing instead to speak of 'the image' rather than of 'the imagination' and of rhetoric instead of poetry, I not only highlight the difference between Kierkegaard and the psychologically-oriented Romantic theory of the imagination but also indicate that issues of aesthetics share important boundaries with interpersonal, social and even political relationships. One measure of the difference between us is that in my final Chapter I draw heavily on the third 'Christian Exposition' in *Training in Christianity*, where Kierkegaard offers us a child's eye view of the Crucifixion. Gouwens looks instead to the fourth 'Exposition' and the discussion of what significance a youthful ideal of perfection might have in a life. My belief is that this discussion is not so much concerned with the capacity of the imagination to produce a picture of human perfection but with how the actual practice of existentially living out one's ideals may have an educative and religiously enriching value for the individual even if these ideals are inappropriate and unattainable for an imperfect human being in an imperfect world – as all ideals of perfection necessarily are (yet these are the natural products of the imagination). The image of the crucified One, by way of contrast, gives a much truer picture of what Christian discipleship is about, being a picture drawn, as it were, from life rather than from the idealising power of the imagination. A similar point may be made in relation to all those who would argue in favour of seeing Kierkegaard as some 'kind of poet'. For the emphasis here must surely be on the 'kind of', since conventional ideas of what 'poetry' involves must be stretched so far to cover Kierkegaard that, to speak in the language of the doctrine of analogy, equivocation wins out over univocity – at which point we must ask why we are hanging on to the term at all?

One answer to this question (with which I would agree) is that although Kierkegaard's view of religion is such as to demand the final sacrifice of poetry, art and imagination, his apologetic concern is precisely for those who live and move and have their being in the realm of aesthetic communication. If he was an *unhappy* lover of poetry and art, he was an unhappy *lover*, and, as a Christian communicator, a particular lover of poets, artists and 'wanderers of the great dream' (Bloy), as Christ was a particular lover of taxgatherers, prostitutes, outcasts and sinners. For it was from the Christ of the Christian gospels that Kierkegaard derived the key elements of his theory of communication, and it was to that same Christ that his writing sought to lead those readers who had eyes to see and ears to hear.

Acknowledgements

In the early 1980s many British (and especially English) theologians were outpacing each other in their attempts to dissociate themselves from such Kierkegaardian vices as existentialism and subjectivity, seeing all that as part of the outdated and bankrupt theology of the much-maligned 1960s. Much has changed since then, but I am still grateful for the help I received from many and varied quarters in the course of my early attempts to reckon with this protean and idiosyncratic thinker. I would particularly like to thank Ann Loades, who supervised my doctoral work on Kierkegaard's thought and who has supported and encouraged me in my ongoing work since then; Julia Watkin of the Kierkegaard Library in Copenhagen University, who has been a constant source of advice and practical help; Bob and Sylvia Walsh Perkins, whose interest in and even enthusiasm for my work has been of incalculable value in sustaining my sometimes flagging morale; and, among many others: Don Cupitt, David Jasper, Arnold Spector, Stephen Sykes, and Peter Vardy, as well as the participants at various conferences, seminars and talks whose questions and criticisms have made me look again at the interpretative views I was expounding. Thanks of a distinctive nature go to Dr T. J. Diffey and to David Jasper for allowing me to work out some of the ideas presented in this book in the pages of *The British Journal of Aesthetics* and the *Journal of Literature and Theology* respectively. Thanks are also due to David Jasper for accepting the first edition of this work in his series Studies in Literature and Religion. Many of my ideas took form in the course of conversation with my friend Ulrich Fentzloff (with whom I first attended lectures on Kierkegaard in Tübingen in 1976); the debt and the friendship are great. Hilary, my partner, had no idea when she married me that she was going to have to share so much of her living space with the great Danish writer with whom she (like, yet unlike, me) has a love-hate relationship. Not quite a *ménage à trois*, but it sometimes (I fear) feels like it! The author and publishers are grateful to Indiana University Press for permission to quote for Kierkegaard's *Journals and Papers*, translated by Howard V. and Edna H. Hong.

References to Kierkegaard's Works

For the sake of consistency I have used the third Danish edition of Kierkegaard's works, making my own translations (though, since I am not a linguist, I have paid careful attention to previous translations). References are given in the text as *SV (Samlede Vaerker)*, followed by volume and page number. Full bibliographical details of this edition may be found at the back of the book. Readers who wish to cross-refer to an English text will find that careful use of the tabular collation of different editions in each volume of *Kierkegaard's Writings* should enable them to do just that. I am hopeful that I have nearly always (and always where it matters) indicated the English title of the text to which I am referring.

As far as Kierkegaard's copious journals and papers go I have used the Howard and Edna Hong translation and edition of *Søren Kierkegaard's Journals and Papers* (See Bibliography for details). Entries are numbered consecutively through the six volumes, and I have given references under *JP (Journals and Papers)* followed by the entry number. In addition I have given the three-part reference (volume, section, number; e.g. I A 6) used in the standard Danish edition of the *Papirer*. Occasionally I have used an entry not found in the Hongs' edition, in which case I simply give the reference in the form used in the Danish edition.

Other forms of reference used in the text are explained in footnotes. All translations from foreign language titles are my own, and I am solely responsible for any errors in such translations.

Introduction: On Reading Kierkegaard Religiously

Kierkegaard: The Aesthetic and the Religious is, at its heart, an attempt to read Kierkegaard religiously, i.e., to read him as an essentially religious author – something he himself called for in *The Point of View for my Work as an Author*. But when it comes to Kierkegaard nothing is that easy, and many commentators have brushed aside the self-interpretation offered in *The Point of View*, pointing out that this work was only published posthumously and that its basic message conflicts with some of Kierkegaard's own claims regarding the independence of the pseudonyms from their creator. Some also go on to argue that, whatever Kierkegaard's authorial intentions, the overall tendency of his work points towards the repudiation of historic Christianity. Such divergent opinions were already to be found amongst Kierkegaard's contemporaries, for whilst some regarded him first and foremost as the author of devotional works that spoke to troubled hearts,[1] others sought to enlist him in the cause of radical secularization.[2] Since then the debate has taken a variety of forms in a variety of contexts. In the inter-war years in Europe the neo-orthodox Kierkegaard confronted the Heideggerian Kierkegaard, and, a generation later, in Paris, the discussion sessions of the 1964 UNESCO Kierkegaard conference were extensively preoccupied with the question as to whether atheistic existentialists and Marxists (in the persons of Jean-Paul Sartre and Lucien Goldmann respectively) could really read Kierkegaard without obscuring or ignoring the vital Christian element in his writing.[3] In our day the question more typically focusses on Kierkegaard's affinity to the literary and intellectual culture of postmodernity, and whether we are to see anything in his writings beyond the glittering trickery of the pseudonymous magic theatre.

This latter question is certainly a part of the background of this study. However, I do not believe that becoming attentive to the literary dimension of Kierkegaard's authorship diminishes its philosophical or religious importance. On the contrary, it is essential to understanding Kierkegaard's unique way of being a religious author.

There are those, however, who seem to see literary and religious approaches as mutually exclusive. Thus, in his contribution to the *Cambridge Companion to Kierkegaard*, Roger Poole proposes a category of Kierkegaard interpretation which he calls 'blunt reading'. Those charged with being 'blunt readers' include most philosophers and theologians, who are said to be guilty of imposing an inappropriate unity on what is an internally heterogenous body of writing. Amongst others, Poole applies this category of 'blunt reading' to the present study. This, it seems to me, reflects a complete mis- (or, I am tempted to say, non-) reading of it. In answering this charge I hope not only to make the polemical point that the category of 'blunt reading' is itself an exceedingly blunt interpretative instrument, but also to say something about what it means to read Kierkegaard as a *religious* author. I shall then develop this further point in response to criticisms of my work by Michael Strawser. But whereas Poole misconstrues the nature of my position, Strawser's comments constitute a perceptive and helpful response to it, and provide an opportunity to clarify the intentionally condensed final section of this book.

Blunt readers, according to Poole, are typically ignorant of the literary background of Kierkegaard's authorship and neglect the fact that many of his works were written by pseudonyms who cannot be identified unambiguously with their author. The need to attend to the literary context of Kierkegaard's work and to the complex formal and stylistic factors at work in it is, I would have thought, one of the most obvious presuppositions of *Kierkegaard: The Aesthetic and the Religious*, since it is largely devoted to showing just how far issues of form, genre and style penetrate into the very fabric of Kierkegaard's writing. I insist repeatedly that the 'what' cannot be separated from the 'how'. I do not approach the threefold distinction between the aesthetic, the ethical and the religious as 'a Hegelian pattern . . . mere *Gestalten* in a kind of phenomenology of the aesthetic',[4] but as corresponding to and requiring distinctive forms of expression (such as drama, the novel and the discourse).[5]

Thus far, it seems that Poole has simply not attended to what I believe is clearly stated in my book. He is, however, correct in seeing that I do seek to interpret the many voices heard in the authorship as contributing to a common conversation that, in the last resort, is of a distinctively religious kind. Where Poole follows Kierkegaard's wish and prayer that, at all times and in all places, we keep the pseudonyms apart, I follow Kierkegaard's no less clearly expressed claim that the authorship came to rest at the foot of the altar, i.e., in the discourses written (as if) for the Friday Communion.[6] However, it by no means follows that this involves what Poole describes as 'a pure and uncontaminated *gnosis*' or that I propose a resolution on '"higher" conceptual ground'.[7] As I argued quite extensively in my study *Agnosis: Theology in the Void*,[8] the thrust of Kierkegaard's religious thought is precisely to problematize 'knowledge' or 'gnosis' of any kind. Being religious in a Kierkegaardian way, I believe, involves the suspension if not the abandonment of any and every claim to 'know' God – a point that is underlined when I draw attention to Kierkegaard's own claim that theology would do better to affiliate itself to rhetoric than to metaphysics. Thus, what the Friday discourses offer is not 'gnosis'. The presence of Christ of which they speak is not 'in' some occult mystical space, but, as a matter of faith, is affirmed as an act of testimony by the concretely existing individual, who continues to be bound by the same ambiguities of experience and interpretation as all other existing individuals. In the immediately preceding section 'The Crucifixion of the Image' I strongly emphasize that 'complete and concrete solidarity with suffering humanity' is the necessary condition of religious thought in our time,[9] and to the extent that Kierkegaard's own work does seem to point to a dualistically-conceived 'other' world, we should not hesitate to critique him.

Of course there are theological readings that impose closure on the texts, subordinating their dynamic variety to a preconceived dogmatic plant. But it is no less possible to pursue a reading that is religious in the spirit of Bakhtin[10] – not so much a matter of providing theological 'answers' but more an exploration of the text's way of posing its guiding questions. The 'religious' element in Kierkegaard, as I conceive it, is not primarily to do with dogmatic content in any conceptual sense, but with how Kierkegaard deploys the paradoxical logic of the 'sign of contradiction' as a means of interrogating the whole field of culture, science and society. The only possible 'finality' would be eschatological, so neither Kierkegaard's text nor its interpreter can deliver a final judgement on the outcome of this interrogation. This, however, does not absolve the reader, living in the meantime, from the responsibility of entering the strife of voices and in full consciousness of the contestability of any single interpretation arguing for that interpretation he finds the most humanly convincing and the best able to do the fullest justice to the widest range of texts.

In the *Søren Kierkegaard Newsletter* (30) of November 1994, Michael Strawser gave an appreciative yet critical review of *Kierkegaard: The Aesthetic and the Religious*, later developing further some of these comments in his own book *Both/And. Reading Kierkegaard from Irony to Edification.*[11] Strawser raises fundamental questions about the way in which Kierkegaard is to be read, and the most basic question of all is simply this: is Kierkegaard a *religious* author?

Now although I am committed to reading Kierkegaard religiously, I think that Strawser and I probably agree that we cannot do justice to the question thus posed by means of any simple 'yes' or 'no' answer. I think that we would also agree that in reading Kierkegaard or any author it is generally a good principle to base interpretation on as wide a range of texts as possible. In the case of Kierkegaard this is notoriously difficult, because the very diversity of the authorship means that different readers will be attracted to different parts of it. The student of modernist literature who feels at home in *Either/Or*, *Repetition* and *Stages on Life's Way* may be less interested in the philosophical and theological issues raised by the Climacan writing, whilst the philosopher who dips into the *Postscript* or *The Concept of Anxiety* for the sake of clarifying Kierkegaard's critique of idealism or concept of freedom may not immediately see much of interest in the various upbuilding or Christian discourses. But if the difference between 'religious' and 'anti-religious' readers of Kierkegaard simply boils down to the fact that each side is reading different texts, then much of the argument evaporates into thin air. My view, however (and Strawser's too, I think), is that the question gets interesting in proportion to the range of Kierkegaard's writings taken into consideration. The argument is not about this text or that text but about the thrust of the authorship as a whole. This is why, for example, the readings of Heidegger and Sartre are particularly challenging to theological interpreters, because they do not hesitate to draw on Kierkegaard's religious and, indeed (in the case of Sartre), Christological writings. Simply to hold up the volumes of upbuilding and Christian discourses as a tangible demonstration of Kierkegaard's religious intentions will not do, for the question still remains as to how we, today, are to read them. Again, I think, Strawser and I are in agreement. Where then do we part company?

In *Both/And* Strawser sets the question up in terms of the categories of irony and edification. If we read Kierkegaard as a fundamentally ironical author, he argues, then the deep certainties that undergird a religious reading are radically destabilized, whereas an edifying reading means that irony is only a transient moment in the overall development of the authorship, a spot of regional unrest in the global providence of a religious life-view (even, perhaps, an apologetic tactic and therefore essentially fake). Strawser's own hypothesis is that irony and edification provide two alternative lines of interpretation that run through every sentence Kierkegaard ever wrote. 'How shall I choose to read Kierkegaard's writings? From irony to edification? From edification to irony? Or both, beginning from either end?' The 'answer', he says, is left 'in the lap of the reader'.[12]

Strawser acknowledges an affinity between his work and my own, in that my account of things 'explains how the relationship between direct and indirect communication is much more intimate than is usually perceived'.[13] He indulges in some sweeping polemics against those to whom he refers as 'Kierkegaardologists' and although I am allowed to count as a partial exception to their collective myopia he concludes that '. . . Pattison does not go far enough . . .'[14] My approach is, after all, too direct, too religious, too Christian.

In his review of the present study Strawser focuses his criticism on my comments about the Friday Discourses. In the concluding section entitled 'A Real Presence?' I state that, for Kierkegaard, the '. . . Communion is the preeminent sign of that relationship of forgiveness, blessing and indwelling in which God, in Christ, becomes an actual and creative presence in human life . . .'[15] I also argue that the materiality of this sign serves as a gesture by which Kierkegaard points beyond textuality and beyond aesthetics to what, for faith, is a real presence.

Noting that the question-mark of the section's title disappears later on, Strawser points out that these signs are themselves 'embedded in textuality, in the text of texts . . .'[16] and goes on to say that the act of communion 'as involving direct sense perception and a keen sense of imagination' can itself be seen as a kind of resurrection of the aesthetic in such a way 'that the question of the real presence is left undecided[.]' (ibid.).

I certainly agree that the presence spoken of and experienced by Kierkegaard in relation to the Friday Communion is not unproblematic or unambiguous. No more than the 'moment' in which time and eternity touch can be made the object of an objective science or an institutionally guaranteed dogma can the 'presence' spoken of here be constituted as an item of public knowledge, and the rhetoric of secrecy is tellingly characteristic of Kierke-gaard's Friday Discourses. The question-mark of the title of my concluding section may disappear, but it is not revoked, and the very brevity of my comments was intended as a clue that what I was saying was suggestive rather than dogmatic. Moreover, the fact that the sign of this presence is Christological draws it into the realm of the sign of contradiction (as Kierkegaard interprets it in *Training in Christianity*: see Chapter 3 below) such that Christ cannot be said to be 'in' the sign in any objective sense. To speak of the Communion as an experience of presence is necessarily to speak subjectively, under the condition of objective uncertainty. Faithful reception of the sacrament is not an act of notional assent to a proposition: it is a gesture of affirmation that in affirming presence negates the possibility of comprehending that presence. The material elements are placed before us as an eloquent refutation of the claims of the general and the universalizable. In being experienced sacramentally, however, the communion is experienced, first, as a gift, as grace bestowed on us from a dimension of 'unincludable otherness' (Buber) and, secondly, as something intrinsically material and bodily. As a sign the sacrament is inescapably entangled in textuality, but, in being believingly appropriated as the singular sign it is, it marks a gesture (no more, no less) of transcendence in relation to its textuality. Like Kierkegaard's auto-destructive novels – *Bildungsromaner* that annihilate themselves in the attempt to articulate a more-than-aesthetic content – the sacramental sign of contradiction works against itself in its own sign character.

There is one further point I should like to make in defending the project of reading Kierkegaard religiously that shows up the differences between Strawser's approach and my own more sharply.

Strawser suggests that we read Kierkegaard in the mode of 'both/and', such that the balance between the ironic and the edifying is infinitely undecidable. What this proposal does not perhaps exclude but certainly does not emphasize is the seriousness that informs Kierkegaard's writings. Let me put my point like this. In facing the reader with the religious requirement, Kierkegaard does not invite us to consider a merely theoretical understanding of existence. He makes, and enables us to make (if we so choose) a venture of interpretation in which the stake is nothing other than our own identity as persons. The religious question is inseparable from the question 'Who am I?'. In asking this question I not only put myself in play, I put myself at risk. Unlike Pascal's wager, Kierkegaard's gamble does not offer a win-win formula. If the religious response turns out to be illusory I have wasted my life. Religion, in this perspective, opens up the real possibility of a tragic understanding of life. As Unamuno, one of Kierkegaard's earliest interpreters, recognised, religion is not the 'answer' to tragedy, the happy ending that makes everything all right. On the contrary, it is religion that reveals the tragic, confronting me with the possibility that my choice, and thus my life, might be 'for nothing'.[17] But that, as Iris Murdoch said, is perhaps the condition of any truly moral act. In the face of this possibility, however, irony calls out for commitment, although commitment will never of itself be able to stand as guarantor for certainty. The nurturing of commitment, self-commitment and commitment in love to others is precisely what I take to be the task of edification. This task is 'beyond' irony, not because it negates irony intellectually, but because it questions the right of irony to immunise itself against critique. Irony is not done away with, for it remains an irreplaceable instrument for the testing of spirits – and every moral or religious assertion that strays outside its own territory is a legitimate prey for irony. The moment that the passion of faith congeals into dogmatic or institutional certainty, irony is free to have a go at it – however, deciding such things is not, of course, the matter of any exact science but of qualitative reading that senses when to give trust and when to withold it. In the course of such reading, I suspect, irony itself may turn out not to be the most precise of terms with which to articulate the fundamental tendency of a non-theological reading and there may also turn out to be concepts (perhaps Kierkegaard's own favoured concept of humour) that signal areas of significant overlap between irony and edification such that the either/or underpinning Strawser's both/and is itself called into question.

In making this defence of my religious reading of Kierkegaard, I do not want to leave the impression that I regard my achievements as an interpreter of Kierkegaard as being beyond criticism. Were I once to begin rewriting the present volume, a very different book would probably emerge from the resulting chaos. I would certainly do things differently now, nearly ten years on from the publication of the first edition. My main feeling, however, is not so much that there is anything 'wrong' with what it says, but that it doesn't say enough. It is, for example, a fundamental thesis of the book that Kierkegaard's categories of the aesthetic, the ethical and the religious are not so much to be understood in terms of psychological states of mind but as forms of communication, requiring correspondingly specific forms of communication (the drama, the novel and the religious address). But these forms do not exhaust Kierkegaard's literary armoury. He also produced a significant body of journalism, culminating in his pamphleteering attack on the established Church. Here we see Kierkegaard writing in what, given some of his own comments about the press, seems to be an altogether alien medium, yet making it his own for specific polemical purposes. As he does so, we see him writing *differently*, precisely because he so well understood that the challenge of public journalistic debate imposes a different set of conditions and constraints and opens different opportunities and possibilities from the task of writing as a single individual for a single 'real' reader. The whole are of Kierkegaard's engagement with popular contemporary culture is also relevant here, revealing relatively unexplored aspects of his authorship – an area I have begun to survey in my recent *'Poor Paris!' Kierkegaard's Critique of the Spectacular City*.[18] But this is only a beginning.

George Pattison, King's College, Cambridge

[1] See, e.g., Frederikke Bremer, *Liv i Norden* (Copenhagen: Eibe, 1849), p.37.

[2] Most famously, of course, his nephew Henrik Lund. Lund fulminated against the Church's appropriating of his uncle's legacy in an emotional speech at Kierkegaard's graveside. See also H. C. Malik, *Receiving Søren Kierkegaard. The Early Impact and Transmission of his Thought* (Washington, DC: Catholic University of America Press, 1997).

[3] See *Kierkegaard Vivant: Colloque organisé par l'UNESCO à Paris du 23 Avril 1964* (Paris: Gallimard, 1966).

[4] Roger Poole, 'Twentieth Century Receptions', in A. Hannay and G. Marino (eds.), *The Cambridge Companion to Kierkegaard* (Cambridge: Cambridge University Press, 1998), p.63.

[5] Although I do point out that in his youth Kierkegaard at the very least experimented with several clearly Hegelian triads as a means of making sense of aesthetics (triads such as epic, lyric and dramatic, or Don Juan, Faust and the Wandering Jew).

⁶ See, e.g., the preface to the *Two Discourses at the Communion on Fridays* published in 1851, included in S. Kierkegaard, *Without Authority*, ed. and tr. H. V. and E. H. Hong (Princeton: Princeton University Press, 1997), p.165.

⁷ Ibid., p.64.

⁸ G. Pattison, *Agnosis: Theology in the Void* (Basingstoke: Macmillan, 1996).

⁹ See below, p.186.

¹⁰ See my paper 'If Kierkegaard is Right about Reading, Why Read Kierkegaard?', in N.-J. Cappelørn and J. Stewart (eds.), *Kierkegaard Revisited* (Berlin: Walter de Gruyter, 1997).

¹¹ M. Strawser, *Both/And. Reading Kierkegaard from Irony to Edification* (New York: Fordham University Press, 1997).

¹² Ibid., p.242.

¹³ Ibid., p.180.

¹⁴ Ibid., p.181.

¹⁵ *See below* p.187.

¹⁶ *Søren Kierkegaard Newsletter*, Number 30, November 1994, p.22.

¹⁷ This emphasis on the tragic also differentiates my understanding of Kierkegaard from religious interpretations such as those of David Gouwens and Sylvia Walsh, and from a philosophical interpretation such as that of Jamie Ferreira.

¹⁸ G. Pattison, *'Poor Paris!' Kierkegaard's Critique of the Spectacular City* (Berlin: Walter de Gruyter, 1998).

1

Idealism and the Justification of the Image

FICHTE AND ROMANTICISM

Images are: they are the only things which exist, and they know of themselves after the fashion of images; images which float past without there being anything past which they float . . . I myself am one of these images; nay, I am not even this, but merely a confused image of the images. All reality is transformed into a strange dream, without a life which is dreamed of, and without a mind which dreams it. . . .[1]

In these words from *The Vocation of Man* (1800) J.G. Fichte gave expression to the disturbing situation to which the sceptical implications of Kantian philosophy seemed to point. In the light of Kant's rigorous and detailed account of the way in which the structures of the human mind themselves determine the form which our knowledge of the external world must take, it was easy to draw the conclusion that knowledge could have no basis in reality itself. The thing-in-itself recedes infinitely away from us, while we remain locked within the limitations of our own categories of thought and representation. Even the simplest mental image of a colour, an object or a scene of some sort (that is to say, even the most apparently non-controversial instances of straightforward empirical knowledge) turns out to be indissociable from that projective mechanism whereby we read meaning into the world rather than (as common sense tends to suppose) the mind reflecting what is *there*. Perhaps space itself, that essential precondition of all knowledge, has no existence outside the mind but is the creation of 'the wonderful power of productive imagination . . . without which nothing at all in the human mind is capable of explanation.'[2]

The Vocation of Man itself takes the form of a dialogue between

1

the philosopher and a higher spirit. In the quotation with which we began it is the philosopher who is speaking and who plainly finds the absence of ultimate certainty regarding the relationship between knowledge and reality to be singularly distressing. The spirit partner in the dialogue, however, is not perturbed:

> You wanted to know of your knowledge. Are you surprised that in this way you discovered nothing more than that of which you wanted to know, your knowledge itself. . . . What has its origin in and through knowledge is merely knowledge. But all knowledge is only images, representations; and there is always something wanting in it – that which corresponds to the representation . . . a system of knowledge is necessarily a system of mere images, wholly without reality, significance or aim.[3]

Taking note of the close correlation between imagination and knowledge in Fichte's argument, we are clearly being pressurised into asking still more forcibly: Is this all? Is there no way past the impasse of ultimate scepticism? Fichte (whom, incidentally, Kierkegaard regarded as a 'noble' thinker) thought there was. Kant had already offered a fresh approach to the question of the existence of God (and thereby also to the ontological grounding of human experience) by pointing to the dynamics of the practical reason and those moral imperatives which require us to regard the world 'as if' there were a God and therefore also a real and serious interest to be pursued in it. Fichte went considerably further. Whereas Kant insisted that the assurances provided by the practical reason could never be constitutive for knowledge, Fichte stated the primacy of the practical reason in such a way as to do away with all doubts. The practical reason is, in his eyes, self-authenticating, and, through it, the world in which and on which it acts is also certain: 'We act not because we know, but we know because we are called upon to act; the practical reason is the root of all reason. The laws of action for rational beings are *immediately certain*; their world is certain only through the fact that they are certain.'[4] It is because the moral sense – conscience – requires that the persons with whom I have to deal are to be treated as real, existent persons (and not mere projections of my productive imagination) that I am bound – literally conscience-bound – to regard the world of consciousness in which such persons appear as real. This conclusion inspires the philosopher of *The Vocation of Man* with enormous confidence. He is fully satisfied that in this way the self, through the practice of virtuous willing, acquires a final and unsurpassable sense of its own meaning and purpose.

> The will is the living principle of reason – is itself reason, when purely and simply apprehended . . . I *am* immortal, imperishable, eternal, as soon as I form the resolution to obey the laws of reason; I do not need to *become* so. The supersensual world is no future world; it is now present. . . . By that resolution I lay hold on eternity, and cast off this earthly life . . . I become the sole source of my own being and its phenomena, and henceforth, unconditioned by anything without me, I have life in myself.[5]

All this provides a highly significant point of reference in relation to what we shall later be seeing of Kierkegaard's thought, as does this further unfolding of the implications of the position Fichte has now arrived at: 'My mind is forever closed to confusion and perplexity, to uncertainty, doubt and anxiety; my heart is closed to grief, repentance and desire. There is but one thing that I know, namely, what I ought to do; and this I always know infallibly.'[6]

Fichte's supposed breakthrough of the Kantian deadlock was not uncontroversial in its own time,[7] but it met with a rapturous reception from those writers and thinkers who were to become known as the Early Romantics (*Die Frühromantik*) who praised Fichte's achievement to the skies. Friedrich Schlegel, one of the movement's leading figures, set the philosopher's *Science of Knowledge* on a par with the French Revolution as one of the key events of the age.[8] But the esteem in which Schlegel and his companions held Fichte did not mean that they were altogether faithful disciples, and they singularly lacked his characteristic ethical vigour. The difference between them has been well summarised by Walter Benjamin, who wrote: 'For Schlegel and Novalis the infinity of reflection is not in the first instance an infinity of progress but an infinity of connectedness.'[9] That is to say that for these Romantic thinkers the self-transcendence of the self, the way in which the self creates for itself a world in and through which to give meaning to its own productive activity, is not characterised by purposive moral commitment (as it was for Fichte) but is more like a never-ending game in which the self simply plays with its own possibilities, exploring the infinite 'connectedness' by which it coheres with its world into a meaningful totality. Above all the Romantics see this play as taking the form of artistic creativity and enjoyment, for it is art which offers the supreme exemplification of the pattern of a self which is unreservedly creative, making, shaping and enjoying its own world, such that, in art, 'In each thought the "I" is the hidden light, in each one finds itself; one constantly thinks only oneself or the "I" . . . [the self] in its higher meaning.'[10] Irony, one of the principal concepts of Early Romanticism, is precisely the consciousness of the self's free and sovereign transcendence over its world. But the distance separating the 'mood' of Early Romanticism from the spirit of Fichte can be clearly sensed if we compare the following passage from Schlegel's novel *Lucinde* with what we have already read from *The Vocation of Man*:

> Really, one should not so culpably neglect the study of idleness, but develop it to an art and a science, yes, a religion! To summarize all points in one: the more divine a man or a man's work is, the more it becomes like plant-life; of all the forms of nature this is the most ethical and the most beautiful. And thus the highest and most perfect life would be nothing but a pure vegetating.[11]

The Early Romantics found their philosophical champion in F.J.W. Schelling, whose work gave systematic rigour to the conviction that artistic creativity is not merely the supreme mode of personal fulfilment but actually discloses the reality of how things really are. Following Fichte, Schelling affirmed the role of an 'intellectual intuition' in which and by means of which the self apprehends itself in its work of self-production, but he also emphasised the aesthetic dimension of consciousness alongside the purely intellectual function. If the intellectual intuition focuses on the priority of the self in creating the world of consciousness, the aesthetic intuition reveals that the self is only a self in, with and under the forms of its self-manifestation. That is to say that in the aesthetic intuition the mind is not merely productive (and, as such, to be characterised as *conscious*, *subject* and *self*) but also product (and, as such, to be characterised as *unconscious*, *object*, *the not-self*) and the aesthetic intuition itself is precisely the intuition of these elements in an indissoluble and primordial unity. In this way it unites the polarities of nature and freedom in a single act of consciousness, as it apprehends the absolute in no other way than as it is made present in the forms provided by the sensuous immediacy of phenomenal being.[12]

We have travelled a long way from the despairing scepticism of our opening quotation from *The Vocation of Man*. The images which consciousness offers for our contemplation are no longer seen as free-floating, rootless or dream-like, but the image itself has the capacity to be in itself a true manifestation of absolute being. If we just *see* the world rightly, we see what it *is*. The dialectic of nature and freedom, of reality and consciousness, is resolved in this unitive aesthetic vision, a vision to which the artist has readier access than the philosopher:

> What we speak of as Nature is a poem lying pent up in a mysterious and wonderful script. Yet the riddle could reveal itself were we to recognize in it the Odyssey of the Spirit, which, marvellously deluded, seeks itself, and in seeking flies from itself; for through the world of sense there glimmers, as if through words the meaning, as if through mists the land of fantasy, of which we are in search. . . .[13]

These ideas spread rapidly across Europe. The story of Coleridge's attempts to bring Schellingian idealism to Britain is well-known, but the influence of Early Romanticism on Scandinavia was both more immediate and more pervasive. Although Danish thought placed more emphasis on the empirical element in knowledge than did the German post-Kantians, Danish philosophers were more receptive to idealism than their British counterparts.

The arrival of Romanticism in Denmark is traditionally identified with a series of lectures given between 1802 and 1803 in Copenhagen by the Norwegian-born philosopher and geologist, Henrik Steffens (1773–1845), an avowed disciple of Schelling and sometime member of the Jena circle in which many of the leading representatives of Early Romanticism moved. Steffens' lectures were not only remarkable in themselves but also had a profound impact on the poet Adam Oehlenslaeger, who was inspired by them to write the poem 'The Golden Horns' (*Guldhornene*) sometimes said to be the first 'Romantic' poem in Danish literature.

Steffens intended his lectures to be preparatory to a series of more technical philosophical lectures and, as such, were intended to make the aims and methods of Romantic idealism accessible to the general public. By 'philosophy' he understood the knowledge of the unity of the finite and infinite worlds, of appearance and reality. Although *knowledge* of this unity was the special domain of philosophy, even the non-philosopher could have some kind of intuition of the infinite harmony of the universe by means of what Steffens called 'premonition' (*Ahnelse*). 'Nobody', he asserted,

> is ever entirely devoid of this premonition. It slumbers deep in the soul of even the most limited of us. It connects us to the whole of nature. It gives everything . . . an higher, more noble significance. It is that which, with the dawning of the day, opens up the radiance and life of nature to every soul, as if an inward sun involuntarily followed the celestial; it raises the infinite multitude of forms from universal darkness; by its means nature's eternal life speaks to our spirit, as if through a mystical cipher which inwardly we understand.[14]

Not only does premonition in this way reveal to us the heart and soul of nature – it also offers a similar insight into the meaning of human history; and it is the poet who, above all others, is best able to communicate such premonitions to us.

> By its operation, times whose habits of thought, whose ways of life, possessed characteristics quite other than our own, become comprehensible to us. . . . It wakens the warriors from their graves, gods and goddesses come among us, every sound from long-vanished ages resounds with its own unique resonance. It conjures the most advanced epochs back into the most obscure. . . . This premonition . . . is called Poesy. No man is utterly devoid of Poesy. No age, not even the coarsest, has ever entirely lost it. It is as if nature's own eternal productivity awoke with the poet. Noble and exalted forms issue forth; a divine, a golden age, illuminated by an eternal sun, arises before our eyes, suddenly, as if by magic. An infinite meaning seems to be concealed behind every form and mystically shines out towards us. We are surrounded by an exalted and glorious radiance; a deep longing awakens in our inmost being and irresistibly draws us to this wonderful and magical world. . . .[15]

Thus the poet, who brings to us an immediate revelation of the eternal in, with and under finite forms, is the maker of 'holy, radiant images of the eternal'.[16] Nor are these images the empty, floating images whose lack of ontological anchorage so distressed Fichte's doubting philosopher: instead they are self-authenticating; windows which open immediately on to the absolute presence of reality itself.

The fascination for the past, for 'long-vanished ages', which characterises Steffens' lectures found an echo in Oehlenslaeger's poem 'The Golden Horns', to which we have already referred. This poem is based on the story of two golden horns discovered at Gallehus in Jutland, one in 1639, the other in 1734. Dating from the pre-Christian era and inscribed with runic symbols, they mysteriously vanished in 1802 and were never found again. A pedestrian explanation is that they were stolen and subsequently melted down, but Oehlenslaeger has another, more poetic story: the horns were gifts from the gods, bestowed on the present age but taken back again because the age could only see in them their material value and not the higher meaning which they have for those who look on them with poetic eyes. This 'Romantic' view of the pagan Nordic past was also highly characteristic of the thought of another leading figure of Scandinavian Romanticism, N.F.S. Gruntvig, whose *Mythology of the North* (1808) gave a Christianised and highly poetic reading of Nordic mythology.[17]

A further philosophical interpretation of Romantic idealism can be found in the thought of F.C. Sibbern (1785–1872), whose main area of interest was in the empirical sciences but who also wrote on aesthetics as well as producing a Romantic novel, *The Posthumous Letters of Gabrielis*, which reflected his unhappy love for Oehlenslaeger's wife, Sophie. Sibbern's lectures *On Poetry and Art* were published in 1834, and although they are much later than the key works of early Danish Romanticism they have been described by the critic Henning Fenger as 'a collective expression of the taste and ideals which the first romantic generation possessed, "the men of 1803".'[18] They are therefore worth examining in the present context of our survey of the view of aesthetics in early Danish Romanticism.

Sibbern argues that art has two roots. On the one hand it is mimetic, reproducing the natural appearance in the medium of ideality. But mimesis is not mere copying; it is rather the representation of nature in a manner informed by human interests and concerns, above all the concern for unity, harmony and truth – 'the whole'. The other root of art is expressiveness, the representation of that which originates in the artist's own inner being. The

'poetry' and 'art' of the title of the lectures refers precisely to these
two roots: poetry to the expressive element in art and 'art' (in the
strict sense) to the mimetic element. These two poles are almost
invariably co-present in any particular work of art. Thus, when art
imitates external nature (as, for example, in landscape painting) it
is akin to 'the simple apprehension of things via the senses',[19] but
it is also always led by a higher, ideal interest:

> The poet and the artist must have an eye for this 'inner' being of
> things, for this proper and essential nature, if he is to represent
> nature as it is in truth. It is to this that the seer's eye must
> penetrate, and from this too that the recreating representation
> must proceed, and therefore we say that it is an ideal rebirth.[20]

The artist never in fact satisfies himself with representing merely
the 'outer shell' of nature, but is always moved by sympathy for
the universal idea moving in both nature and humanity alike. As
with Schelling's concept of aesthetic intuition and Steffens' concept
of premonition, 'sympathy' is conceived as a bond uniting both art
and nature, and it is through a parallel sympathy that the recipient of
the artwork (the audience, the reader, the listener, etc.) apprehends
and participates in the 'ideal rebirth' of aesthetic experience.

Similarly, although expressive (or, as Sibbern also calls it, lyrical)
art springs directly from the inner ideality of the artistic consciousness, it is not, or should not be, one-sidedly idealistic. Instead it
uses the materials of imitative art to give form, substance and
objective shape to its creations. The artist must be true to nature,
he must 'immerse himself in the world, in nature and in history'.[21]

The essentially idealistic nature of art means that it should not be
dismissed as 'lower' than philosophy. Like philosophy art pen-
etrates to the primal (*Ur*-) or fundamental (*Grund*-) ideas which
give meaning to the world, even though it represents these ideas
in individual or concrete form.

> Here we see that deeper content (*Gehalt*) of life and of humanity,
> which science makes the object of its investigations, appear in its
> real presence. . . . But the work itself shall not be a summation
> of investigation and reflection, of scientific development and
> classification. [Instead] it is to bring the object itself before us in
> the totality of its concrete actuality, but in an ideal rebirth, in an
> ideal representation.[22]

Pleasure is an essential accompaniment of aesthetic experience: 'That only can be said to have an *aesthetic* effect which works by means of the pleasure with which it fills us in the immediate impression, so that we thereby relate ourselves to it in a purely contemplative manner.'[23] One implication of this is that we can draw a clear line of demarcation between aesthetic and religious categories. It is, for instance, said to be quite inappropriate to judge hymns aesthetically since it is not the primary aim of a hymn to please. In the novel *The Posthumous Letter of Gabrielis* Sibbern had made a similar point, contrasting the teaching of the Bible with works of philosophy and art:

> In all those other noble and profound thoughts and images there may move a deep philosophy, there may be developed a rich and penetrating view of life, there may live an infinitely noble soul and heart. But in the words of scripture there moves an holy God. . . . In those other realms, in philosophy or poetry, there is a profundity in ideas, but in these works the Spirit of the Lord is stirring; those are begotten of genius and profundity, but these are spoken as by Him who has authority.[24]

This may seem fairly straightforward. However, one of the reviewers of *On Poetry and Art* (Dean Tryde, who was to conduct Kierkegaard's funeral) complained that Sibbern had not sufficiently emphasised the distinction between the higher ideality expressed in art and the divine being of God.[25] Nonetheless it is also worth pointing out – especially in relation to our investigation of Kierkegaard's engagement in these issues – that not only does Sibbern draw explicit attention to the need to draw a proper boundary between the aesthetic and the religious, but he was also the first Danish philosopher to develop a critique of Hegelianism, a critique which included a discussion of what he regarded as Hegel's failure to distinguish between the needs of a personalistic faith and the programme of speculative philosophy.[26]

HEGELIANISM

The relationship between Hegelianism and Romanticism is highly complex, especially when we are examining them simultaneously in the German and in the Danish context. Against the Hegelian view itself we cannot see Hegelianism as representing a straight-forward linear advance on Romanticism. The Romantics did not simply fade away under the impact of Hegel's systematic and highly rationalistic critique of Romantic philosophy. Many of them, including, for example, Schelling and Sibbern, stayed around to develop a critique of Hegel which was not merely a restatement of earlier Romantic positions but which, at least in certain respects, anticipated such later developments as we shall find in Kierkegaard himself. Moreover, there are strong differences between German and Danish forms of both philosophies. If Danish Romanticism showed itself to be more appreciative of empirical science than its German counterpart (and consequently placed less emphasis on the 'absolute' creativity of the 'I' or self), Danish Hegelianism showed less interest in history, economics and politics than Hegel himself. The leading Danish Hegelians had distinctive aesthetic and religious concerns and, as we shall see, deviated from Hegelian 'orthodoxy' at several key points.

We shall, however, start with Hegel himself, with the *caveat* that we are here only seeking to highlight those elements of his thought which relate most directly to our theme of 'the aesthetic and the religious' – although even with this limitation it will be necessary to simplify to the point of oversimplification.

Like other idealists Hegel regarded art as representing a fusion of an ideal or spiritual content with a material form. In this way art transcends nature, but does not (unlike logic) turn away from 'sensuous individuality and immediate determinateness . . . the work of art stands in the middle between immediate sensuousness and ideal thought. It is *not yet* pure thought, but, despite its sensuousness, is no longer a purely material existent either, like stones, plants and organic life.'[27] Art works with matter, but it reduces matter to the status of instrumentality, as a vehicle in and through which a supersensuous reality is to shine forth. In this respect (and here Hegel deviates from the typical emphasis of Romantic thought) art is *only* the *immediate* form of absolute truth, which truth can also be known in higher and more appropriate forms, namely religion and philosophy.

In the course of the history of art Hegel discerns a movement from those forms of art in which the material element predomi-nates, to higher forms in which the essential spiritual reality of art is more apparent, until art reaches the point at which it transcends itself, and other modes of spiritual existence and expression are called for which art is unable to furnish. The key stages of this history are called by Hegel the symbolic, the classical and the romantic forms of art respectively. Symbolic art, which he identifies with the ancient religious art of India, Persia and Egypt, is art in which the material, sensuous element obscures the transmission of the ideal meaning or truth it contains. Typically such art represents the divinity in the form of an animal or some other sub-human shape, and Hegel sees the culmination of this stage of art in the figure of the sphinx, in which 'out of the dull strength of the animal the human spirit tries to push itself forward, without coming to a perfect portrayal of its own freedom and animate shape, because it must still remain confused and associated with what is other than itself'.[28] But the riddle of the sphinx – and this, for Hegel, is the meaning of the Oedipus legend – is resolved in the emergence of the humanism of the Greek city-state, and the belief that it is human consciousness itself which is the measure of all things.

Art now enters its classical phase, in which the absolute Idea is still represented sensuously but in a manner altogether appropriate to its supersensuous content: the human figure. For 'the human exterior is not only living and natural, as the animal is, but is the bodily presence which itself mirrors the spirit.'[29] The inner has now found a far more suitable vehicle by which to represent itself to itself in an appropriate outer form. In the sculptural masterpieces of Ancient Greece Hegel finds the highest expression of this classical ideal of a perfect balance between form and content. But this is nonetheless a synthesis which contains the seeds of its own dissolution. 'The sublimest works of sculpture are sightless. Their subtle inner being does not beam forth from them, as a self-knowing internality in that spiritual concentration of which the eye gives intelligence.'[30] There remains a whole realm of inwardness, feeling and thought which such art is unable to express. The new form of art which makes such expression possible is what Hegel calls romantic art. The breakdown of the classical synthesis and the emergence of romantic art is a key moment in Hegel's thought and is also highly instructive with regard to Kierkegaard's own critique of art, and we shall therefore examine it in some detail.

The dialectic governing the relationship between classical and romantic art is determined by two main factors: firstly, the process of *Erinnerung*, a term which carries the double connotation of *internalisation (Er-innerung)* and *recollection (remembrance* or *memory)*; and, secondly, the theological dynamic centred on the Christ-event and the development of the Early Church. By the way in which he dovetails these two elements Hegel arrives at an overall view of aesthetics which combines both philosophical and re-ligious factors – the weight which should be given to each having been a constant point of discussion ever since.

Erinnerung is the mechanism which leads from sense to thought, which reflects on, recollects and internalises in thought the process or history by which the human subject of that history has come to be what it is. In this way *Erinnerung* is the means by which Spirit appropriates itself in and through the recognition of its own creative agency in history, that is to say, recognises that history is the process of its self-creation. As such it presupposes a prior stage of unconscious self-formation, a period of sensuous life outside the domain of pure intellectual self-consciousness. This unconscious, sensuous phase, however, also acquires a human meaning pre-cisely through that act of recollection which incorporates it into the total history of consciousness. It is in this sense that we are to understand Hegel's famous remark that philosophy 'appears only when actuality is cut and dried after its process of formation has been completed . . . the Owl of Minerva spreads its wings only with the falling of the dusk'.[31]

Classical art in this way can be said to recollect or internalise the meaning of symbolic art by revealing the human subject of that earlier, less self-conscious form of art. The pinnacle of classical art is thus the depiction of the beautiful human figure in the three-dimensional form of sculpture. Yet it cannot be said that the medium of sculpture is sufficient to give full expression to the interior, spiritual interest of the human subject. Art, Hegel suggests, requires a still more interior medium – and this medium is language. So, in place of the stone pantheon of classical statuary a new pantheon is created whose 'element and habitation' (*Element und Behausung*) is language.[32] The first form which the new art of language takes is the epic poem, the work of the bard (Homer, for example) whose achievement is to translate into language the myths and legends of the gods and heroes previously represented in stone. 'His pathos is Mnemosyne, meditation and developed inwardness, the internalization of what was previously immediate essence.'[33] Yet there remains something lacking in the bardic work, for such a poet does not speak or write what issues from his own spiritual essence, but about the deeds of gods and heroes whose lives are quite other than his own. To put it another way: in the epic poem the hero is spoken of, he does not speak. A higher form of language is therefore required which will overcome the duality between actor and speaker – and this, Hegel says, is the language of tragedy. Yet, once again, even this art fails to give a complete expression of the essential freedom and creativity of spiritual existence. For in tragedy the hero is inevitably depicted as constrained by and subject to the power of the gods. Consequently a further step is needed in which the conception of human destiny as subject in this way to external determination is done away with and the Spirit is allowed, finally, to find its own proper voice. This takes place in classical comedy, for in the comedy heaven is depopulated, the gods are relativised, and the drama is seen to be a human concern in which the actors are able to step out from behind their masks. There is, however, a strongly negative element in that the world of comedy is a world which has left behind the old gods but has not yet found new gods, and the newly-emergent human subject whose consciousness it represents is unable to establish or affirm any kind of absolute value or meaning. The question then is: is it possible for art to find new gods, a new substantive content, without violating the insight which has been (albeit negatively) gained into the decisive role of human freedom in the life of the Spirit?

Hegel answers this question in terms of the Christological perspective which now comes to play a key part in his aesthetics. In the revelation of the incarnate God we see that the divine power formerly construed as external to human consciousness is not really external at all. Substance *is* subjectivity.[34] (That is, the human subject *is* the substantive element in the history of consciousness.) The impact of this discovery has powerful implications for art, since it gives to art a new thematic, throwing open as it does the whole realm of suffering, passionate human life to the work of artistic figuration. This is the dawn of what Hegel calls *romantic* art in the broad sense. Although the ultimate content of this new art is not derived solely from purely aesthetic categories (since it is set in motion by what occurs in the religious rather than in the aesthetic realm) its advent signals an enormous enrichment of the content of art. For Hegel argues that whilst the entire external world is relativised and robbed of its claims to ultimate significance because of the depth of inwardness revealed in Christ,

it follows by the same token that any and every external phenomenon is now available for aesthetic exploration and expression. Art
is no longer limited to the purely beautiful ideal forms of classical
art, but its subject-matter is widened to a 'multiplicity without
bounds'.[35]

With romantic art, new artistic media come into prominence:
painting, music and poetry are developed to an extent unprecedented in previous stages of art. This is no accident but has to do
with the appropriateness of these media for exploring the new
dimensions of subjective inwardness opened up by the Christ-
event. They are, for Hegel, typically *Christian* forms of art – thus,
he sees it as no mere coincidence that it is precisely in the Christian
Middle Ages that painting experiences such a prodigious expan-
sion and transformation. Yet it is not in music and painting but in
poetry that the whole dialectics of art reach their climax and
conclusion.

Poetry, like all art, trades in figures and images. It does not,
however, deal with them in their external form as such, but as
re-presented within the spiritual medium of language. It is therefore appropriate that the whole previous history of art is recapitu-
lated (*recollected*) within the history of poetry: in its most primitive
forms it is still burdened with the weight of externality, offering (in
the *epos*) 'sculptural pictures for our imagination'.[36] Lyrical poetry,
on the other hand, is inner feeling coming to consciousness of itself
in no other way than through self-expression in language. Drama
unites both these modes, the epic and the lyric, with tragedy
giving greater emphasis to the epic and comedy greater emphasis
to the lyrical element.

Because poetry belongs to language and language in turn is
essentially rational, poetry deals with experience in the light of
universal principles and thoughts. Like philosophical speculation
it aims to structure experience within the context of a well-formed,
rational world. Moreover, the extent to which it is able to achieve
this aim will depend on the extent to which society itself is subject
to rational regulation. Thus, as opposed to the Romantic ideal of
poetry as immediate expression, and against the Romantic prefer-
ence for a mythical or medieval past, Hegel's aesthetics affirm the
philosopher's confidence in the essential rationality of art and the
superiority of the modern, bourgeois world.

But if art is to be evaluated according to the extent to which it is
truly rational, then it would seem likely that art itself will have to

take second place to those forms of consciousness in which the claims of rationality are even more directly expressed, above all philosophy itself. This is indeed Hegel's conclusion. At its highest point of development art 'transcends itself . . . and passes over from the poetry of imagination to the prose of thought'.[37] Art turns out to be only the 'immediate' form of the absolute, hindered by the vestiges of externality and materiality which cling to even the most advanced forms of art. Art is thus surpassed by religion (which Hegel calls 'picture-thinking')[38] and philosophy, in which thought is finally at one with itself in its proper medium.

An important moment in the history of this transcendence of art is the Protestant Reformation, when 'religious ideas were drawn away from their wrapping in sense'.[39] Since the Reformation and the Enlightenment 'the peculiar nature of artistic production and of works of art no longer fills our highest need . . . Thought and reflection have spread their wings above fine art.'[40] And, Hegel says, art, 'considered in its highest vocation, is and remains for us a thing of the past. . . . Art invites us to intellectual consideration, and that not for the purpose of creating art again, but for knowing philosophically what art is.'[41] Finally: 'no matter how excellent we find the statues of the Greek gods, no matter how we see God the Father, the Christ and Mary so estimably and perfectly portrayed: it is no help; we bow the knee no longer.'[42] In the Reformation the religious content of romantic art, the preaching of faith in the God incarnate, breaks loose from the aesthetic mould in which the Middle Ages had set it. In the Enlightenment (though one-sidedly) and in Hegel's own thought, philosophy itself comes to a final and unsurpassable knowledge of that truth which even faith can only express imperfectly. This does not necessarily mean that there is no longer any need for either art or faith. It is once again a matter of recollection: art and faith continue, but they continue precisely as they are recollected within the perspicuous self-knowledge of philosophy (philosophy itself not having any peculiar intellectual content, but taking for its content the whole history or phenomenology of consciousness).

If we now turn to those Danish Hegelians whose thought belongs to the immediate background of Kierkegaard's thought, we find many of the Hegelian themes restated. At the same time there are highly characteristic differences. It is, from the point of view of this present study, significant that the men most associated with the introduction of Hegelianism to Denmark were a dramatist and a theologian: Johann Ludvig Heiberg (1791–1860) and Hans Lassen Martensen (1808–84), and their commitments led them to give a noticeable twist to Hegel's own version of absolute idealism.

Heiberg was 'converted' to Hegelianism in 1824[43] and produced several (not very substantial) philosophical essays in the Hegelian mould. A convenient summary of his intellectual programme can be found in the short book *On the Meaning of Philosophy for the Present Age*. In this work he describes the present age as being in a situation of crisis and transition, an age in which religion, art and poetry have lost their power of conveying 'immediate certainty concerning the divine and eternal'.[44] It is, he argues, only philosophy which can bring an end to this crisis, for although art and religion express the same substantial content as philosophy, they obscure this truth on account of the accidental nature of their form. Yet, in such figures as Dante, Calderón and Goethe, Heiberg hailed the possibility of a genuinely speculative art, and this concept of speculative art was further developed in his more narrowly aesthetic writings to which we now turn.

As a dramatic poet Heiberg is particularly associated with a series of vaudevilles, musical comedies of great sophistication, ingenuity and wit. In his critical writings he set out, with the aid of Hegelian logic, to justify the literary status of these plays. The key to his argument lies in his analysis of the various genres of poetic art. He dismisses as 'dilettante' any approach which ignores the proper boundaries of literary genres, thereby failing to recognise that content and form can only relate to each other in the highly specific manner determined by the particular genre of the work in question. Thus, for example, *The Barber of Seville* and *The Marriage of Figaro* are not two different forms expressing the one content, but the content itself is altered when there is such a significant shift of form. On the same principle, the supernatural element which may well have a place in epic poetry is inadmissible in the theatre, where the 'material actuality and sensuous reality make every spectator a sceptic'.[45]

Following a well-established precedent Heiberg then goes on to distinguish between the plastic and the musical forms of art, the former being objectified in space, the latter in time. Every actual work of art, however, will be a mixture of both, a fact which is, above all, true of poetry. Poetry is thus 'art's art', in the same way (Heiberg says) as logic is 'philosophy's philosophy'. In a clear departure from Hegel he states that in its original form poetry is predominantly musical (the lyric) and, in its second stage of development, plastic (the epic). Drama unites the two and is thus 'poetry's poetry'. But within drama itself the same duality of plastic and musical continues to recur. Thus *character* is a musical element, whilst *situation* is essentially plastic – since character develops in time but situation 'is momentary, at least at its highest point'.[46] But in the *action* of the play they are united, although in tragedy it is character and in comedy it is situation which takes precedence. When it comes to vaudeville, Heiberg argues that all these factors are united in such a way that the musical element is taken up into and determined by situation. In this way vaudeville stands at the very summit of aesthetic sophistication.

Heiberg's view of criticism flowed from his categorisation of artistic genres since, he said, 'every work which answers to the requirements of the genre to which it must be assigned is good, and if it answers perfectly to its concept, then it is a masterpiece . . .'.[47] This principle was not only axiomatic for his own practice as a critic, however, but also throws considerable light on Kierkegaard's literary criticism, as we shall see – and, indeed, on his theory and practice of indirect communication.[48]

Heiberg uses his theoretical artillery to launch a devastating attack on the Romantic theory of poetry, particularly on Adam Oehlenslaeger, the poet of 'The Golden Horns'. The starting point for this assault was a review of Oehlenslaeger's play *The Vikings in Byzantium*. Heiberg criticised the play for an inappropriate use of monologue, declaring this to be an undeveloped lyrical element, unadapted to the specific demands of dramatic poetry. Oehlenslaeger, he asserts, is essentially a lyrical poet whose genius is not up to dramatic production. His best dramatic pieces belong to what Heiberg calls 'immediate or abstract drama'.[49] For although he *is* a genius, he is a genius without reflection. He 'stands on the level of immediacy, and has thus still not awoken to that struggle with the external world which is called reflection'.[50] He is, in addition, totally without irony, but irony is an essential presupposition of all modern drama. When Oehlenslaeger responds to these criticisms by saying that feeling and spirit are worth far more than the coolly critical detachment which alone is capable of taking an interest in such niceties, Heiberg is ready with his answer. Thus, when Oehlenslaeger says '"Let us not therefore coldly hold on to the *form*, but to the *spirit* in a poem," he must be told that it is precisely the form by which we come to know the spirit . . . and the spirit which does not reflect itself in some form does not exist from our point of view.'[51] When Oehlenslaeger goes on to say that 'immediate grief and laughter teach us more than a hundred cold demonstrations', Heiberg tells him that this is exactly what we would expect a poet to say – but a critic cannot allow this to pass itself off as the basis for critical evaluation.[52]

Pride of place in the table of aesthetic genres (even taking precedence over Heiberg's beloved vaudeville) belonged to what he called 'speculative drama'. Poetry, Heiberg asserts, 'is in its highest development speculative . . .'.[53] We have already noted his respect for such speculative poets as Dante, Calderón and Goethe, but he was also prepared to make his own efforts in this direction, notably in the 'speculative comedies' *Fata Morgana* and *A Soul After Death*. The latter was not, strictly speaking, a stage play but a play for reading (although it was staged in 1891), but *Fata Morgana* proved to be a theatrical fiasco. Nonetheless these two pieces are well worth looking at, not only because they help us to understand just what Heiberg's project of fusing Hegelian philosophy with poetic practice meant, but also because they represent the kind of thinking about the relationship between religion and aesthetics which was so important in the immediate background of Kierkegaard's early authorship.

SPECULATIVE COMEDY

Fata Morgana opens with a group of fishermen's wives anxiously awaiting the return of their menfolk.[54] They are alarmed by the appearance in the sky of a mirage over the distant city of Palermo, which vision they ascribe to the power of the fairy Fata Morgana, who represents the power of illusion. The mirage has a special impact on one Clotaldo, who, alone among the men of the village, takes no part in the coral-fishing which is their livelihood. He has travelled as a troubadour in Provence, where he fell in love with Margarita, the daughter of the Duke of Palermo, in whose fiefdom the village lies. What Clotaldo sees in the mirage is an image of the beautiful illusion of art, and, he asks, 'is a beautiful deception not worth more than that which the world foolishly calls truth? Oh! He who only grasps after actuality – *he* is deceived by a false appearance. The eternal is the beautiful image which has neither flesh nor blood, neither marrow nor bone, but is the light thought of the heavy world, dark actuality's clear vision in the sky.' (I,1) From this we learn that he is a romantic dreamer, and the 'story' of the play could well be described as the story of the conversion of this 'Romantic' to Hegelianism.

Clotaldo's father eventually returns with corals of exceptional value. He wants his son to take these to Margarita as a wedding-present – for she is now to be married. He does not (of course) know of Clotaldo's love for the Duke's daughter and cannot anticipate the effect which this mission has on the young poet. Clotaldo is downcast at the news of the impending nuptials, particularly as the groom, Count Alonzo, is a rather unpleasant character; on the other hand, he is elated at the thought of seeing (even if it is only seeing) his beloved again.

Act Two takes us to the fairy-isle to which Fata Morgana has gone to meet her sister, Alcina. Clotaldo, we learn from her, is actually of royal descent and the fairy is disturbed because of a prophecy which says that one member of this royal line will one day destroy her illusory power. She explains to Alcina how she has used her magic to capture humanity in a web of manifold illusions, luring them on to the pursuit of what is merely transient: knightly honour, sensuality and the struggle for daily bread. However, she fears nothing from Clotaldo, addicted as he is to poetry and love, for 'among all the blossoms of illusion which grow in the heaven of dreams there are surely none which fade as quickly as these two'. (II,3) She also tells her sister that Clotaldo, on his way to Palermo, has been overpowered by robbers. They have taken his precious corals, but she has given him instead a magical pearl, which is to entangle him still further in her spells.

In Act Three we find Clotaldo duly sunk in admiration of the pearl, in whose depths he sees a vision of the lovely Margarita. But then she herself actually appears, and he realises that, compared with the reality of her presence, the image in the pearl is as nothing. It is, he says, 'only an image', but 'he who sees the true object praises the image no more, even if it is represented as accurately as it is here . . . my dreaming nature was chained to the image in the pearl. . . . [But now] I feel myself set free in spirit, when I offer up illusion's phantasm for the true appearance.' (III,2) Margarita, we may be sure, feels similarly – but Morgana's sylphs (who have been spying on the loving couple) flee in alarm back to their mistress. There is still, however, the problem of Margarita's fiancé, Count Alonzo, but his treachery is soon to be exposed.

When Clotaldo presents the pearl to the Duke he is knighted as a reward for this noble gift. 'With this sword,' he declares, 'I shall be reminded of the struggle which is to be carried out on behalf of actuality; and the poet shall not himself be ensnared in his realm of images, but shall struggle for the actual truth.' (III,7) Now, the pearl has the property that whoever looks into it will see in it their deepest wishes. The scheming Alonzo, for example, sees in it the ducal crown which he himself covets. This leads to a quarrel breaking out between him and the Duke over possession of the pearl. The Duke denies Margarita's hand to Alonzo, who storms off, vowing to seize both pearl and throne. He soon returns to do just that, but Clotaldo, who now understands the nature of the pearl's magic, shatters it with his sword. Where the pearl had been, a rose bush grows up, the image of a truth 'which has no mere external beauty, but whose spirit is in its [invisible] scent'. (IV,6) Out of this 'true image' comes a sylph who explains to Clotaldo that he is really of royal ancestry and warns him that Margarita has in the meantime been captured by Morgana and taken to her fairy palace in the sky. But Clotaldo has now decisively broken with the whole web of illusion in which he and the other figures of the drama had been entrammelled, and the dénouement begins.

Clotaldo resolves to journey to Morgana's palace. Three winged figures – Trochē, Iamb and Molossos – who represent the technical aspect of poetic art (remember Heiberg's disparagement of Romantic appeals to feeling) come to his aid and so he sets out to rescue his beloved (true Beauty) from Morgana, mistress of illusion. The final encounter takes place on a bridge spanning the two wings of the sky palace. He has already taken Margarita and holds her in his arms when he is accosted by Morgana.

MORGANA: What does this defiance mean? What superior claim do you have?

CLOTALDO: This – that I can now encounter the false delusion with contempt. You are Queen of Illusion; therein lies your strength – is it not so? And since I was bound heart and soul to illusion's world – because love had entrapped me by its power, as had poetry too – you believe that I am yours eternally and can never free myself. But your thinking is mistaken; your understanding does not understand that over against the false there stands the true, the divine appearance.

Your visions borrow their truth from earthly nature, from the transient being which lies behind the wall of actuality; mine take their truth from the Spirit, which has impressed its image in the clay in order to lead it back to the light in which it was [heretofore]. Love is no delusion, though it goes in a robe of clay; poetry consists of truth, even if it consists of images. (V,3)

Furious, Morgana causes the bridge to collapse beneath Clotaldo, but he remains standing, upheld by his invisible winged servants (true poetry is not dependent on immediate inspiration but on technical command and form). Morgana's palace now collapses, and the scene returns to earth, where Alonzo's uprising has been crushed and all ends happily.

The play was premiered on the occasion of the King's birthday in January 1838 and was thus offered not only as a vindication of Hegelian aesthetics over against the 'illusion' of Romanticism, but also as a celebration of the actual, earthly monarchy, the rationality of the real. Yet though this intention, together with the work's polemic against a purely Romantic aesthetic, is broadly in line with Hegelian doctrine, it is clear that there are also significant divergences from the rule of the master – in the play itself and in the overall thrust of Heiberg's aesthetic theory. Hegel's stated aim in his *Aesthetics* had been to give a *philosophy* of art, and he specifically eschewed the attempt to lay down laws of taste or to supply rules for the working artist. Heiberg, however, did not keep such a clear line of demarcation between theory and practice. He seems rather to have taken Hegelianism as a programme for his own poetic productivity. But in terms of Hegel's own principles this would appear to be getting art to perform tasks which can only be done by religion and philosophy. Heiberg's version of Hegelianism is also singularly lacking those historical and theological interests and commitments which informed Hegel's own work. For Heiberg everything seems to be narrowed down to logic and aesthetics.

It seems that these differences were largely unnoticed by other Danish Hegelians. Among these H.L. Martensen was particularly prominent. A theologian (who, in 1834, had been taken by Kierkegaard as his tutor), Martensen was nonetheless profoundly engaged in aesthetic and philosophical issues. In a lengthy review of Lenau's *Faust* for Heiberg's journal *Perseus* (*A Journal for the Speculative Idea*) he criticises both Lenau's and Goethe's handling of the

Faust idea. He sees the legend of Faust as having an essential relation to Christianity, since it depends on the recognition that evil is a spiritual reality, rather than simply consisting in the power of the material world to limit or obscure spiritual existence. Because evil is in this way spiritualised, the conflict between good and evil can take place at any and every level of spiritual life, including the purely intellectual or theoretical plane. This, in fact, is where the conflict portrayed in Faust (man and play) belongs. For Faust 'represents the striving of the human race to establish a Kingdom of the intellect without God'.[55] *Faust* is 'apocalyptic poetry', 'in that it portrays religion as the absolute power in world history triumphing over the worldly principle; in that it reveals the nothingness of the finite and the vanity of the world, it is an anticipation of the day of judgement'.[56] As previous examples of such apocalyptic poetry Martensen cites the *Book of Revelation* and Dante's *Divine Comedy*. *Faust*, however, presents its apocalyptic theme in a more interior, more spiritual manner than either of these. 'Faust is the expression of thinking self-consciousness which turns from faith to doubt and, through doubt (which has become the principle of thinking) is brought to despair.'[57] In this way the drama of Faust has a profound, though contrastive, relation to the Protestant Reformation. Faust is the counter-image of Luther. But, Martensen says, no adequate poetic version of Faust has yet been given. He concludes that

> The real poetic portrayal of the Christian myth of Faust . . . must therefore be still awaited. This will first be able to be produced . . . when the Protestant poet, whose gaze does not merely turn outwards towards nature and history, but spontaneously turns towards the intellectual world itself, completely grasps this *attrait* of his genius, when, with clear self-consciousness he feels his prophetic call, his art's universality.[58]

Was this the summons which led Heiberg, one year later, to stage *Fata Morgana*? Not a 'Faust' story, admittedly, but nonetheless an attempt to give poetic form to the reality of the intellectual world itself. Whatever the answer to this question, Martensen certainly found in the play the exemplification of his idea of apocalyptic poetry – and he responded with due adulation.

In his enthusiastic review of the play he developed his theory of apocalyptic poetry further. Poetry, he says, must be rooted in the actuality of the world, even though it sees this actuality in the light of its own idealism. The present age, however, has a uniquely developed degree of self-consciousness; it is itself idealistic, itself systematic: 'it is the period of systems, not only in the more strict sense of philosophical and scientific systems, but of religious, poetic, political, yes, even industrial and mercantile systems'.[59] In Kierkegaard's work we might read such a sentence ironically – but there is no irony in Martensen's enthusiasm for the 'period of systems'. It is, he goes on, this reflective, systematic world which art must represent, if it is to be a true mirror to the age.

> To make this [the speculative idea] visible to us – *as far as this is at all possible for art* – is poetry's highest task. Only speculative poetry can be the poetry in which we would be able to find a more than partial, a total satisfaction, because not only is it, like all poetry, a mirror which reflects the diverse ideal strivings and expressions of the human race, but it reflects too the Ideas and ideals which govern life.[60]

The poet who is to do all this must have both visionary genius and technical command. The former can be found in Romanticism, the latter in Goethe – but where is the speculative unity of the two?

It must, Martensen says, be looked for in comedy. Tragedy is tied to external distinctions between good and evil, but comedy allows us to distinguish between essence and phenomenon, reality and appearance, 'Comedy rests on the contrast between the true and the inverted world, which latter in all seriousness believes in its own reality – but when this is held up against the light of the idea it is dissolved and evaporates as [mere] phenomenon.'[61] This is precisely the conflict to be found in *Fata Morgana*, the conflict between true and false appearances. Fata Morgana herself represents the false ideality which leads to disappointment with ideality as such. Yet all ideality is ultimately rooted in human freedom and therefore 'one can say that every man himself creates his own Fata Morgana.'[62] One of his few criticism of the play is that it does not bring this point out clearly enough, that is, that Clotaldo's struggle is really with himself.

Heiberg's other apocalyptic drama *A Soul After Death* was to meet with equal acclaim from Martensen. It first appeared in a volume entitled *New Poems* (1841) and concerns the adventures of a newly-deceased soul, a member of the Copenhagen petit-bourgeoisie. He makes his way to Heaven (as his family and the clergyman are sure he will), but things don't turn out as expected. Saint Peter demands that he undertakes a purgatorial pilgrimage, journeying to the sites mentioned in the gospel narrative. The soul does not like this idea. For a start he can't remember them all and, anyway, he'd rather go to America. Surely, he says, Peter is being over-literal – isn't it the spirit of the scriptures that counts? And doesn't the spirit always transcend the capacities of verbal expression? 'That is so among you,' Peter replies, 'but not in Paradise . . . the more clear the Spirit is, so much the less does it economize on the word. He who cannot express his thought in words does not enter Heaven.'[63] But God is incomprehensible, insists the soul. So why do you want to seek him? counters Peter. Eventually the soul agrees that it would be best if he tried his luck elsewhere and he sets off for Elysium. Again, however, he runs into difficulties, since his classical learning is even more deficient than his knowledge of the scriptures.

At last, without knowing where he is, he arrives at the gates of hell. Here he is met by Mephistopheles, and is relieved to discover that here at least is somewhere where anyone can enter – though none may leave. Indeed, his lack of deep thought is even an advantage, for, Mephistopheles says, 'here is surface but no depth'.[64] Hell is described as the Kingdom of Immediacy, a realm of existence without meaning, purpose, history, coherence or form. 'My friend,' Mephistopheles assures him, 'you don't need to delve into all this. It is something no one understands'.[65] Precisely: because in immediacy there is nothing to understand, nothing for the mind to grasp. This is that view of hell which Heiberg had previously ascribed to Dante: 'Hell is for him precisely that self-sufficiency based on immediacy which is merely isolation from everything, neither itself moving towards anything, nor itself necessary for anything else.'[66]

When the soul asks after the name of the place, Mephistopheles is quite consistent in saying that the name doesn't matter, it is only a sound without meaning. That is all language is in hell. But when Mephistopheles is eventually forced by the soul to utter this meaningless sound, the soul is disagreably surprised. Yet, Mephistopheles replies, this is where he has really lived all his earthly life, 'only people are not so accustomed to call that flabby phlegmatic earthly existence which puts all its trust in reality and doesn't even get the glimmering of . . . an idea'.[67] The soul is soon persuaded that hell is, in fact, the best place for him and that he will feel quite at home there, especially since so much of his familiar Copenhagen life will also be there – including his favourite newspapers and the works of F.C. Sibbern and Hans Christian Andersen. Moreover, he is comforted by the thought that his wife will doubtless soon join him. He is at last happy to enter and take part in the common task of hell – to fill a bottomless barrel with water, an apt symbol for the ceaseless, purposeless activity of hell. 'I am so busy with so many things,' complains Mephistopheles, but for all his busyness he gets nowhere and does nothing.[68]

Martensen's review of *New Poems* emphasises that hell, like other dimensions of spiritual life, is a state which can exist *here* just as much as in the hereafter. Thus Heiberg's identification of hell with the world of middle-class Copenhagen is compared favourably with Dante's discovery of elements of contemporary Florence in the Inferno or Swedenborg's visions of Paris and London in the spirit-world. In such instances the two worlds, this world and the next, the finite and the infinite, become transparent to each other. In the case of *A Soul After Death* the truth about Copenhagen which this mini-apocalypse reveals is that it is under the sway of triviality. The play, Martensen says, is 'a contribution to the metaphysics of triviality'.[69] The trivial here is identical with the non-dialectical, the one-dimensional.

> True science and poetry, like faith, see all objects in a *double perspective*, they see them at one and the same time in the form of eternity and in the form of temporality. Triviality [on the other hand] has no copula by which to link finite and infinite, natural and supernatural, thought and experience, *a priori* and *a posteriori*.

Heiberg, he adds, even represents an advance on Dante. For Dante's categories are moral and religious – but not metaphysical. He fails to grasp adequately the distinction between essence and appearance, truth and falsehood, in which comedy is at home. Likewise Dante's Heaven lacks a genuinely Christian humour. In such a humorous Heaven the blessed spirits

> play with the phenomena of their temporal consciousness which, in all the detail of its empirical reality, in all its infirmity and transience, they will have with them in Heaven, because it must serve them as poetic material by means of which their spirit

will lay on for itself the enjoyments of its infinite freedom and blessedness.

In other words, the souls in Paradise will not only find God, but will also find the world again (compare Hegel's doctrine of recollection). In terms of the distinction between tragedy and comedy, tragedy can only go as far as the image of divine judgement but comedy can go on to affirm a good ending, when God will be all in all. 'The "humorous" which belongs exclusively to Christianity includes not only the whole of irony, the poetic nemesis on the fallen world, but also the fulness of love and reconciliation. It comprises the pain of the whole world, but overcome in a rich depth of joy.'

Martensen's enthusiasm was echoed by Dean Tryde, the more conservative, personalistically-minded theologian who had previously chided Sibbern's failure to make due allowance for the divine transcendence and personality. Heiberg's play, he wrote, 'is an actual Apocalypse, an actual insight into the condition into which souls enter after death'.[70] Nonetheless, and *contra* Martensen, he insists that there are aspects of empirical reality which have no place in heaven. 'Can the madman who has been healed be reminded of his undeserved insanity without deep sadness? Certainly never with pleasure.' The voice of God speaks through conscience, and conscience separates and distinguishes between different aspects of this world's reality, approving this but disapproving that. The implication of this, however, is that the total reconciliation between idea and appearance promised by the Hegelians cannot be carried through in its entirety.

NIHILISM

Even though Hegel in certain respects relativised the place of the image over against the 'higher' functions of reason and thought, Hegelianism, like Romanticism, did offer some kind of justification or vindication of the image as a means by which to interpret and communicate the real. The image carries an essentially rational meaning which is fundamentally the 'same' as the truth with which philosophy is concerned, albeit the image expresses that truth in an inadequate manner. The power of the image to interpret life was, however, to be much more seriously challenged by the literary and philosophical generation which followed Hegel. Both Romanticism and Hegelianism held to an ideal of harmony and unity in the light of which the conflicts and discords of existence could be seen to be merely apparent. In the 1820s and 1830s this ideal was increasingly threatened. The left-wing Hegelians and the 'Young Germany' movement challenged the cosmic and historical optimism of the older generation. Even if, as for Marx, history was still seen as moving towards a unifying goal, that goal could only be realised through conflict and violence – but, others were asking, perhaps there is no goal, no 'answer' to the question of existence.

> Why does the just man drag himself,
> Bloody and suffering, beneath the weight of the cross
> While, joyous as a victor,
> The wicked man trots by on a noble steed?
>
> Who is guilty? Is perhaps
> Our Lord not quite so powerful?
> Or does he himself perpetrate these crimes?
> Oh, that would be contemptible.
>
> So we go on asking
> Till, with a handful of earth,
> Our mouths are finally stopped –
> But is that an answer?[71]

That was Heinrich Heine who, with Byron, was one of the leading exponents of this new outlook, irreverent and iconoclastic. For many it seemed that if there were to be any fulfilment awaiting human beings it could not be the fulfilment of a transcendent destiny but the material fulfilment of human needs for food, drink and sex. As David Friedrich Strauss's 'speculative Christology' made clear, the 'idea' of Christ, the God-man, could no longer be understood theologically, but as a symbol for the human race's discovery of its own practically infinite capacity for mastering its material environment and realising its material and social possibilities.[72] Feuerbach's reduction of Christianity pointed in the same direction. Henceforth 'Man' (and the masculine form is appropriate in this context) was not to set his sights on heaven but on the emancipation and enjoyment of his material life in a material world.[73] Strauss and Feuerbach remained basically optimistic thinkers, but for others (especially artists and writers) the disappearance of the transcendental world became the cause of considerable unease. Although Danish thought had, typically, been less extreme than that of Germany, this same spirit was apparent here too. As Richard Summers has put it, 'a new movement arose in Danish literature which took up the themes of disappointment, frustration and despair expressed by contemporary European youth'[74] – and this, we must emphasise, was precisely the period of Kierkegaard's own spiritual and intellectual youth, the context in which his own early thought took shape.

Of particular importance in this respect was Poul Martin Møller (1794–1838), generally acknowledged to have had a significant influence on Kierkegaard's development both as a teacher and as a friend. Møller did not himself share the mood of those he regarded as nihilists, but was quick to recognise the force of their ideas and to realise that this was not just a matter of youthful brashness but the manifestation of a pervasive tendency in modern thought. Although, as the Danish critic Uffe Andreasen has shown, Møller regarded Schopenhauer as the archetypal nihilistic thinker, he believed that the seeds of nihilism were deeply embedded in both Romanticism and Hegelianism. In a striking anticipation of the argument of Kierkegaard's dissertation *On the Concept of Irony*, Møller traced contemporary nihilism back to Fichte and to Schlegel's interpretation of Fichte's thought. Irony, he wrote, 'is a consequent development of the fruitless struggle to construct a self-enclosed ethical system from the standpoint of the individual. This method must necessarily end with the loss of all content, with moral nihilism.'[75]

Møller's own thought is strongly personalistic, but he does not view the human person solely from the standpoint of his or her rational capacities. He maintains that the full development of personal life depends on the acceptance of a proper 'life-' or 'world-view' and he regards such a position as being compounded of three main elements. First, there is the conformity of the self to a realm of higher, ideal experience; secondly, the grounding of the personality in ordinary, empirical experience; and thirdly, participation in the historic, communal life of Christianity. This is a significantly different way of thinking about the self from that put forward by Hegel, especially in the emphasis Møller gives to experience. In what is intended as a clear rebuff to Hegelianism he states that if anyone will now say that true science, or the pure concept in its immanent movement, has nothing to do with the realm of experience, then we will . . . assert that such pure science – as they call it – is a one-sided form of knowledge, and can only become true knowledge if it be permeated by experience.[76]

Since, in his view, Hegelianism does not allow for this experiential element it cannot give a proper place to the concept of personality.

Møller also rejected the notion of finality or comprehensiveness in philosophy. Whereas Hegel believed that philosophy could provide a total interpretation of reality, Møller held that the task of philosophy could never be completed, that philosophical work was always open-ended and could only be expressed through a sequence of individual viewpoints. It was this approach to philosophy, for instance, which he admired in the Greeks. His own writing was, quite consistently, extremely unsystematic. Most of his surviving work is 'occasional', much of it is unfinished and was not published in his own lifetime, whilst a considerable part of his philosophy is to be found in the aphorisms which he called 'Strøtanker' (straw thoughts) and which, he acknowledged, were 'half poetry, half prose'.[77]

His most complete theoretical work was the essay *On the Possibility of Proofs for Human Immortality*, published a few months before his death in 1838. Here he sets his face firmly against what he regards as the *a prioristic* methods favoured by the German idealists. There is *no* philosophical vantage-point (such as Fichte's 'intellectual intuition') or method (such as Hegel's dialectical logic) which can provide a once-for-all foundation for philosophical knowledge. The rootedness of a thinker's concrete world-view in experience not only means that we must always be open to the possibility of new developments but also indicates that philosophical reflection is always already contextualised, and must be related to specific traditions of thought.

Purely on his own, as a single individual, no one would come to consciousness of religious concepts: he who believes that he has put aside external authority, and solely by the free self-activity of thought has gained a new result, which is his purely personal possession, has nevertheless . . . always received a significant impetus from the tradition, without which his thought would have lost itself in subjective, fruitless fancy.[78]

This 'tradition', however, is not construed as narrowly identical with the doctrinal tradition of Christian theology: it is rather that blending of Christian doctrine with the wider tradition of faith and practice embodied in Christian society, a kind of 'Christian culture'.

The three elements which make up the life-view are synthesised through what Møller describes as 'an experience of an higher kind', in which the individual whose horizons have been suitably shaped by Christian culture apprehends for himself 'the presence of the supersensuous in the sensuous'.[79] Thus

> The Christian tradition, empirical experience, as well as the higher experience in which the supersensuous encounters us in a real form at particular times and places, give the discrete points which must have their place in a proper world-view; and the systematic, philosophic exposition only expresses with formal perfection that knowledge which is first present in an immediate way and in an inarticulate form.[80]

This respect for the concreteness of empirical experience and the role of the great 'given' of the Christian tradition is also found in another Danish critic of Hegel, F.C. Sibbern. In what was the first sustained attack on Hegel in Denmark, Sibbern had drawn attention to Hegel's lack of interest in natural philosophy and the empirical sciences, and criticised him for turning Christian faith (which Sibbern regards as first and foremost a matter of living, personal devotion) into concepts, *credere* not *fides*. 'The Kingdom of the Christian fulfilment,' he wrote, 'is something other and more than a *Reich des Wissens*, or than a realm which is to find its Kingdom of God *in a philosophy*.'[81]

Møller's distinctiveness lies in his recognition that the kind of unity which his favoured 'world-view' comprises, is increasingly problematic in the modern world; that contemporary thought seems to be set on a course in which the ideal and the real are being torn apart, and the Christian tradition is no longer strong enough to bring them together again. At the beginning of the *Immortality* essay he wrote:

> I will not deny that I nurture a doubt as to whether the basic view, for whose defence these pages give a provisional contribution, can, by any amount of effort, be vindicated in the present time. It is very possible that negation [that is, nihilism] has still

not reached the point which must be reached, so that it can be made apparent that the desolation it brings with it is not the sphere in which the human spirit is at home. But it is something: those who do not share the peculiar passion for destruction may nevertheless seek to build themselves an ark in which they can establish themselves in the hope of better times.[82]

This judgement not only reflects Møller's view of the philosophical situation – it also pervades his attitude towards the contemporary literary world. For he himself was not solely a philosopher: he was also a highly-regarded poet, novelist and critic. In accordance with his overall philosophical viewpoint he held that the 'immediate way' of figurative and imaginative expression was no less relevant to our understanding of the human situation than the rigours of technical philosophy. In this respect it is striking that he even interrupts the philosophical argument of the *Immortality* essay to insert an anecdote about a bookkeeper and a theological student who are discussing a new book about immortality. Moreover the kind of world-view which he regards as the foundation for all true philosophy is also serviceable as a foundation for good literary practice. Here too, however, he had to admit a doubt as to whether such a position could come to expression in the contemporary cultural climate. Instead of the harmonious ideal of the early Danish Romantics, the 'men of 1803', he identified the Wandering Jew, Ahasverus, condemned to wander the earth forever, as a more representative image of the modern situation. In a small collection of aphorisms entitled *Ahasverus* Møller sketches the philosophy of the Wandering Jew, the man who has seen it all before and who cannot but see through the vanity of all human striving. The following are two typical examples of these aphorisms:

"Your ignorant priests believe that there is an absolute difference between good and evil, but they do not observe that I stand precisely at the zero-point on life's thermometer."

Ahasverus wills nothing. He regards himself as infinitely higher than those who will anything.[83]

The prevalence of the nihilistic mood symbolised in Ahasverus, the inability of the present age to recognise and hold on to the sources of a wholesome world-view, leads to an ever sharper division between those who still treasure the ideal of a harmonious religion-culture and those who are gripped by what Møller calls the 'peculiar passion for destruction'. In his poem 'The Artist Amidst the Tumult' he tells the story of a sculptor whose house and studio are invaded by an insurrectionist mob. When he refuses to join them in their rebellion they wreck his studio, destroy his work and accuse him of cowardice. Thereupon he goes berserk, seizes a bludgeon and lays about him. He plays a leading role in quelling the disturbances and is personally congratulated by the monarch – but he can see nothing to congratulate himself on.

> I am at home in my art
> As a master in his trade;
> I would rather forget
> My bloody work today.
> Its remembrance will darken
> The radiance of my world of images
> And cast a loathsome hindrance
> In place of my visions' dance.
> In my studio, that place of stillness
> I say 'farewell' to the world,
> And I will never act the judge
> Nor slay my fellow men.
> On the blackboard of memory
> This day's deeds
> Will be scrawled, spectre-like
> In a hateful hand.[84]

The artist rejects the violent republicanism of the left – but nor is he concerned to celebrate the established order in the manner of Heiberg's *Fata Morgana*. Instead, he retreats to the inner stillness of his studio, the 'ark' in which he awaits 'better times', gleaning what fragments of light he can from among his darkened images. In such a situation he may well be tempted to renounce even art itself – a temptation addressed in another of Møller's poems:

In melancholy hours I often bewail
You, you nineteenth-century rational man.
Poetry's flower has withered in your fields,
You seek the promised land in a wilderness.

Your child is an old man who never jokes,
His music, the ringing of the chimes of rebellion;
. . .
You are right: it's all up with my poetry,
Now I overturn Art's despised altar.
. . .
And yet – what is life, if the artists flee,
If only seriousness remains, dwelling beneath a roof of ice?
A pitch-dark house, without light or lamp,
And the lime-tree before the door with its coal-black branches.[85]

Art can no longer pretend to offer the key to universal knowledge, as the Romantics had claimed, nor can it maintain an alliance
with the all-consuming spirit of rationalisation, as in Hegelianism:
but amidst the ruins of a broken tradition it may still provide some
kind of refuge for the human spirit, a solitary light in the 'pitch-
dark house' of modernity.

Such a view of the conflict between art and the 'wilderness' of
modernity has been a pervasive theme of much modern art, visual,
musical and literary alike. If Møller's ideals point back towards an
earlier, more optimistic generation, his realisation of the impossibility of carrying through the idealistic programme points forward
to many of the crises of nineteenth- and twentieth-century art.
More immediately, it anticipates crucial themes in the thought of
his pupil and friend, Søren Kierkegaard. As we now prepare to
move to Kierkegaard's own understanding of the aesthetic and the
religious we may note, finally, that for Møller the conflict between
art and nihilism is not merely a theoretical issue. In a poem such as
'The Artist Amidst the Tumult' it is clear that a social and political
dimension is also invoked. If nihilism threatens the eclipse or
banishment of the image this is not simply a notional or 'cultural'
event. The crisis of the image is inseparable from the crisis of
violence and terror which Møller sees as endemic in the new era of
modernity, a violence and a terror which he sees as being theoreti-
cally anticipated in the subjective idealism of Fichte and Schlegel
and, equally, in the negative dialectics of the Hegelian system.[86]

We could go much further in filling in the details of the literary
and intellectual background to Kierkegaard's thought. It was a
time of great ferment and great achievement in Danish culture,
perhaps helped rather than hindered by the smallness of the

Danish scene. Certainly it is possible for us to see in the Danish microcosm the same forces which were sweeping and transforming European culture and politics, miniaturised, individualised, and expressed with force and clarity. It was an auspicious moment for the appearance of a thinker concerned with the fundamental dynamics of religion and modernity, and of art and faith.

2

The Genealogy of Art

KIERKEGAARD, HEIBERG AND MØLLER

As we now begin to explore Kierkegaard's understanding of the relationship between the aesthetic and the religious, we shall start by locating his position in relation to those thinkers and theories which were the subject of the preceding chapter. By setting his work in this context we shall be able to identify assumptions, usages, concepts and themes which show that he was very much a man of his age. This is true even of certain features of his thought (such as the psychological reduction of art which we shall be examining later in this chapter) which reveal a distinctive radicality and brilliance. At the same time we may ask at what point and in what ways Kierkegaard 'goes beyond' his predecessors. The answer to this question, I shall argue, lies in the emergence of his theory and, still more importantly, his practice of indirect communication. In other words – and this might at first seem to be merely stating the obvious – it is precisely Kierkegaard's pseudonymous authorship itself, its form, its style, its content, which makes his work so different and which has brought it about that we today read Heiberg and the rest chiefly on account of Kierkegaard, rather than reading Kierkegaard simply as one more sub-heading of 'Danish literature and aesthetics in the second quarter of the nineteenth century'. For now, however, I shall limit myself to attempting to see him in context, to see how his own position and methodology were shaped by the horizon of contemporary idealist aesthetics. In doing so it will be worthwhile recalling that the cultural world to which Kierkegaard belonged was extremely small. This is true of the German scene and it was even more true of Denmark. In the early nineteenth century, Copenhagen was a city of only 100 000 inhabitants, while a book which sold 500 copies was considered a bestseller.[1] All the Danish thinkers and writers who have been discussed so far lived and worked within the confines of a very narrow social band and were mostly known to each other personally as well as through their work. Sibbern, Heiberg, Martensen, Tryde and Møller were all known to Kierkegaard and, though such factors will necessarily take second place when it is a matter of analysing ideas, this personal element undoubtedly played a role in Kierkegaard's reaction to them. We can, for instance, easily see that the peculiar asperity of many of his comments about Heiberg owes not a little to questions of personality.

Kierkegaard's first published work was an article which appeared in Heiberg's newspaper *Copenhagen's Flying Post*, satirising female emancipation in a rather silly and 'undergraduate' way. This was shortly followed by three rather more serious articles in the same paper attacking aspects of political liberalism. Closely related to these is the talk given to the University Student Association in November 1835, dealing with issues of journalism and politics.[2] The tendency of all these is markedly anti-liberal, a tendency reflecting Heiberg's own position. Teddy Petersen, who has edited a collection of Kierkegaard's early polemical writings, suggests that one of Kierkegaard's main aims in writing these articles was 'to demonstrate his literary and polemical abilities to Heiberg'.[3] Kierkegaard appears to have been gratified by the fact that both another newspaper and Poul Møller thought that the first of the political articles was actually *by* Heiberg himself.[4] Kierkegaard's association with the Heiberg faction at this point was itself the subject of satire: in a series of anonymous broadsheets he was lampooned as Heiberg's 'amanuensis',[5] whilst some commentators have seen Hans Christian Andersen's story 'The Lucky Galoshes' as containing a caricature of the Heiberg household with Kierkegaard appearing as the family's parrot.[6] Kierkegaard's connection with Heiberg is also indicated by his turning down an offer of money from George Carstensen, founder of the Tivoli Gardens, to write an article against Heiberg. Instead Kierkegaard defended Heiberg against Carstensen *en passant* in one of his own articles.[7]

There is therefore reasonable evidence in support of the view that Kierkegaard's literary debut was as a young and talented member of the Heiberg circle. But what was it about Heiberg that attracted him? The situation has, I believe, been well summarised by Frithiof Brandt, who wrote that

As an aesthetician, Kierkegaard was spiritually akin to Heiberg in the highest degree and understood how to appreciate his work as few others did. He found in Heiberg a philosophically supported theory of criticism, which understood the genres of art and their logical characteristics. Furthermore, he found in Heiberg's person that elegant and witty urbanity which was his ideal in his aesthetic youthful years; he found, in general, that highly cultured spiritual aristocracy which was his own.[8]

It is striking (though not surprising) that this estimation emphasises precisely the *aesthetic* dimension of Kierkegaard's attraction to Heiberg. As a further comment on Brandt's assessment we might also add Kierkegaard's own tribute in *The Concept of Irony*, where he compares Heiberg's mastery of dramatic irony to that of Goethe: 'As a poet, Professor Heiberg occupies the same standpoint [as Goethe], and while nearly every speech he has ever written can provide an example of irony's inner economy in the play, there also manifests itself through all his plays a self-conscious striving, which assigns each part its place in the whole.' (*SV* 1, pp.327f.)

It will therefore be appropriate to look for Heiberg's influence on Kierkegaard in the aesthetic sphere itself, where we can find a clear appropriation and development by Kierkegaard of key elements in Heiberg's critical practice. In the 1835 address to the University Student Association Kierkegaard defined the 'task of reflection' as being 'to investigate whether or not the idea has gotten the properly corresponding form'. (*JP*,5116/I B 2) Although in this same passage he also takes pains to repudiate the extreme formalism which forgets that 'form is not the basis of life, but life is the basis of form', his definition of the 'task of relection' as being the investigation of the correlation between idea and form is very much in the Heibergian mould and also provides the key to his own practice as a critic. We shall be looking at his various critical writings in more detail in Chapter 4, but in ail of the works he discusses, ranging from *Don Giovanni* through to French comedies, he can be seen to be seeking formal appropriateness as the hallmark of aesthetic excellence.[9]

Even at the purely aesthetic level, however, his relation to Heiberg was not unproblematic. When Heiberg wrote what Kierkegaard regarded as a haughty and uncomprehending review of *Either/Or*, the *Journals* reveal something of the young author's anger and frustration. 'Professor Heiberg is also accustomed to "preside at the Day of Judgement" in literature. Have you forgotten what happened to Xerxes? He has even taken with him the

scribes who were to record his victory over little Greece.' (IV B 41)
A similar rancour motivates Kierkegaard's description of Heiberg's
readiness to respond to the requirements of the age as a kind of
literary prostitution; 'For some years now Professor Heiberg has
sat all dolled-up in the window of literature and waved to those
going by, especially if it was a dressed up man and he heard a
small "Hurrah" from the next street.' (IV B 49) And, in the same
mood, Kierkegaard writes of himself as a 'wild young horse', while
Heiberg is merely a 'paradeur'. (IV B 37)

When Heiberg later made a condescending and misplaced reference to *Repetition*, the *Journals* show a second bout of anti-Heiberg
polemics, which were to be incorporated into the remarkable but
little-known book *Forewords*.[10]

Yet, quite apart from the element of personal pique in these and
similar notes, there were aspects of Heiberg's thought which were
almost inevitably bound to alienate Kierkegaard, whose preoccupation with religious questions (above all, the problematic of
finding and living out an authentic personal faith) goes back to the
earliest strata of his *Journals*. Thus, Heiberg's extension of comedy
into the realm of metaphysics and apocalyptic aroused Kierkegaard's amusement, suspicion and, ultimately, contempt. 'Perhaps', he asked, 'Professor Heiberg believes that Christianity is a
subject for vaudeville?' (IV A 105) As we have seen, Heiberg's
practice, and the enthusiasm of such theological commentators as
Martensen and Tryde, did indeed seem to point in that direction.

> It may now be just about two years ago that Herr Professor, from
> being the witty, jocular, hilarious poet of vaudeville, who some-
> times seemed to be a bit unorthodox in matters of faith, the
> triumphal polemicist, the aesthete of well-measured step, be-
> came Denmark's Dante, the brooding genius who, in his apoca-
> lyptic poem, gazed into the secrets of eternal life – became the
> obedient son of the Church, from whom the reverend Diocesan
> clergy expected everything that would serve the best interests of
> the Church. (IV B 46)

Was Heiberg now, as 'a serviceable critic, an officious opinion,
let it none too obscurely be understood' to 'undergo a new metamorphosis and reveal himself as the one who was to make clear the
riddles of theology'? (IV B 119)[11] A concise summary of the resulting confusion was later to be provided by the pseudonym Johannes Climacus, who wrote:

I have read Prof. Heiberg's *A Soul After Death*, indeed I have read it together with the commentary by Dean Tryde. I wish I had not done so, for in reading a poetic work one enjoys oneself aesthetically and does not demand the uttermost dialectical accuracy, which is appropriate for a reader who seeks to order his life in accordance with such guidance. If a commentator compels one to seek such a thing in a poem, then he has not helped the poem. (*SV* 9, p.143)

The concept of speculative drama is comic enough – but in a quite unintended and self-ironising way:

He who would set his hope upon a speculative drama serves poetry only insofar as he serves the comic. If a wizard or a sorcerer were to bring such a thing to pass, if by the assistance of a speculative thaumaturge (for a dramaturge would not suffice) it were to satisfy the requirement of the age as a *poetic* work, this event would indeed be a good motif for a comedy. (*SV* 8, p.211)

Kierkegaard's reasons for this revulsion were not, however, purely aesthetic. His questioning of the cultural/philosophical synthesis which undergirded Heiberg's project related to a deeper questioning of the whole basis of Hegelianism and, indeed, of idealism in general. To illuminate this questioning further we now turn to Kierkegaard's relation to Poul Møller, who, as we have seen, had been among those Danish philosophers most critical of Hegel.

If the keynote of Kierkegaard's relation to Heiberg was the admiration of an aspiring young literary lion for the established 'Pontifex Maximus' of Danish literature,[12] his relation to Møller seems to have been one of much deeper personal warmth; and if he shared with Heiberg a concern for formal considerations, he shared with Møller a sense for darker but, perhaps, more substantive questions, a premonition of the radical collapse of the Christian tradition and a recognition of the need to take seriously what one reviewer of *Either/Or* described as 'the rending and dissolution which, like a stream of dissonances, is heard from many of our age's most gifted children'.[13] Again like Møller, Kierkegaard saw in Ahasverus, the Wandering Jew, an apt symbol of the modern consciousness, whilst at the same time sensing the deeply problematic nature of any attempt to restore a brighter and more optimistic philosophy.

Møller, as we saw, had traced the origins of contemporary nihilism back to Fichte's subjective idealism, and especially to the appropriation of Fichte by the Early Romantics – and this was, in essence, the argument which Kierkegaard was to deploy in his Master's dissertation *The Concept of Irony*.[14] Here he declaims against the 'acosmism' and 'docetism' of Fichte's position, arguing that it denies the validity of real, historical existence. By ascribing to the 'I' an almost infinite power of self-creation, Fichte opened the door to a doctrine of the self's absolute and untramelled autonomy – a doctrine taken up by the Romantics in their cult of artistic genius. But, Kierkegaard argues, the world will come to lose all solidity and coherence for the ironic individual who makes this stance his own, and his life will become a meaningless sequence of fragmented moods. The supposedly omnipotent creative personality of the ironist himself is dissolved into airy vacuity, a sequence of events which the Romantic idealisation of the *Taugenichts*, the good-for-nothing, unwittingly reveals. Far from being lord and master of his moods the ironist becomes their victim, and such reconciliation as he manages to bring about between Idea and appearance, ideality and reality, only operates on a purely poetic level: it is *imagined* and not real, an exodus from reality and not a true reconciliation. Only a religious attitude is able to bring about 'the true blessedness in which the subject does not dream, but in infinite clarity possesses himself, is absolutely transparent to himself'. (*SV* 1, p.306)

Now, all these were criticisms which a Hegelian might equally have made, and the extent of the 'Hegelianism' of *The Concept of Irony* have been much discussed.[15] What can scarcely be questioned, however, is that with *Either/Or*, and the abandonment of the academic format of *The Concept of Irony*, Kierkegaard is able to give a far more thorough, more concrete and (in some ways) more sympathetic exposition of Romantic nihilism. In Part I of *Either/Or* – in the 'Diapsalmata', 'The Rotation Method' (which expounds the thesis that boredom is the most significant principle in human life) and in the gatherings of the 'Symparanekromenoi', a fictional fraternity whose name has been interpreted by one translator as 'the fellowship of buried lives'[16] – we hear again the voice of Ahasverus, the philosophy of the 'zero-point'. In a passage such as the following we see the extreme results of irony's self-negation:

Men may well assert that God's voice is not in the raging storm but in the gentle breeze; but our ears are not shaped to hear gentle breezes, but rather to devour the roar of the elements. And why should it not break forth more violently still and make an end to life and to the world and to this short address, which at least has the advantage over other things that it soon comes to an end. Yes, let that vortex, which is the innermost principle of the world . . . break forth, and with vehement wrathfulness bring down the mountains, nations, creations of culture and mankind's clever achievements, let it break forth with the last dreadful shriek which, more surely than the final trumpet, will signal the downfall of all things. . . . *SV* 2, p.156

The beautiful images of Romantic art are no more than a 'painted veil' thrown across this wild vortex. But – and this is the point I wish to emphasise here – Kierkegaard is not simply concerned to show irony its place with true Hegelian magisterial assertion. Instead, with Møller, he senses in himself the sting of such nihilism and is compelled to recognise that it is not merely a deviant or arbitrary phenomenon, but a serious and urgent manifestation of the impending 'storm-cloud of the nineteenth century'.[17]

In his first book-length publication, *From the Papers of One Still Living*, which is essentially an extended review of Hans Christian Andersen's novel *Only a Fiddler*, Kierkegaard commends a 'life-view' closely modelled on the 'life-' or 'world-view' previously described in connection with Møller. But he too sees this 'life-view' as being under attack from the nihilistic tendencies of the age. The book opens with a swingeing criticism of these tendencies, particularly as they are manifested in movements such as the 'Young Germany' movement in literature. Politically, the same principles, the same assumption of a split between the ideal and the real, have even more sinister consequences. Such political nihilism 'begins, like Hegel, with nothing: not the system, but life itself; and the negative moment by which and in the power of which all movements occur (the immanent negativity of Hegel's "concept") is lack of confidence, which undeniably has such a negative power (and this is the good thing about it) that it must end by destroying itself'. (*SV* 1, pp.23f.)

We can see here that Hegel has joined Fichte and the Romantics as being intellectually implicated in the development of nihilism –

although this development will not be able to be limited to the intellectual plane. In this respect it would seem that Kierkegaard is regarding the left-wing Hegelians as being very much the authentic heirs of at least one aspect of Hegel's thought. As the criticisms levelled by Sibbern and Møller had already shown, Hegelianism's absorption of all elements of givenness into the self-development and self-recollection of Spirit and its construction of reality as a historically-realised projection of the dynamic Idea, implied a scepticism no less drastic (though admittedly less obvious) than that of Fichte and the Romantics. As Kierkegaard was to argue in the *Concluding Unscientific Postscript*, all idealism is essentially sceptical.[18] Moreover, there is no great distance from theoretical scepticism or Romantic irony to the kind of negative aspects of modernism which, like Møller, he regarded with great unease: rationalisation, systematisation, standardisation – or, in his own favoured expressions, 'reflection' and 'levelling'.[19]

All this, however, has direct implications for the making and reception of works of art. Whereas Heiberg held that reason, as the actual ground of the image, could serve to re-animate the image in such a way that art could find a new role for itself in expressing and celebrating a fully rationalised reality, Møller and Kierkegaard did not believe that true art could flourish or even, perhaps, survive in a rational, critical age. Good art can only take shape within the aura of immediacy, it must have about it something spontaneous and intuitive. But all of this is precisely what the 'period of systems' (Martensen) destroys, as surely as the rationalisation of agriculture in the Enlightenment destroyed the ancient woodlands of Europe. (*SV* 1, p.23)

Is there, then, no option but to endure the gradual (or even rapid) erosion and dissipation of cultural values by the 'spirit of the age'? Here, at least, Kierkegaard goes further than Møller; for if Møller could not see beyond the possibility of attempting to make some kind of cultural ark, a refuge for the life of the spirit 'until this tyranny be overpast', Kierkegaard pointed towards a radical and original religious resolution of the problem: 'if it is true,' he wrote, 'that the time of immediacy [that is, the time of poetry and art] is past, then what matters is to gain the religious, nothing in between can help'. (*SV* 8, p.214) We shall return to this issue later,[20] but now we turn to his early journals, to see how he developed a theory of art in which, via Romanticism, art itself comes to exhaust its own possibilities in such a way that the dialectics of art themselves point to the need for a religious resolution of the aesthetic crisis of modernity.

ROMANTICISM AND THE CRISIS OF ART

If it is correct to see Kierkegaard's early reflections on art and on the relationship between art, culture and religion as having been framed within the horizons of the kind of theorising represented by Heiberg and Møller, then it is highly unlikely that Kierkegaard himself is going to be categorisable as a 'Romantic' in any easy or obvious sense. On the contrary, his view of Romanticism is, from the very beginning, marked by a certain epistemic distance. Although he respects and admires the achievements and the outlook of the 'men of 1803', and their ideal of informing the intellectual comprehension of life with the warmth, passion and enthusiasm of imagination and feeling, he has clear doubts as to the sustainability of their project in the circumstances of the 1830s and 1840s. His very earliest writings show that he regards Romanticism as, in a sense, already history, an object of concern and enquiry and, moreover, as a movement which has, in its more extreme forms, spawned a multitude of undesirable consequences. In a manner not dissimilar to that of Hegel, who spoke of art as 'a thing of the past', chiefly significant as an object of philosophical reflection and evaluation, Kierkegaard approached Romanticism (and, for both Hegel and Kierkegaard, Romanticism means the absolutisation of the aesthetic standpoint) in search of an understanding. Like Hegel he seeks to show how, in Romanticism, the dialectics of art point beyond themselves, requiring a shift into another sphere or dimension of consciousness; like Hegel he sees the fate of art as being circumscribed by a historical development in which the dynamics of interiorisation, the Christ-event and the overcoming of the 'unhappy consciousness' of the Middle Ages (and, also, of Early Romanticism) played major roles. But whereas Hegel looked in the direction of an objectively valid system of knowledge, recapitulating in a logically rigorous form the inner meaning of art, Kierkegaard looked instead to what Hegel called 'subjective Spirit', that is, psychology. For Kierkegaard it was in the crises and exigencies of individual, personal life that the religious decision chiefly came into play, setting a definitive barrier to the claims of art and aesthetics. What he offers is, in effect, a genealogical reduction of art, which in several respects anticipates Nietzsche's genealogy of morals and religion.[21] But this is not the end of the story, since such a reduction would simply replace one form of objectification (metaphysics or logic) with another (psychology). His later, 'indirect' assault on the aesthetic consciousness would, in fact, explode the categories of existential psychologism as thoroughly as it demolishes Hegelian claims to objective metaphysical knowledge. We are not, yet, however, equipped to develop this statement further.[22] Instead, we shall, for the present, confine ourselves to Kierkegaard's early journals, where we can study the germination and flowering of a psychological understanding of art and of Romanticism which – though he himself would 'go beyond' it – was to continue to resonate throughout his authorship.

The interpretation of the early journals and papers is fraught with difficulties. They contain a great variety of entries, from fragmentary jottings through to extensive drafts for plays, novels, lectures, and newspaper articles. Many commentators have seen these documents as being (at least in part) the first-person testimony of a Romantic youth, the record of a 'Romantic Kierkegaard', repudiated and repressed by, but ever haunting, the mature 'Christian Kierkegaard' who, for all his polemics against the aesthetic, remained under the magical spell of art.[23] My reading of these papers, by way of contrast, sees them as being *about* Romanticism, rather than as an expression of Romantic ideals. In particular I concur with those commentators who argue that the standpoint from which Kierkegaard developed his critique of Romanticism was, however deficiently, Christian and theological at bottom, though dialectical and psychological in method and form. At the same time, I would wish to minimise the extent to which these papers can in any way be read as extracts from a poetic autobiography, calling on Henning Fenger's thorough demythologising of earlier attempts to use this material to construct a biographical portrait of Kierkegaard himself.[24] The character of these writings – though it doubtless contains some personal material – is that of a writer's notebook, a sketchpad, a laboratory, a workshop, a cross-section of 'work in progress'. It is the record of the formation of a literary, philosophical and religious writer, a *persona* who exists for us precisely in his writing, rather than outpourings from the confessional or the psychiatrist's couch. Let us, then, turn now to the texts themselves, and allow them to guide our further interpretation.

In one of the earliest entries we find Kierkegaard spelling out the
basic connection he sees as holding between art and ideality.

> The reason I cannot really say that I positively enjoy *nature* is that
> I do not quite realize *what* it is that I enjoy. A work of art, on the
> other hand, I can grasp, I can – if I may put it this way – find that
> Archimedean point, and as soon as I have found it, everything is
> readily clear for me. Then I am able to pursue this one main idea
> and see how all the details serve to illuminate it. I see the
> author's whole individuality as if it were the sea, in which every
> single detail is reflected. The author's spirit is kindred to me; he
> is very probably far superior to me, I am sure, but yet he is
> limited as I am. The works of the deity are too great for me; I
> always get lost in the details. (*JP*,117/1 A 8)

He goes on, in the same entry, to consider the significance of the
blindness associated with such poetic figures as Homer and Ossian. He takes this to mean that the artist does not merely copy
nature in an external sense, but apprehends beauty by means of an
'inner intuition'. It is the *Idea*, not the external appearance which is
the true source of artistic beauty – a view which, as Sibbern's
lectures *On Poetry and Art* show, was almost a commonplace in
early nineteenth-century aesthetics. At the same time this passage
has important links with other entries from this period where we
find the issue of how to find unity within multiplicity recurring in
various contexts. Theologically, the question occurs in the debate
between predestination versus Manichaean dualism; scientifically,
it has to do with how to provide a unified theoretical explanation
for a mass of empirical details; ethically, how is the individual
going to find an idea capable of giving unity to his life's disparate
strivings?[25] In all these cases, however, the problem of finding the
'Archimedean point' is seen as insoluble and, as such, a source of
doubt and despair. But art is different. In art we *can* find it, we *can*
recognise the idea which gives coherence and meaning to the work
as a whole: the aesthetic 'idea' corresponds to our own receptive
and interpretative capacities because it is an idea springing from
another human being, from one like unto ourselves. Art – as
against nature, divinity or life – is on the right scale. As such it
becomes the source of a 'harmonious joy', (*JP*,5199/1 C 123) and
Kierkegaard echoes Sibbern's talk of an 'ideal rebirth' by saying
that when a work of art successfully integrates its various parts

into an organic whole then it is a case of 'what is sown is perishable, what is raised is imperishable'. (*JP*,5361/II A 312)

As a model of such aesthetic balance and harmony he commends Goethe's *Wilhelm Meister*, in which he perceives a 'well-balanced guidance which pervades the whole.' ((*JP*,1455/1 C 73) The unity of the novel reflects both the firm hand of authorial control and the thematic and philosophical unity of the 'Fichtean moral world-order' represented in the novel. In this way the book is 'truly the whole world seen in a mirror, a true microcosm'.

The intuition of the ideal unity in the art-work brings about what Kierkegaard calls the 'transfiguration' of life. A striking example of what this might mean comes in this account of the joys of reading fairy-tales:

> When I am weary of everything and 'full of days', fairy tales are always a refreshing, renewing bath for me. *There* all earthly, finite cares vanish; joy, yes, even sorrow, are infinite . . . one completely forgets the particular, private sorrows which every man can have, in order to plunge into the deep-seated sorrow common to all. . . . (*JP*,5287/II A 207)

Art thus acquires a privileged position within consciousness, since it is able to create and communicate a sense of unity which natural science, existential experience and theology can only postulate as a *desideratum*. But how far does this privilege extend? Here Kierkegaard is decidedly non-romantic. The privilege of art is precisely its limitation. The unity which art offers quite simply does not resolve the question of unity in other spheres of life, and so the wholeness which poetry and art achieve cannot be looked for in the world. The 'poetic morning-dream of our life' is related to reality as Moses is related to Joshua – the one *sees* the Promised Land, but it is only the lesser figure, the epigone, who actually enters it. (*JP*,859/II A 165) Or, it is like Pharaoh's dreams: when he dreamed first of lean cattle and then of wasted corn he progressed from a lesser to a more appropriate symbol of famine – but his dreams remained dreams which he himself was unable to understand. In the same way, poetry may approximate to life, but without touching it. (*JP*,3651/II A 551) This distance may be even more dramatically expressed, as when Kierkegaard ponders on a mood which is essentially akin to aesthetic experience:

One dozes, as it were, in the totality of things (a pantheistic element, without producing strength as does the religious) in an oriental reverie in the infinite, in which everything appears to be fiction – and one is reconciled as in a grand poem: the being of the whole world, the being of God, and my own being are poetry in which all the multiplicity, the wretched disparities of life, indigestible for human thought, are reconciled in a misty, dreamy existence. But then, regrettably, I wake up again, and the very same tragic relativity in everything begins worse than ever. . . . (*JP*,1019/II A 125)

This passage, which contains a strong allusion to the aesthetic vision of Friedrich Schlegel,[26] makes it clear that such a vision, such a reverie, is powerless to resolve the actual conflicts of existence to which the dreamer must inevitably return. The consequence of such an essentially 'pantheistic' attitude is 'obviously the evaporation of the person brought about by the luxuriousness, the poetic world that the individual projects, in which authentic conscious existence is surrendered and everything is poetry, in which the individual is at most like a flower woven in a damask cloth'. (*JP*,3890/II A 464) In the poetic universe the joy and harmony of aesthetic experience are brought at the price of a dissociation of the self from the real world, the loss, rather than the finding, of the self. In a fragmentary entry Kierkegaard speaks of 'the purely aesthetic' as a 'misty, dreaming, fairy-like existence' (II A 618) – a state for which von Eichendorff's evocative line is normative: ''' – Träume ich denn, oder träumt diese phantastische Nacht von mir?''' (II A 405)[27]

It is, however, not just that the aesthetic, if over-indulged, is able to bring about such a volatilisation of the personality or to perpetuate the split between a merely imaginary harmony and an actual situation of anarchic fragmentation – it is rather that the aesthetic is itself the product of such a split. It is at this point, then, that we can see Kierkegaard's investigations taking a distinctly genealogical turn.

When one understands Brorson's words
When the heart is most oppressed
Then the harp of joy is tuned
not religiously, as they were written, but esthetically, then he

has in them a motto for all poetic existence, which necessarily must be unhappy. (*JP*,800/III A 12)

Poetry and art are, in consequence, intensely ambiguous. On the one hand poetry 'is the cord through which the divine holds fast to existence', but the poet's own lot is 'annihilation of their personal existence as being incapable of enduring the touch of the divine'. This ambiguity can be summed up by saying that 'The poetic life in the personality is the unconscious sacrifice . . . it is first in the religious that the sacrifice becomes conscious and the misrelation-ship is removed.' (*JP*,1027/III A 62) The poet's problem is not that he suffers, nor even that he suffers in excess of the average human being: it is rather that poetic production itself obscures the reality of suffering and thereby prevents the application of religion's radical cure. This cure, though, does not so much remove the suffering as enable a conscious and willed acceptance of it to take place, thereby making the sacrifice conscious. As with Pharaoh's dreams poetry can approximate to an awareness of its situation, but it can never express it directly. Nonetheless, cultural history from the Middle Ages down to the present does show an ever-increasing reflection by art on its own dark roots.

Kierkegaard pays particular attention to three aesthetic ideas which he regards as having a more than usual revelatory force in this connection: Don Juan, Faust and the Wandering Jew. These, he says, are 'three great ideas representing life in its three tend-encies, as it were, outside of religion . . .'. (*JP*,795/1 A 150) These tendencies, moreover, are seen as part of a dialectical development in the direction of an ever more explicit consciousness of the nullity of life 'outside of religion', representing (respectively) sensuous-ness, doubt and despair. Despair is only implicitly present in the figure of the amorous Don who, as the representative of sensuous immediacy, lacks self-consciousness. Faust, the personification of doubt, is a more clearly intellectual figure, yet even he does not have a complete understanding of his own situation. That is left for the Wandering Jew, the man who has freely chosen the way of defiance and who (in the words of E.T.A. Hoffman, excerpted by Kierkegaard) '". . . through the brightest bustle of the world, without joy, without hope, without pain, in dull indifference (which is the caput mortuum of despair) wanders as through an inhospitable and comfortless desert."' (I C 60) This whole develop-ment also has a definite historical dimension, since, although all of

the ideas in one sense belong to the folk-consciousness of the
Middle Ages, Don Juan belongs to this period in a pre-eminent
way, while Faust (as Martensen also maintained) is a parody of the
Reformation (*JP*,1968/II A 53) and the Jew is essentially a figure of
the modern world. (*JP*,737/I A 181) It is, finally, important to note
that all his remarks on these three representative figures indicate
that he conceives of them primarily as *aesthetic* ideas. At several
points this aesthetic connection is quite apparent, as when he
discusses which aesthetic media are most suitable for the different
ideas (lyric, epic or dramatic) (*JP*,1179/I C 58), when he takes both
Goethe and Lenau to task for misconstruing Faust in their rework-
ings of the Faust legend[28] or discusses Don Juan in the context of
Mozart's *Don Giovanni*. (*JP*,4397/I C 125) As *aesthetic* ideas they are
able to show art's ever more clear insight into and expression of its
own nullity when cut off from the divine ground of religion. The
Wandering Jew not only represents 'Modern Man' in his alienation
from God: he also stands for the thoroughly godless artistic situation of the modern world, the fate of an art without meaning or
purpose.

Kierkegaard also brings us to this same point by a more systematic analysis of what we may call 'the dialectics of Romanticism'.
One may, of course, apply a dialectical method to any phenomenon, but Romanticism (according to the early journals) is a particularly suitable case for such treatment since it is in itself highly
and characteristically dialectical. Whereas in classicism the inner
idea is able to find a thoroughly appropriate external expression
and thus, in a sense, come to rest in its expression, Romanticism
represents a situation in which a clear distinction or duality has
emerged between inner and outer, idea and form. In Romanticism
both art and life manifest themselves only by 'a constant pendu-
lum movement'. (*JP*,1545/I A 225) Romanticism will thus appear to
be restless (*JP*,3806/I A 203), lacking integration (*JP*,16/I A 135),
incapable of being given a permanent stable form. (*JP*,3815/I A 294)
Indeed it does embody a conception of life as struggle, as a
constantly self-surpassing striving (*JP*,5131/I C 85), 'a continual
grasping after something which eludes one'. (*JP*,3816/I A 303) No
single image or expression can satisfy the Romantic consciousness
for 'the whole idea cannot rest and be contained in the actual
expression', (*JP*,3807/I A 214) since the expression gives only 'the
image of the shadow'. (*JP*,3816/I A 303) In all of this, Kierkegaard
acknowledges, Romanticism shows itself to be dialectical in the

very specific sense of representing the second 'moment' of the Hegelian dialectic, in which reality reveals itself in irreducibly dualistic forms. (*JP*,1565/I A 225)

This dialectical character can be seen in many features of the medieval world, the Romantic period *par excellence*.[29] The duality of medieval life appears in such phenomena as the separation between scientific and poetic languages (*JP*,2698/I A 213), between monastic and chivalric ideals (*JP*,2745/I A 267), between celibacy and courtly love (*JP*,2581/II A 429), between clergy and laity. (*JP*,2702/I A 284) In another respect the dialectical aspect of medieval life can be seen in the characteristic patterns of Gothic architecture and scholastic method (*JP*,755/III A 92) or in the contradictory features of chivalric sagas and narratives.[30] An unmistakable manifestation of the innate duality of the medieval consciousness is the figure of the licensed fool, the dialectical counterpart of the knightly hero. In the *personae* of Sancho Panza, Leporello and Wagner we find him accompanying the great representative figures of Don Quixote, Don Juan and Faust respectively. (*JP*,4387/I A 122) At this point we can also see the ironic and self-ironising tendency of the medieval dialectic. This cannot be avoided, since every development which takes place in a dialectical or dualistic period will necessarily be one-sided and must end in self-contradiction or self-parody.[31] Thus, the children's crusade can be regarded as 'history's sarcastic comment on chivalry'. (*JP*,2701/I A 281) This tendency to self-ironising, however, means that the despair figured in the *persona* of the Wandering Jew is inherent in Romanticism, although in the medieval world itself it was held in check by the stabilising force of social and ecclesiastical cohesion.[32]

On the other hand, the more the subjective aspect of the Romantic spirit comes to the fore, the clearer will be its essential despair. To explore this subjective aspect (as interpreted in Kierkegaard's early journals), let us now look at the dialectic of moods in Romanticism.

The typical Romantic mood is one of yearning or longing, a longing which is said to be 'the umbilical cord of the higher life'. (*JP*,4409/II A 343) Kierkegaard cites the situation of Ingeborg in *Frithiof's Saga* as being archetypally Romantic, when she sits on the seashore watching the departing sail of Frithiof's vessel. (*JP*,3800/I A 136) Such a mood is hard to define, but Kierkegaard concurs with Jean Paul in likening it to the illumination of an area by moonlight or to the tone waves in the echo of a ringing bell, of a stroked string – a trembling sound that swims, as it were, farther and farther away and finally loses itself in us and still sounds within us although outside of us it is quiet. (*JP*,5135/I C 88)

Romantic longing is just such an oscillation between presence and absence, between the given and the possible. Thus the Jutland Heath and the Arabian Desert are both said to be typically Romantic landscapes, since their very monotony and uniformity allow the mind to float indeterminately in the realm of the possible. (*JP*,3797/I A 131; *JP*,2279/II A 68) Hunting and fishing are likewise Romantic sports whose interest depends on possibility, as opposed to the 'classical' sport of athletics which has to do with discipline and control. (*JP*,3798/I A 132) We can see the same tendency in the 'wandering' characteristic of the Middle Ages, with its wandering knights, scholars, troubadours, friars, etc. (*JP*,3814/I A 262; *JP*,4927/II A 428)

The mood of longing is also reflected in premonition (*Ahnelse*), a concept which, as we have seen, occupied a key place in Henrik Steffens' account of consciousness. According to Kierkegaard, premonition is 'the homesickness of earthly life for the higher, for the perspicuity which man must have in his paradisic life'. (*JP*,92/II A 191) (Compare this with the definition of longing as 'the umbilical cord of the higher life.') But whereas for Steffens premonition was the mode of apprehending the holy unity of the world, Kierkegaard sees it in a more ambiguous light, relating it to evil as well as to good. This, he says, can be seen in folklore, 'permeated' as it is 'with a profound, earnest melancholy, a presentiment [*Ahnelse*] of the power of evil . . . All presentiment [*Ahnelse*] is murky and rises all at once in the consciousness or so gradually fills the soul with anxiety that it does not arise as a conclusion from given premises but always manifests itself in an undefined something'. (*JP*,3551/II A 32) Indeed, it may not merely serve the apprehension of some external evil but also lead the soul itself into guilt and despair:

just as it can have a deterring effect, it can also tempt a person to think that he is, as it were, predestined; he sees himself carried on to something as though by consequences beyond his control.

Therefore one ought to be very careful with children, never believe the worst and by untimely suspicion or by a chance remark (a flame of hell which ignites the tinder which is in every soul) occasion an anguished consciousness in which innocent but fragile souls can easily be tempted to believe themselves guilty, to despair, and thereby to make the first step towards the goal foreshadowed by the unsettling presentiment [*Ahnelse*]. . . . (*JP*,91/II A 18)

It may also relate to the past as well as to the future. In this respect it can arouse the anxious consciousness of original sin (the Danish term for which means, literally, hereditary sin, thus construing it as an inheritance from the past so that the individual is seen to stand within an inherited history of sinfulness). And this anxious consciousness of original sin may also contribute to luring the soul into evil. There is a clear and important correspondence in all this between premonition and anxiety. (*JP*,3557/V B 53:9)

Premonition is also akin to melancholy, another typical Romantic mood. Melancholy is the consciousness of absence, incompleteness or loss. As such it can be a quality of a landscape, as in Kierkegaard's description of Gurre Lake, a lake gradually being overgrown by rushes: 'Here around Lake Gurre there rests a quiet melancholy; the region lives, so to speak, more in the past.' (*JP*,5095/I A 64) It is a mood which embraces the young man of the Gilleleie journal, who is pictured meditating on his departed loved ones until aroused by the cry of a gull: 'the seagull's harsh screech reminded me that I stood alone, and everything vanished before my eyes, and I turned back with a heart full of melancholy to mingle with the world's crowds – without, however, forgetting such blessed moments'. (*JP*,5099/I A 68)

Longing, premonition and melancholy all reveal something of the Romantic sense of time. Romanticism is, typically, dissatisfied with the limitations of temporality: 'the romantic Middle Ages comprehend only one side of eternity – the vanishing of time.' (*JP*,832/II A 100) The same dissatisfaction infects the nostalgia of modern Romanticism for a lost age of chivalry, a nostalgia which Kierkegaard believes to be self-frustrating. (I C 86) The sense of time is also another point at which we can see a clear contrast between the classical and Romantic spirit: 'The classical is present tense; the romantic is aorist.' (*JP*,17/I A 137) The Romantic feeling for time informs the musicality of Romanticism. In Molbech's *Lectures on the More Recent Danish Poetry* Kierkegaard read and noted that music is the most romantic of all arts 'for it exceeds all other art in dealing with the infinite, the inexhaustible, the unfathomable in the soul, but here only through feeling, immediately intuited . . .'. (*JP*,5135/I C 88) Like the basic Romantic mood itself, music can never be precisely defined. Even the perfect tone is not logically or mathematically definable, but is a constant oscillation between the mathematically perfect and imperfect. (*JP*,1024/II A 711) Romantic poetry itself has an essentially musical quality. (*JP*,2304/I A 250; *JP*,5137/I C 89)

All this betrays the fundamentally dialectical character of Romanticism. As such it is unable to achieve a definitive affirmation of meaning or truth; conscious of the dark flux of time, it has an evil premonition, an anxiety, coiled in its heart, and in this anxiety it intuits its ultimate succumbing to guilt and despair. The phenomenology of Romantic moods which we have just sketched gives a figurative and oblique expression to this consciousness. The issues come to a head, however, with the analysis of irony and humour.

Irony and humour are often described by Kierkegaard as being two aspects of what is essentially the same existential situation, with irony as the objective and humour the subjective pole of the dissociation between ideality and reality, between self and world.[33] Or: 'humour is irony carried through to its most powerful vibrancy'. ((*JP*,1699)/II A 136) They are like the two ends of a seesaw, with irony lying below and humour lifted above the point of balance. (*JP*,1671/I A 154) That is to say that the ironic individual suffers under his separation from reality whereas the humorist rises above it. In this respect irony remains entrammelled in the dialectical phase of existence (that is, it corresponds to Romanticism), whilst humour is closer to the concept of character in its transcendence of the ambiguities and contradictions of dialectics. (*JP*,1676/I A 239) Unlike irony, humour is not founded on the self-projective dynamism of the Idea (or the 'I') but on the Christian revelation, presupposing as it does the Christian negation of the world in its entirety. Humour understands that

everything which hitherto had asserted itself in the world and continued to do so was placed in relation to the presumably single truth of the Christians, and therefore to the Christians the kings and the princes, enemies and persecutors, etc., etc., appeared to be nothing and to be laughable because of their opinions of their own greatness. (*JP*,1674/I A 207)

Whereas irony simply plays off one aspect of the world against the other, humour relativises the world in its entirety. Thus Kierkegaard pictures 'a travelling humorist who is making preliminary studies, preparatory work for a theodicy – he travels about seeking as far as possible to experience everything in order to prove that everything is a disappointment'. (*JP*,1736/III A 98) In this respect the humorist has a certain resemblance to Ahasverus, the Wandering Jew. He is entirely solitary, like a beast of prey (*JP*,1719/II A 694) or like Robinson Crusoe on his desert island, for humour is 'absolutely isolated, independently personal'. (*JP*,1699/II A 136) The humorist has a clear insight into the essential agony of the human situation which the ironist (or the poet) cannot achieve.

> When an ironist laughs at the whimsicalities and witticisms of a humorist, he is like the vulture tearing away at Prometheus's liver, for the humorist's whimsicalities are not *capricious little darlings* but the *sons of pain*, and with every one of them goes a little piece of his innermost entrails, and it is the emaciated ironist who needs the humorist's desperate depth. His laughter is often the grin of death . . . (like the dead man's grin which is explained as the muscle twitch of rigor mortis, the eternally humorous smile over human wretchedness). . . . (*JP*,1706/II A 179)

The humorist's 'desperate depth' not only puts him on a different level from the Romantic ironist, it also puts him altogether outside or above the merely aesthetic standpoint: 'humor is not an esthetic concept, but life . . .'. (*JP*,1699/II A 136) It follows that it can only achieve an ambiguous and (aesthetically) unsatisfying expression in literature; that aesthetic harmony of idea and form which is gained at the cost of severance from the actuality of life eludes the humorist. In this respect the fragmentary and obscure literary inheritance of J.G. Hamann (Kierkegaard's constant paradigm of the standpoint of humour) is typical.[34] Similarly the humorist is far removed from the systematising ambitions of the philosopher who 'believes that he can say everything', since 'he lives in the abundance and is therefore sensitive to how much is always left over . . .'. (*JP*,1702/II A 140) Like the Christian revelation itself its truth is always concealed even in the very act of communication – a point which foreshadows Kierkegaard's own concern with 'indirect' forms of communication. (*JP*,1682/II A 78)

Yet there is also a tremendously positive side to humour. If

humour sees through the vanity of the world it is 'also the joy
which has overcome the world'. (*JP*,1716/II A 672) Over against
irony, the world of the humorist is a world in which, as 'Paul says
of the relationship of Christianity to Judaism: "All is new."'
(*JP*,1711/II A 608) The Christian humorist is like a plant whose
roots alone are visible, while his flower unfolds before a higher,
invisible sun. (*JP*,1690/II A 102) His apparent pessimism is an
incognito, his pain the mask concealing a higher joy: 'Humor is
lyrical (it is the most profound earnestness about life – profound
poetry, which cannot form [*gestalt*] itself as such and therefore
crystallizes in baroque forms . . . the *molimina* of the higher life).'
(*JP*,1690/II A 102)

The Christian nature of humour is testified historically as being
characteristic of the medieval Church (*JP*,1698/II A 114), manifesting itself in such phenomena as 'der Narrenpapst, der Kinderbischof,
der Abt der Unvernunft'. (*JP*,1687/II A 85) Yet when it is most truly
itself, humour cannot be objectified or institutionalised in this way,
but is intensely individual and personal.

Who, then, is the humorist? As an observer of the human
situation he is someone who has lived through and seen through
the nullity of the unhappy consciousness of Romanticism which is
also the unhappy consciousness implicit in all forms of aesthetic
experience and expression. Like the poet, the 'unconscious sacrifice', he also suffers; but like Prometheus his suffering is something for which he can make himself fully and consciously
responsible. He is essentially beyond the dualistic consciousness,
manifest in both historical and individual life, which is unable to be
at one with either itself or its world. Even when he is despised,
rejected and misunderstood by the world he does not lose sight of
the invisible sun which illuminates his inner existence and makes
sense of his suffering. This inner confidence enables him to confront the utter relativising of all aspects of life, fit to survive in the
bare deserts of modernity. He is a suitable companion for Ahasverus on his lonely path of despair, but he does not himself
despair, does not grow hard against either himself or others. He is
a sign, pointing to the Christian resolution of the crisis of art in the
modern world, able to pity the withered flower of poetry in the
barren fields of the nineteenth century (Møller) because his own
life is turned towards God, like a hidden flower, hid with Christ in
God.

The journal entries which we have been examining here all

predate the inception of Kierkegaard's mature authorship. They show that he was, from the very beginning, not only concerned with finding a way in which to express his own personal crises and dilemmas, but with seeking an understanding of art and of the fate of aesthetic ideals in the modern world. In the dialectics of Romanticism we are invited to see how the aesthetic consciousness itself prepares the way for its own downfall, especially in the way in which Romanticism gives voice to feelings of melancholy, premonition and anxiety. These dialectics, however, are also worked out on a historical time-scale in such a way that the ultimate crisis of art and of Romanticism is in a quite unique way a matter for 'the Now': now that the despairing voice of nihilism is making itself heard with unprecedented clarity, the way of art itself is brought into question in a hitherto unknown manner. The search for an understanding at this point becomes the requirement of a decision – whilst the figure of the humorist indicates the direction in which that decision will lead.

Before moving any further in that direction, however, let us go back one step and look more closely at what I have referred to as Kierkegaard's genealogical reduction of art, a reduction which is adumbrated at several points in the early journals, but which was to continue to play a not-insignificant role in the mature authorship.

THE GENEALOGY OF ART

Kierkegaard's *Either/Or* was his first major pseudonymous work. Its first volume opens with a collection of 'Diapsalmata', highly poetic aphorisms expressing the philosophy of aesthetic despair. The first of these contains one of Kierkegaard's most powerful images, alluding to the legend of the tyrant Phalaris who had a brazen bull in which he roasted his enemies alive, while a system of carefully contrived pipes transformed their screams into music.

> What is a poet? An unhappy man who conceals deep pains in his heart, but whose lips are so fashioned that when the sigh and the cry pass out of them they sound like beautiful music. His situation is like that of the unfortunate person who was slowly tortured by a soft flame in the Ox of Phalaris, whose screams could not reach that tyrant and so affright him because he heard them as sweet music. (*SV* 2, p.23)

But art is not merely the sublimation of suffering in beautiful images, for the artist is, as we have already seen, precisely an *unconscious* sacrifice, who does not understand and therefore cannot escape from his situation of suffering and alienation. Moreover, just as neurotic anxiety is compounded by the subject's attempts to evade recognising the actual causes of his behaviour and thought, so the suffering of the artist is in part to do with his unwillingness to expose his need of healing. His addiction to beauty reinforces and perpetuates his inability to see that split between ideality and reality which gives his images their peculiarly intense allure. Even when, as in aesthetic nihilism, the artist proclaims a philosophy of despair, this proclamation remains existentially ineffective. Thus, to stay with *Either/Or* I, the essay 'The Rotation Method' commends a philosophy of ultimate boredom and meaninglessness. Boredom, the essayist tells us, is the supreme principle of life, and the motor-force of history.

The Gods got bored, therefore they created human beings. Adam got bored because he was alone, therefore Eve was created. From that moment boredom entered into the world, and increased in extent precisely in proportion to the increase in population. Adam got bored alone, then Adam and Eve got bored *à deux*, then Adam and Eve and Cain and Abel got bored *en famille*, then the multitude of peoples in the world grew and the peoples got bored *en masse*. To distract themselves they got the idea of building a tower, which was so high that it reached up into the clouds. This idea is just as boring as the tower was high, and a fearful proof of how boredom had got the upper hand. Then they were scattered across the world, as one nowadays travels abroad, but they continued to get bored. (*SV* 2, p.264)

So, what is to be done? For the author of the essay there is no final 'answer' to boredom. Instead, the *ennui* of existence is to be kept at bay by the subtle manipulation of remembering and forgetting such that the monotony of life is broken up into a multiplicity of experiences. This is the 'rotation method' whereby the aesthetic personality constantly shifts from one viewpoint to another, not neglecting the most arbitrary or capricious. In this way an almost infinite variety of perspectives can be brought into play in even the most banal or trivial situations.

One sees the middle part of a play, one reads the third part of a book. In this way one gets a quite different pleasure from that which the author has been so good as to intend for one. One enjoys something absolutely accidental, one observes the whole of existence from this standpoint, and lets its reality be wrecked on it. (*SV* 2, p.276)

The philosophy of post-modern aesthetics?[35] In any case, it is fitting that this essay immediately precedes 'The Seducer's Diary', since the Seducer himself can be regarded as a pre-eminently skilled practitioner of the method. He is, as is well known, no Don Juan, no masterful sensuous presence, but a man of intrigues for whom the 'interesting' aspect of a relationship is of much greater value than mere sexual gratification. A long, complex and delicately nuanced process of psychological manipulation is what gives him most enjoyment. He seduces by means of words and ideas rather than by glamour or potency. The 'stage' on which he carries out his seduction is the interiority of the victim's consciousness, and his aim is to create an 'interesting' situation on this stage which he can then relish – being as much a spectator as an actor. Indeed, the alarming associations of the title 'the Seducer' should not mislead us. This is no Miltonic Satan nor yet a Hercules of the bedroom. This is a man incapable of genuine relationships, incapable of love, friendship and contentment, a narcissist, a *voyeur*. What incites him is the possibility of extracting an image from a situation, which he can then take away and enjoy in the privacy of his own mental world, without having to confront the reality of the Other. Unable to allow for the irreducible otherness or autonomous freedom of those he manipulates, his view of life is essentially pornographic. He is sheer perspective, a sequence of ideas with no intrinsic or sustainable relation to reality.

Once again, as in the early journals, the sense of a gap between ideality and reality arouses anxiety in those associated with the Seducer. Victor Eremita, the pseudonymous editor of *Either/Or*, writes of the anxiety felt by 'A' himself in relation to 'The Seducer's Diary'. ('A' is the 'name' of the aesthetic young man whose papers, including the Diary – which he claims to have purloined from the Seducer himself – make up the first part of *Either/Or*.) 'The mood which governs A's introduction [to the Diary] in a manner betrays the poet. It is actually as if A himself had grown afraid of his poem, which, like a disturbing dream, continues to cause anxiety even as

it is being told.' (*SV* 2, p.14) 'A' himself describes the world of the
Seducer as a 'nebulous realm, a dream-world, where every moment one is scared by one's own shadow'. (*SV* 2, p.287) Such
anxiety (or *angst*) is an implicit acknowledgement of the unan-
swered claims made by reality on the poetic consciousness. A
persuasive and brilliant description of the genesis of the *angst*
which must inevitably haunt the poet is given by the Assessor
William in Part II of *Either/Or*, as he seeks to challenge 'A' into
taking a more serious view of life. The Assessor takes as an
example the Emperor Nero, whose life of absolute power and
dissipation

> however depraved it may be, has nonetheless matured his soul,
> and yet, despite all his understanding of the world, despite all
> his experience, he is still a child or a youth. The Spirit's immedi-
> acy cannot break through, and yet it requires a breakthrough, it
> requires a higher form of existence. But if this is to happen, then
> there will come a moment when the splendour of the throne, his
> power and dominion, will grow pale, and he does not have the
> courage for this. Now he catches at pleasure, all the cunning of
> the world must be used to devise new pleasures for him, for he
> can only find rest in the moment of pleasure, and when it is over
> he gasps with weariness. . . . Then the Spirit in him gathers
> itself like a dark cloud, its wrath broods over his soul and it
> becomes an *angst*, which does not cease, even in the moment of
> enjoyment. See, therefore his eye is so dark that none can bear to
> look at it, his glance flashes so angrily that it causes anxiety,
> because behind the eye lies the soul, that is like a deep shadow.
> One calls the glance 'royal', and the whole world goes in awe of
> it, and yet his innermost being is *angst*. . . . He is a riddle to
> himself, and *angst* is his essence. . . . (*SV* 3, pp.174f.)

Thus Nero, and thus the poet. A more detached explanation of his
predicament follows shortly:

> There comes a moment in a person's life, when immediacy is, as
> it were, mature, when the Spirit requires a higher form, when it
> will grasp itself as Spirit. As immediate Spirit, a person is
> interdependent with all other forms of earthly life, but now the
> Spirit will, as it were, recollect itself out of this dispersion and
> become transparent to itself: the personality will become conscious

of itself in its eternal validity. If this does not happen, if the
movement is prevented, it is forced back, and thus melancholy
enters in. (*SV* 3, p.177)

It is at this point, the point when the dialectical phase of consciousness has run its course and requires a reintegrative movement, that we find the absolute frontier between the aesthetic and
the religious. We might call it the moment of choice, a moment
towards which the aesthetic points, though not able to encompass
it itself. The threshold of this moment – and we have already had a
number of clues regarding this – is also the subject of *The Concept of
Angst.*[36] For *angst* too exists in the tension between the ideal and
the real, between the unconditional freedom of the human subject
and the phenomenal conditionedness of human life as it is lived.
As such, *angst* is the condition, or state, out of which the subject
must, in freedom, become responsible for itself, in faith or in sin,
becoming or failing to become itself.

> *Angst* can be compared to dizziness. He whose eye looks down
> into the abysmal depths grows dizzy. But the cause is as much in
> his looking as in the abyss itself, for it would not have happened
> if he had not looked down. Similarly, *angst* is the dizziness
> caused by freedom which occurs when the Spirit wills to bring
> about the synthesis, and freedom looks down into its own
> possibility. . . . (*SV* 6, p.152)

Angst contains the premonition of the freedom which the human
subject is called to be. Yet, because this freedom is a transcendent
characteristic of personhood, irreducible to any set of finite causes,
conditions or appearances, we can never, in fact, define exactly the
content of *angst*. In *angst* we find ourselves related to that which
does not (at least, as yet) exist, what is only possible, a lack, an
absence, a void, an abyss, a nothing. 'If we now ask more closely
what the object of *angst* is, then the answer must as usual be that it
is nothing. *Angst* and nothing stand in a constant reciprocal relation to one another.' (*SV* 6, p.183)[37]
The transcendent character of freedom, and its relation, in this
very transcendence, to nothingness, can be illuminated from
another angle if we consider the way in which Kierkegaard con-
strues the task of becoming subjective (that is, becoming the
freedom we are) as interdependent with the human longing for an

eternal happiness. For though the human person is, from a Christian point of view, to be understood in and through its destiny as the prospective recipient of such a happiness, we, as existing human beings, cannot claim to be already in occupation of an eternal standpoint. We can only relate to eternity from the (shifting) standpoint of creatures who know only the tension of temporal existence, and who are permeated by the annihilating flux of time. But time too (as philosophical idealism as well as popular devotion has long maintained) corresponds to nothingness. There is therefore an analogy between the relation of *angst* to freedom and the relation of time to eternity, as these issues concern existing human beings. Moreover, in the same way that the Romantic consciousness itself betrays a dawning recognition of *angst*, so too it (Romanticism) brings into play a sense of the 'vanishing of time', the negative reflex of the self's relation to eternity.[38]

Whether we define the self in terms of freedom or eternal happiness, however, it does not have any immediate participation in the plenitude of its destiny. To attain fulfilment it must traverse the dual abyss of *angst* and time. If this is to be taken fully seriously it means that we must face the question as to whether we are in any way justified in believing in absolute meaning, absolute value, absolute reality, absolute truth at all – or whether we are altogether and in every way transient, mutable and contingent beings, journeying from the wild vortex of *Either/Or's Symparanekromenoi* to death and extinction.

But what has this to do with the genealogy of art? Much in every way. For insofar as art offers a plenitude of experience, a communion of ideas, it pre-empts the actual requirement laid on the self to pierce the mystery of nothingness in which the secret of human life lies hidden, and this act of pre-emption is scarcely innocent. Instead of embracing and living the vision of the void, art seeks to conceal and to avoid that vision, giving to 'airy nothing/A local habitation and a name'.[39] But freedom and fulfilment can only be won in and through a paradoxical resolve which affirms the full seriousness of mortality, refusing the reification and objectification of what transcends image, language and logic alike. Art is in this way a paradigmatic case of the human subject's flight from freedom, an almost irresistible mechanism of repressing the consciousness of what we are called to be. The 'meaning of art' is precisely the void itself, nothingness, *angst* – but this is exactly what art itself is unable to realize or to express. Yet art is

not the only example of such radical self-deception in human life –
it is only the best, the clearest, the most transparent. Kierkegaard
thus extends his genealogical reduction of the aesthetic to many
other phenomena: the clergy of the Established Church who are
derided as 'poets' (a charge which has nothing to do with the
literary quality of their sermons);[40] the bourgeois philistine, the
sort of character portrayed in Heiberg's *A Soul After Death*, is also
essentially 'aesthetic';[41] so indeed is the age itself, not to mention
Established Christendom in its entirety.[42] For in all of these instances we can see a masking and a mystification of those issues
which most need to be faced if human life is to accomplish its
religious destiny. In this respect art is very much a mirror to the
age – though in a sense quite different from that intended by
Heiberg and Martensen. But if art cannot communicate the mystery of human freedom, if its 'holy, radiant images of the eternal'
turn out to be illusory, then what can be used for such communication? *How* can faith, freedom and eternity be represented in such
media of communication as are available to human beings? To
answer these questions we turn now first to the theory and then to
the practice of what Kierkegaard called 'indirect communication'.

3

The Dialectics of Communication

TOWARDS A RHETORICAL THEOLOGY

We have surveyed the immediate background of Kierkegaard's thought with regard to the relationship between art, philosophy and religion and we have indicated something of his own standing *vis-à-vis* the various positions represented in this background. We have also seen how his early journals offer the outline of an ambitious account of the dialectics of the aesthetic consciousness, showing (in a manner not too far removed from that of Hegelianism) how that consciousness develops towards an increasingly dialectical, interior, subjective and, ultimately, despairing standpoint. At this point Kierkegaard's own distinctive psychological perspective comes into play and he indicates that the resolution of the contemporary malaise of aesthetic nihilism can only be found in an individual, personal faith, such as that which he characterises as 'humour'. At the same time the origin of the aesthetic consciousness itself is shown to be in a form of 'unhappy consciousness', a failure to respond adequately to the profound psychological and spiritual contradictions of human existence. This is then the basis for a psychological reduction of aesthetics which is carried over into the mature authorship and which points to the state of *angst* as both the ground and the limit of the aesthetic consciousness. Much more could be said about this aspect of Kierkegaard's critique of aesthetics, its terms and concepts could be defined more closely and its relation to other forms of psychological reductionism (notably Nietzsche's and Freud's critiques of religion) highlighted. However, I want now to suggest that, interesting as this might be, it is not where the real cutting edge of Kierkegaard's treatment of these issues lies. This is, instead, to be found in both his theory and his practice of Christian communication, a theory and a practice in which the tension between what he called 'direct' and 'indirect' forms of communication is particularly prominent. To look at the issue in this light is to move away from an interpretative position which must inevitably come to grief on the notorious and vexatious problems of Kierkegaardian 'individualism'. For his view of individual life was both extremely sombre and, from a theological point of view, verging on the unorthodox in the extent to which he seems to depreciate the totality of the individual's sensuous-somatic life. It is for this reason that a psychological interpretation often proves discouraging to potential readers.[1] But his case against 'the aesthetic' does not depend solely on the validity of his psychological theory. Instead, as I have suggested, it has more to do with his understanding of the forms and dynamics of communication. Let me use two quotations to indicate the direction in which my argument now lies, the first from the journals, the second from the *Concluding Unscientific Postscript*: 'A new science must be introduced: the Christian art of speaking, to be constructed *admodum* Aristotle's Rhetoric. Dogmatics as a whole is a misunderstanding, especially as it has now been developed.' (*JP*,627/VI A 17) And: '*In objective terms it is* WHAT *is said that is emphasised; in subjective terms* HOW *it is said*.' (*SV* 9, p.169)

What is the 'misunderstanding' of dogmatics to which the first quotation refers? It is, I suggest, a view which sees dogmatics as having to do primarily with *knowledge*, a view which, in many respects, is widely shared both by those who see dogmatics as needing an intellectual foundation within the realms of 'natural' reason or experience and by those who see it as an autonomous 'theological science'. The current development of dogmatics which Kierkegaard particularly deprecates here will therefore have to do with the way in which, under the influence of idealism, the scientific (*wissenschaftlich*) element of dogmatics had been especially brought into prominence. This might, in the first instance, seem to be directed against the Hegelian attempt to explicate the basis of Christian doctrine metaphysically, but it would apply equally to all attempts to accentuate the knowledge component of dogma, including those which adopt a historical or (most pertinently) a psychological approach. Psychology, in Hegelian terms 'the doctrine of Subjective Spirit', is, after all, just as much a part of 'the System' as logic or aesthetics. Though concerned with subjective life it is nonetheless 'objective' in that it takes subjective life as an object of investigation, analysis and description. It is for this reason that Kierkegaard is so insistent that the psychological enquiry *The Concept of Anxiety* does not and cannot *as a psychological work* deal with such dogmatic concepts as sin.[2]

Equally, the repudiation of this 'misunderstanding' of dogmatics differentiates Kierkegaard's project from that of Romantic idealism. For although Romanticism seems to champion imagination, intuition, feeling and art over against the rationalistic emphases of Hegelianism it nonetheless interprets these as media by which we gain access to the true nature of things. The aesthetic intuition, as Schelling put it, is to serve as 'the organon of philosophy',[3] as a means of breaking the epistemological dilemma bequeathed by Kant. Similarly, Steffens' concept of premonition was offered as a way by which 'Nature's eternal life speaks to our spirit, as if through a mystical cipher which inwardly we understand.'[4] Art was, in short, seen as a true and adequate expression of the Idea, the transcendental 'I', a mirror in which that Idea gives itself to be intuited by human minds. To put it another way: the aesthetic intuition is ontologically secure, a true and unsurpassable revelation of Being.

It is in the light of such reflections that we might read the second of our quotations: '*In objective terms it is* WHAT *is said that is emphasised; in subjective terms* HOW *it is said.*' Now this might very well seem to invite an existential reading as some kind of exhortation to consider the matter in hand with passion, concern and 'fear and trembling' rather than with an eye to theoretical exactitude. Again, however, though we *can* find such exhortations in Kierkegaard's work that is not the only, nor even the most important thing, he is saying here. If we connect it to his concern to introduce 'a new science . . . the Christian art of speaking, to be constructed *admodum* Aristotle's Rhetoric' then the emphasis on the HOW appears in a more formal, methodological aspect. We might, for instance, go on to relate this distinction back to the kind of approach to aesthetics advanced by Heiberg and, to a certain extent, taken up by Kierkegaard himself; an approach, namely, which seeks to bring about the maximum congruence between content and form and which regards any mismatch between them as a sign of literary bungling. The requirement to emphasise the HOW thus involves the further requirement to give proper heed to the *form* of religious or subjective communication. It is *not* an open invitation to unstructured 'self-expression'. It also illustrates from another angle why it would be a mistake to reduce Kierkegaard's critique of aesthetics to the level of descriptive psychology, for such an approach would mean that Kierkegaard was merely offering us a

new WHAT instead of encouraging us to pursue more rigorously
the significance of the HOW. To emphasise the formally rhetorical
concern with the means and methods of communication, and to
examine the way in which this concern gives his work its very
specific and unique shape is, however, to pursue his own plea on
behalf of the HOW all the way. In particular I shall argue, both in
this and in subsequent chapters, that his authorship leans heavily
on the Heibergian idea of an essential interdependence of content
and form and that the form of his aesthetic works is in fact
subverted – deliberately subverted – by the religious content to
which such aesthetic forms are unable to do justice. The principle
behind such a procedure is enunciated succinctly by the pseudonym Johannes Climacus: 'The more perfect the contrast of form,
the greater the inwardness . . .'. (*SV* 9, p.202) This, however, is to
anticipate. For the present I wish to make only one further point: to
see Kierkegaard's concern for rhetoric, for communication, as
central to his authorship is to abandon once and for all any attempt
to portray him as a philosopher of individualism and to render
illegitimate all charges of solipsism and acosmism which might
relate to such supposed individualism. For concern about communication (certainly concern of the kind which Kierkegaard
showed) points to a view of the individual as being 'always already'
a member of a community of persons, situated in a specific cultural
and historical situation, constantly receiving and transmitting
messages through words, images and gestures. It is this view of
the individual as involved in intricate and manifold networks of
communication which gives to Kierkegaard's critique of the aesthetic its distinctive and urgent shape and his call to 'become an
individual' in a radical and interior sense is inseparable from the
requirement to fulfil our obligations as communicators who have
an appropriate responsibility towards the other participants in the
process (including, we may add, God, as supreme instigator and
respondent of all communication).

I have been at pains to stress the originality and distinctiveness
of Kierkegaard's approach to communication. That is not, however, to say that it is entirely without precedent. We may, for
instance, recall that the position of the humorist, outlined in the
preceding chapter, was said to be communicable only in a fragmentary and oblique manner on account of the transcendent
premises which the humorist's position presupposes. A model of
such an authorship was that of J.G. Hamann, for Kierkegaard the

humorist *par excellence*. Hamann described one of his own works as a 'rhapsody in cabbalistic prose' and its uniquely provocative mixture of philological erudition and epigrammatic pith makes quite peculiar demands on the reader.[5] Another possible model for Kierkegaard's own authorship might be found in Schleiermacher's *Vertraute Briefe über die Lucinde (Confidential letters on Lucinde)*. These contained Schleiermacher's qualifiedly approving response to Schlegel's novel *Lucinde* and was presented in the form of a series of letters circulating among a group of friends on the subject of the novel. Kierkegaard wrote of it:

> It is probably a model review and also an example of how such a thing can be most productive, in that he constructs a host of personalities out of the book itself and through them illuminates the work and also illuminates their individuality, so that instead of being faced by the reviewer with various points of view, we get instead many personalities who represent these various points of view. But they are complete beings, so that it is possible to get a glance into the individuality of the single individual and through numerous relatively true judgements to draw up our own final judgement. Thus it is a true masterpiece. (*JP*,3846/I C 68)

The novel *Lucinde* was of particular importance to Kierkegaard, and as many of the issues which it raised for him recur throughout his 'aesthetic' authorship it is not implausible to see Schleiermacher's work as contributing, at least in part, to the formal as well as the substantial aspects of that authorship.[6] Schleiermacher himself, however, is only one example among many in Romantic literature of the fusion of literary and philosophical forms. The ideal romantic novel contained a variety of genres (*Lucinde* itself being a case in point) and it would be no surprise to readers to find the discussion of serious philosophical and religious issues juxtaposed to passages of humour, narrative or verse. The preeminent example of such a book would be Goethe's *Wilhelm Meister*, a work which Kierkegaard, like the Romantics, admired greatly.[7] The decision to treat religious and philosophical questions in a literary 'aesthetic' form was, it could be said, a well-established way of making those questions more relevant, more alive to the reader. Thus, Kierkegaard had written out in his journals the following quotation from Schubarth's lectures *On Goethe's Faust*:

thus, instead of the Absolute being a subject for philosophy, where it always remains stiff, dry, dead, unenjoyable and occasions crazy combinations, its concept properly belongs to poetry, which alone is capable of securing its validity and which first makes it living, effective, true, as also delightful and cheerful, through the boundless enthusiasm of the imagination. (I C 97)

In a similar vein he was favourably struck by Poul Møller's use of lighthearted anecdotal material in his essay on immortality. It is, Kierkegaard wrote,

very interesting; perhaps it will become the usual thing to mitigate the more strictly scholarly-scientific tone with lighter portions which, however, bear forth life much more fully, and in the area of knowledge will be somewhat comparable to the chorus, to the comic portions of romantic dramas. (*JP*,5201/II A 17)

However we may look for a more remote yet more obvious model for the mixture of literary, figurative writing with philosophical enquiry in a writer to whom Kierkegaard was especially heavily indebted: Plato. As Nietzsche was to write,

Plato has furnished for all posterity the pattern of a new art form, the novel, viewed as the Aesopian fable raised to its highest power; a form in which poetry played the same subordinate role with regard to dialectic philosophy as that same philosophy was to play for many centuries with regard to theology.[8]

It was, after all, Plato's Socrates who was to provide Kierkegaard with the main focus of his master's dissertation *On the Concept of Irony* and he was repeatedly to allude to Socrates' 'maieutic' approach to teaching, that is, being the midwife who brings others' thoughts to birth (or, on occasion, to Socrates' self-description as a 'gadfly', stinging the sophists into an encounter with truth).[9]

We shall return shortly to this Socratic model, but, important as this influence undoubtedly was, we cannot entirely explain Kierkegaard's understanding and practice of communication in terms of any of the models we have cited. Together they point out something of the direction he was to take, but – and this is almost a truism if we take sufficient note of the highly figurative quality of his writing – his authorship was to be a quite distinct exercise in raising religious issues in an aesthetic (or apparently aesthetic – let us not prejudge) way.

Kierkegaard's work contains a number of passages, ranging from short journal entries to complete books, where the *theory* of Christian communication stands in the foreground. It will be our concern in the remainder of this chapter to summarise and comment on the most important of these. First, however, two words of caution are in place. Although his writings on the theory of communication often seem to suggest that his whole authorship was created with a very definite, very precise theoretical foundation in place from the beginning this is not the case. This is recognised by Kierkegaard himself.

> I dare not say of myself that I have had a clear panorama of the whole plan of production from the outset; I must rather say, as I have continually acknowledged, that I myself have been brought up or educated and developed in the process of my work, that personally I have become more and more committed to Christianity than I was. (*JP*,6231/II A 218)

Kierkegaard did not set himself up as a teacher of the age: rather he was only a teacher insofar as he was also a learner, only an author insofar as he was himself his own reader. It is indeed one of the keys to understanding his rhetorical strategy to recognise precisely this: that the author/teacher is not greater than the reader/learner and that the processes of Christian communication and of communicating Christianity can only take place in mutual freedom.

The second caution is simply that just as the theory of communication to be found in Kierkegaard's work cannot be said to predate that work, so it cannot be said to exhaust the complexity of that work. Like all theories it simplifies and in doing so runs the risk of oversimplification – a point about theories of which Kierkegaard was very well aware but which he himself could not entirely escape.

THE POINT OF VIEW AND THE LECTURES ON COMMUNICATION

We shall begin with *The Point of View* which, though not the first of the theoretical works on communication, has an attractive simplicity, corresponding to its intention to explain Kierkegaard's work as an author to his contemporaries at large (though it was not, in fact, ever published in his own lifetime). In this respect it provides a convenient starting-point for our enquiry and a useful introduction to the more difficult texts.

The Point of View sets out to rebut the possible misapprehension that the authorship began as an aesthetic authorship and then gradually became religious, a misapprehension which is said to reflect the common assumption that religion is something especially suitable for older people. Against such a reading Kierkegaard argues that not only did he write the second part of *Either/Or* before the first part – that is to say, that he had the ethical 'answer' to aesthetic nihilism in place before he set out to create a representative 'aesthetic' text – but that the publication of the first two *Upbuilding Discourses* three months later confirms this original religious purpose. '*Either/Or*', he says, 'was, in the strict sense of the term, written in a monastery.' (*SV* 18, p.90) Of the relationship between these works he says that 'With my left hand I held out *Either/Or* to the world, with my right the *Two Upbuilding Discourses*; but all, or as good as all, took with their right hand what was in my left.' (*SV* 18, p.91) With the publication of *Fear and Trembling* later that same year the religious note was decisively struck: a claim for which Kierkegaard appeals to the support of no less eminent a witness than Bishop Mynster, primate of the Danish Church, who had warmly commended the author of *Fear and Trembling* as an example that by no means all the best minds of the generation had espoused the causes of agnosticism and atheism. 'From now on . . . the serious observer, who had religious presuppositions at his disposal, the serious observer to whom one can make oneself understood from afar, and to whom one can talk in silence . . . had to become observant of the fact that this was surely a unique kind of aesthetic production.' (*SV* 18, pp.91f.)[10]

More interestingly, from the point of view of our present enquiry, Kierkegaard then goes on to explain *why* his authorship had to take an indirect form, *why* it had to look 'aesthetic' though it was really religious. This explanation begins with a sweeping indictment of the present situation of the Danish 'Christian culture' – an indictment which can be readily extended to the whole situation of 'established Christendom'. 'Christendom,' he asserts, 'is a monstrous illusion.' (*SV* 18, p.93) Today, perhaps (and partly on account of Kierkegaard), this thought is commonplace, but to him it was a wounding discovery that though society regarded itself as 'Christian' and though the majority of its members would also regard themselves individually as 'Christian', most people live most of their lives in categories altogether alien to the spirit of Christianity. The thought itself was scarcely original. We have, for instance already seen how Heiberg satirised precisely this situation in his poem *A Soul after Death*: but though Kierkegaard could also make good use of satire his religious concerns led him to make a much more serious and impassioned response than that found in Heiberg's ironic comedy. On the other hand, he realised that to take up the stance of an enthusiastic revivalist or reformer is to foredoom oneself to failure in the task of bringing about a true Christian awakening. For the so-called 'Christian' society is used to dealing with such people. It knows very well how to avoid them or how to make them appear one-sided or exaggeratedly fanatical. No, the religious writer must first establish his credibility in worldly categories if he is to have any attention paid to his work. As far as the modern world is concerned this means that he must work 'in aesthetic, or at most aesthetic-ethical categories', (*SV* 18, p.95) because these are the categories in which most nominal Christians actually live.

What is in play here is the principle that 'If one is truly to succeed in bringing a person to a definite point, one must first and foremost pay attention to finding him there, where HE is, and begin there.' (*SV* 18, p.96) And this, he says, carries the further corollary that 'truly to be a teacher is to be a learner. The lesson begins with you, the teacher, learning from the learner, putting yourself in a position to understand what he has understood . . .'. (*SV* 18, p.98)

This is the key to the indirect method of communication, which might therefore seem (unchristianly) to involve a deliberate deception, but, Kierkegaard says, 'One can deceive someone in the cause of truth . . . deceive them into the truth.' (*SV* 18, p.104) Thus the indirect method 'in the service of a love for truth prepares everything dialectically for the one who is to be ensnared; and now, as love always does, bashfully withdraws in order to witness the confession he, that is, the recipient of the communication, now alone before God, makes to himself, that he has thus far lived in illusion'. (*SV* 18, p.95) The recipient of the communication, the reader, must in this way follow the clue hidden in the name of the pseudonym Victor Eremita: he must win through to an understanding of the text in solitude, without the support either of authorial guarantees or of the received opinion of fellow readers. Thus, the decision as to whether or not these works are to be read 'religiously' is left to each reader. We shall later on examine in greater detail how Kierkegaard effectively effaced his own authorial presence by using recognised literary forms to deal with issues which such forms are (in his view) essentially unable to handle, thereby setting up a tension which only the response of the reader can resolve.

What justifies such a tactic is the actual character of the present age itself. It is precisely because the age itself is essentially aesthetic that the use of deception is not merely permissible but necessary. For if the teacher is to start where the learner is then he must start with the aesthetic – even though the aesthetic is incapable of expressing the religious truth which is the goal of his teaching. At the conclusion of the preceding chapter we saw how Kierkegaard was able to extend his psychological reduction of 'the aesthetic' from the sphere of poetry and art to such characteristic figures of the contemporary world as the cleric (representing established Christendom) and the bourgeois philistine – even though such persons may have little taste or aptitude for aesthetics in the narrow sense. Let us now briefly examine further his view of the age in which he lived and the implications of this view for aesthetic and religious communication.

A key element in his understanding of the modern world is the concept of levelling. Levelling means the sceptical and abstract equalisation of all human relationships and institutions, the dissolution of all historical, organic concretions in social life. Even when the bourgeois order permits such institutions as the Church and the monarchy to survive, this is a mere façade, since the bourgeois outlook, based as it is on rationalistic and prudential self-interest, is quite opposed to the principles of authority and faith which such institutions originally stood for. The bourgeois society 'lets everything remain standing but cunningly steals away its meaning'. (*SV* 14, p.71) In this way the Communists and aesthetic nihilists are only shouting from the rooftops what their bourgeois parents already know in secret. In the situation where levelling holds sway, the situation where the spirit of reflection and rationality has made everything ambiguous and questionable, all authority is, *qua* authority, suspect and mistrusted. To attempt to assert any kind of authority (politically, religiously or culturally) is perceived as a breach of the spirit of abstract equality, as an attempt to make oneself better than the others – thereby provoking a renewed manifestation of levelling. 'Modern Man' (to use a term which is no longer current but which is appropriate to this context) will, simply, not be told what to do, since his supreme value is autonomous self-determination. He is 'the rebel', 'man in revolt', '*l'homme revolté*'. The religious teacher cannot therefore step forward and assert a direct authority. He must, instead, make himself unrecognisable but

> none of these unrecognisable ones dare help directly, express himself directly, teach directly, take decisive action as the leader of the masses (instead of negatively helping the individual to act decisively by supporting him where he himself is); this would be cause for dismissal, because he would then be dabbling in human sympathy's short-sighted inventiveness, instead of obeying the orders of the divinity . . . for all the individuals who are to be saved . . . must make the leap [of faith] by themselves and the divinity's infinite love will not then become for them a second-hand relationship. (*SV* 14, pp.98f)

It is – at least in part – for such reasons that direct communication will not do – or, rather, will only do if it is prepared for and enacted in the most careful possible way. The assessment of the contemporary situation in art as nihilistic and the assessment of the domination of contemporary society by the spirit of levelling thus work together, if not to determine then at least to shape the context in which Kierkegaard's view of religious communication was formed.

There are, however, more intrinsic factors affecting the form of such communication, factors which have to do with the structure of communication as such and with the specific content of Christian communication. As we approach the closer analysis of these factors we turn to another of Kierkegaard's 'theoretical' writings on communication: the substantial set of notes for a series of *Lectures on Communication* which were, apparently, planned for an audience of theological students, but which were never delivered. These notes postdate both the *Philosophical Fragments* and the *Concluding Unscientific Postscript* and therefore presuppose the critique of Hegelian (and other forms of) idealism found in these works. They also attempt to give a more systematic presentation of the implications and the scope of the methods of Socratic midwifery which play a large part in the *Fragments*.[11]

In these lectures Kierkegaard aimed to draw a fundamental distinction between the communication of knowledge and the communication of capability. Referring again to the confusion of the modern world he remarks that it is precisely the inability of the present age to make this distinction which constitutes one of its chief errors. As might be expected, ethical and religious communication are said to be first and foremost concerned with the communication of capability, though with regard to Christianity a certain element of knowledge is also said to be necessary. However, the overall thrust of Christian communication 'is not in the direction of knowledge but of capability; the knowledge which is communicated in this communication is a preliminary'. (*JP* I, p.307) What does this mean?

Ethical communication is communication of capability (or, as he also refers to it here: 'oughtness-communication') *par excellence*: 'the emphasis must fall absolutely upon "You shall" . . .'. (*JP* I, p.285) The ethical teacher is not concerned to put knowledge *into* the learner but to draw out from him his own capability or potentiality. Several of the analogies which he employs to make this point have a distinctly military character. Thus:

> The corporal sees the soldier *kata dunamin*, i.e. potentially in the farm boy, and therefore says: I will have to pound the soldier out of him. On the other hand the soldier studies a manual of field tactics; in regard to the instruction contained therein, the corporal might say: I will have to pound this into him. (*JP* I, p.285)

The former instance is a case of ethical communication, the latter a case of communication of knowledge. There is no requirement on ethics to offer any kind of knowledge-communication, there is nothing to 'pound into' the learner, since it is assumed that the subject matter of such communication is universal: the ethical is precisely that which may be required of every rational human being unconditionally, equally valid for each and every one of us. It is, for example, this view of the ethical which underlies Kierkegaard's argument in *Fear and Trembling* that Abraham's consent to the divine instruction to sacrifice his son involved a religious suspension of otherwise universal ethical principles (in this case the universal prohibition of murder, *scil*. infanticide).[12]

But if Christianity requires some element of knowledge to be communicated what might this be? This is not stated in the lecture notes themselves but it is clearly minimal. In the *Philosophical Fragments*, for instance, Johannes Climacus had stated that

> The historical fact that the God has been in human form is the main thing, and the rest of the historical detail is not even as important as if, instead of the God, we were talking about a human being. . . . Even if the contemporary generation had not left anything behind them but these words: 'We have believed that in *anno* such-and-such, the God showed himself in the lowly form of a servant, he lived and taught among us, and then died' – it would be more than enough. (*SV* 6, p.93)

It might, perhaps, be unwise to take this as Kierkegaard's last word on the matter. In various of his religious writings he was himself to sketch in far more of the detail of Christ's earthly life. Nonetheless, as he was to suggest in a particularly striking manner in *Training in Christianity*, the knowledge-element in the Christian element is nothing that even a fairly young child could not grasp quite easily.[13] Once this minimal knowledge-element is mastered, Christian communication, like ethical communication, has to do essentially with communication of capability; '. . . a knowledge about Christianity must certainly be communicated in advance. But it is only a preliminary.' (*JP* I, p.289) What follows then is what Kierkegaard calls reduplication, the translation of what is communicated at the level of knowledge into existential actuality. This is in fact more difficult. The difference between these two levels being like 'the swimming instructor who in a safe and "quiet" hour explains the motions of swimming to his pupils but when he says; Let us now dive in, they say: No thanks.' (*JP* I, p.287) This step is vital, but, Kierkegaard believes, it has been generally lacking. 'Until now, from generation to generation, men have taught Christianity as a knowledge (the first course) and then the next course, again, as a knowledge.' (*JP* I, p.280) Knowledge has triumphed over oughtness-communication, over actuality and reduplication. This, as we have already suggested, is not materially affected by whether the knowledge in question is metaphysical, historical or psychological. Even more significantly the requirement of reduplication concerns the teacher just as much as it concerns the pupil: 'To teach in actuality that the truth is ridiculed, etc., means to teach it as one ridiculed and scoffed at himself. To teach poverty in actuality means to teach it as one who is himself poor . . .'. (*JP* I, p.286) This was to become one of the central arguments in his latter 'Attack on Christendom' when he pilloried the clergy of the State Church for preaching about the suffering, poverty and cross-bearing characteristic of the Christian life from a position of affluence and social acceptability.[14]

As well as 'pounding in' this essential distinction between ethical communication and knowledge-communication the lectures also broach what Kierkegaard claims is his own most original contribution to Christian thought: 'My service in using pseudonyms consists in having discovered, Christianly, the maieutic method.' (*JP* I, p.280) Let us then look more closely at what this means.

The term itself relates back to the practice of Socrates as recorded by Plato (Gk *Hē maieutikē*: midwifery) as Kierkegaard acknowledges in the opening pages of the *Fragments*. 'He [Socrates] was and remained a midwife, not because he "had no positive teaching", but because he saw that this role is the highest, which one human being can take on in relation to another.' (*SV* 6, p.16). The assumption underlying Socrates' maieutic practice is, as Kierkegaard emphasises, that each individual is already essentially in possession of the truth and therefore does not so much need to be *taught* the truth as to be *reminded* of the truth he already knows. Ultimately the logic of this position leads, as in Plato, to a full-blown doctrine of recollection in which the pre-existence of the soul is affirmed in such a way that, as in Wordsworth's line, 'Our birth is but a sleep and a forgetting.' The difference between ignorance and knowledge is, on this account, simply a matter of degree. Such a position is, however, incompatible with the Christian view of the 'fallen' situation of humanity and the need for salvation, redemption, atonement, conversion, repentance and rebirth before the human being can enter into a fully affirmative relation to the truth about herself. It would seem, then, that the maieutic method cannot be used in the context of Christianity – or can it?

Interestingly, Kierkegaard was not (as he claimed) the first to have discovered 'Christianly' the maieutic art. Augustine had already expounded such a method in various of his writings – but the contrast between them is instructive. In Augustine's *The Teacher*, for example, a dialogue concerned with the nature of signs, knowledge and reality, Augustine argues that all speech essentially serves the purpose of reminding: 'So, too, speech serves us only to remind, since the memory in which the words inhere, by recalling them, brings to mind the realities themselves, of which the words are signs.'[15] In the conclusion to the dialogue it is made clear that comprehension of truth is not brought about by teaching in words but by the direct relation to truth which is part of the essential structure of every rational soul.

> Regarding, however, all those things which we understand, it is not a speaker who utters sounds exteriorly whom we consult, but it is truth that presides within, over the mind itself; though it may have been words that prompted us to make such consultation. And He who is consulted, He who is said to *dwell in the inner man*, He it is who teaches – Christ – that is, *the unchangeable Power of God and everlasting Wisdom*. This Wisdom every rational soul does, in fact, consult. But to each one only so much is manifested as he is capable of receiving because of his own good or bad will.[16]

Thus, 'If we know, we recall rather than learn', led by the 'Teacher within', the 'hidden Oracle' so that the 'teacher' in a human sense is not really such at all but 'only a prompter'.[17] There is an argument here as to what extent Augustine was, in such texts, still under the influence of his former Platonic beliefs, but such a concept of an essential inner relation to truth did establish itself and survive in Christianity and, with it, the possibility of a Christian maieutic. But is such a position tenable in the context of, for example, the Protestant emphasis on the total obliteration of the image of God in man occasioned by the fall and the concomitant assertion (in Kierkegaard's own well-known phrase) of an 'infinite qualitative difference' between the divine and the human? That is the question which Kierkegaard's (re-?)discovery of a Christian maieutics addresses.

The possibility – and indeed the point – of such an art hinges on the relationship between teacher and learner, author and writer. Where the communication of knowledge is concerned the maieutic relationship is irrelevant. Conversely, since Christianity (as Kierkegaard understood it) assumes that the learner is factically outside the pale of truth it is not possible to speak of 'reminding' the learner of a truth he already knows. What is left? Simply to remind the learners (readers) of their own responsibility for their standing *vis-à-vis* truth. This may seem little enough but it requires a dramatic break with the overwhelming mass of those literary and social pressures in the modern age which militate against such responsibility. Our age is dishonest, subject to 'The tyranny of the daily press, periodicals, brochures', etc. (*JP* I, p.277) We lack a proper naivety or, as Kierkegaard also calls it, primitivity, caught in an ever-increasing swamp of secondary literature and second-hand ideas: 'Nowadays one becomes an author by reading – not by his primitivity, just as one becomes a man by mimicking others – not by his primitivity.' (*JP* I, p.277) Crucially this means – and we may recall the diagnostic account of the 'evaporation' of the personality in aesthetic experience – the loss of a deep and genuine sense of self-identity. 'One of the tragedies of modern times is precisely this – to have abolished the "I", the personal "I".' (*JP* I, p.302) It is this which Kierkegaard's own Christian maieutic seeks to restore *indirectly* by means of the pseudonyms:

> Therefore I regard it as my service that by bringing poetized personalities who say *I* (my pseudonyms) into the center of life's actuality I have contributed, if possible, to familiarize the contemporary age again to hearing an *I*, a personal *I* speak. . . . But precisely because the whole development of the world has been as far as possible from this acknowledgement of personality, this has to be done poetically. The poetic personality always has a something which makes him more bearable for a world which is quite unaccustomed to hearing an *I*. Beyond this I admittedly do not go. I never venture to use quite directly my own *I*. But I am convinced that the time will come when an *I* stands up in the world, someone who says *I* directly and speaks in the first person. Then, for the first time, he will also in the strictest sense rightly communicate ethical and ethical-religious truth. (*JP* I, p.302)

How can the fictive personalities of the pseudonyms become the occasion for the renewal of authentic 'primitive' personal responsibility in the reader? The key to answering this question, I believe, lies in the fact that the pseudonyms are not, first and foremost, *characters* in books but *authors* of books. In the pseudonymous works there is no 'real' author to take responsibility for the 'fictional' characters. Consequently the burden of responsibility is passed back to the reader – a move which, as we have already noted, is signalled by the name of the first pseudonymous editor: Victor Eremita.

The programme of Christian maieutics which Kierkegaard sets out in the lectures on communication is not, therefore, aimed at leading learners (readers) to the truth and it cannot recall to them or prompt them to take note of a truth which they already essentially have. What it can do, however, is to make them take note of their responsibility for their own comportment towards the truth, a move which, logically at least, is a prior condition of the further question as to whether they are living 'in' the truth or 'outside' it, growing towards it or departing from it, acquiring it or losing it. The Christian midwife, however, has no authority in relation to such issues.

Kierkegaard was, religiously, worried by the ambivalence inherent in this attempt to restore a sense for primitive personal impressions *indirectly*. He suspected that there could even be something demonic about it since it could seem to absolve the author of the pseudonyms from himself enacting precisely that kind of responsibility towards which he is manoeuvring his readers.

There are several issues tangled up here. Insofar as Christian communication involves an element of knowledge (however subordinate) this would seem to point towards the necessity of some measure of directness in all authentically Christian communication. Moreover, because of the specific nature of the Christian message the Christian communicator, like the learner, must humble himself under that message and show ('reduplicate' in Kierkegaard's vocabulary) its effects in his own actual life. And, finally, there is a further twist in that the knowledge element itself is of a highly ambiguous nature: the Christian proclamation is the proclamation of a paradox, of what defies simple and direct appropriation. To unpick this tangle we shall now proceed to another text where issues of communication are paramount, the *Book on Adler*, before turning, finally, to a closer examination of the ultimate Christological focus of Kierkegaard's reflections on communication as presented in *Training in Christianity*.

THE BOOK ON ADLER

Adolph Adler was a contemporary of Kierkegaard's who, in December 1842, while serving as a parish priest on the island of

Bjornholm, claimed to have received a personal visitation from Jesus Christ. In this revelation Christ ordered him to burn his earlier philosophical (Hegelian) writings and dictated to him a new doctrine concerning the fall, instructing him in future to hold fast to the Bible. Adler made these claims public in the foreword to a collection of sermons and addresses which he published in June 1843, most of which, he asserted, were written under the direct guidance of Jesus Christ himself so that he (Adler) was merely an instrument of divine revelation. These claims – especially in the light of some of the disturbing doctrines and assertions made in these writings – naturally attracted the attention of the Church authorities. In 1844 Adler was suspended from office and invited to respond to questions challenging his state of mind at the time of these revelations, the appropriateness of such 'supposed external revelations' and the false and offensive nature of many of the claims made in the 'Sermons' and 'Studies' he had published. These questions and his response to them were published by Adler himself in 1845. The case, foreseeably, ended with Adler's dismissal.[18]

Kierkegaard was throughout interested in the story, especially since he had been approached personally by Adler who saw in him a potential ally. But Kierkegaard was critical from the beginning, and the book which he wrote on the case (not published in his own lifetime) set out to distinguish sharply between their respective positions. He argues that it is clear from Adler's own presentation of the case that, granted he had indeed had the experiences he claimed to have had, he simply did not understand what it meant to be the recipient of a revelation and that his behaviour and writings were altogether inappropriate for someone who had received a direct communication from God. His own book, he says, is 'an ethical investigation' into the concepts of *revelation* and *authority* which lie at the heart of the case. As in *The Point of View* and the *Lectures on Communication* he sets the discussion of these issues firmly in the context of a critical *Auseinandersetzung* with the spirit of modernity, seeing Adler as a typical representative of the confusion of the modern world when it comes to religious matters. Julia Watkin has therefore appropriately entitled her recent Danish edition of the book *The Religious Confusion of the Modern Age*.[19] For the issue is not just an issue of one man's religious deviancy since it illustrates the basic religious character of the present age, raising the question as to how genuine religious communication is possible in such an age.

Kierkegaard begins by looking at the obligations which are incumbent on anyone who seeks to challenge the existing order of things, the 'establishment'. These include the obligation that the burden of proof must lie with those who seek to undermine, challenge or overturn the prevailing traditions, conventions and institutions which guide and shape society and culture. The person who sets out to be the exception to the rule, 'the extraordinary', must be aware of their 'dangerous responsibility'. (*BA*, p.54) Such a person must also take full account of the nature of the situation which they are addressing. As far as the modern world goes this means recognising its reflective, rational, critical character, especially when the issue at stake is a religious issue. 'Our age is reflective; it can scarcely be thought that the divine governance itself is not attentive to this.' (*BA*, p.56)

It is not *a priori* impossible that God might give a direct communication to an existing individual in 1842: the question is whether that individual's subsequent behaviour and account of himself is appropriate. For instance, does such an individual show the silence, the patience, the 'faith, humility and . . . daily self-dedication' (*BA*, pp.62ff.) which are characteristic of the truly religious life? Also, does he make himself *repulsive* in such a way that the issue is seen to be the truth for which he stands rather than some kind of cult of personality? Is he merely asserting a claim as leader, or potential leader, of yet another sect or faction – or is he prepared to endure the ruination of his own career, status and personality in order, if necessary, to bring into prominence the message itself?

At this point Kierkegaard draws a contrast between the Aristotelian and the Christian concepts of the miraculous. For Aristotle a miracle is a breach or a failure in the smooth working of the laws of nature and, as such, abnormal. But Christianity sees the miraculous as being something higher than nature, higher than the normal. The true dialectic of the miraculous, Kierkegaard concludes, is the unity of these in such a way that it is precisely in the suffering (e.g. of Christ or of the martyrs) which represents failure from the point of view of a system of natural teleology that God is revealed. 'The Miracle' is 'the Miracle' and therefore *higher* than the norm precisely by the way in which, naturalistically regarded, it falls *below* the norm. This means that what might count as evidence in a normal situation is completely irrelevant. The authority of the established order, the testimony of history, the attempt to make the issue of faith a question of reasonable probability – something to be argued over, discussed, weighed up – none of this matters in the slightest. In other words, as we have seen, the communication of faith is not primarily a knowledge-communication and cannot take the sort of form which would be appropriate in the case of a knowledge-communication. For the content of faith is simply the paradox 'that the eternal once existed in time'. (*BA*, p.76) To believe, to acquire faith, is to become contemporary with that time, a step which is still possible eighteen hundred years after Christ because since it is a matter of the *eternal* in time all time is equally near and equally far from such an event: 'To believe in an eminent sense corresponds quite correctly to the Miracle, the Absurd, the Improbable, that which is foolishness to the understanding, and it is therefore precisely for that reason that it is absolutely indifferent as to how long it is since the event occurred or whether it is today.' (*BA*, p.90). A corollary of this is that the possibility of offence is just as 'live' an issue as the possibility of faith, for it is 'contemporaneity's tension to have to be offended or to grasp faith'. (*BA*, p.86) Once a paradox, always a paradox – a truth which must be reflected in the manner of the communication.

If Adler had grasped all this he would, Kierkegaard believes, have resigned his post, and thus have made himself *lower* than the establishment (the norm). But no: instead, he sought to hold on to his office and to remain a member or representative of the establishment while at the same time putting himself *above* its laws by virtue of his singular claims. Even worse, the manner in which he went about this, his arguments on his own behalf and his other subsequent writings, showed the confusion of his ideas as to what revelation really is and what the communication of revelation really requires, a confusion in which he is all too plainly a faithful representative of the modern age.

As far as content is concerned Adler's 'revelation' is not unique except for the manner of its being communicated to him. His claims on this score mean that he is putting himself in the position of an apostle and his writings in the position of inspired writings. However, when he is asked directly by the Church authorities, 'Have you had a revelation?' Adler prevaricates. He cannot, he says, deny 'that an event took place through which I was seized by faith'. (*BA*, p.106) But, Kierkegaard points out, to be 'seized by faith' is a very different thing from being commissioned to take a specific message to the world. Adler has, in effect, confused the situation of being an apostle with the situation which, it might be presumed, ought to be the situation of every Christian, for every Christian ought to be 'seized by faith'. Adler appeals for support to the Bible, but, Kierkegaard replies, the question is not *what* Jesus communicated to him (that would be a straightforward knowledge-communication) but whether it was *Jesus* who communicated it to him. Adler confounds matters still further by expressing the hope that if people find the manner in which he has set out his ideas imperfect then they will regard his work so far as being the first, inevitably fumbling efforts of a child trying to communicate something important for which he has not yet found the right words. But again Kierkegaard is ready with a rebuke. For if these words were really given by divine dictation then to say that the ideas could be better expressed is little short of blasphemy. Later Adler makes the further request that his readers regard his account of the divine visitation and his characteristic dogmatic utterances as 'points of reference' (*Holdningspunkter*) 'which have been necessary for me so that in the beginning of my enthusiasm I could have a form in which to hold fast the Christian content'. (*BA*, p.118) With such pleas and requests, however, Kierkegaard sees Adler as simply perpetuating the mistaken assumption of modern dogmatics that scripture (revealed truth) is no more than a kind of 'immediacy', a mere external form capable of being superseded by a more comprehensive and more comprehending exposition of divine truth.

In short, then, Adler has allowed the paradox involved in revelation to become something relative, something that by virtue of a better form, a better explanation, might in time become less paradoxical, more readily assimilable by the human mind, losing its potential for causing offence whilst remaining an object of faith. But then, in Kierkegaard's view, it is no longer the paradox. What Adler has done (and his later writings which bring in the further self-description as a 'genius') is to have 'moved the sphere of the paradox back into the aesthetic'. (*BA*, p.137) 'When the sphere of the paradox is done away with or retrospectively illuminated by the aesthetic, then an apostle becomes neither more nor less than a genius, and so, Good Night, Christianity.' (*BA*, p.138) Adler has sought to reduce revelation to an event exemplifying his own authorial 'idea' by treating it in this way and has thereby dissipated the absolute into the flux of such relative relationships as those characterising author and reader. He has given his work the wrong sort of authority. In this, however, he is, once again, a typical representative of the age.

> Such thoughtless eloquence can just as well hit on praising Paul as a stylist and literary artist, or even better, since it is known that Paul in addition practised a trade, assert that his work as a tentmaker must have been so masterly that no carpet-maker before or since can have made anything so perfect – for if one simply says something good about Paul then all is well. But, as a genius Paul cannot bear comparison with either Plato or Shakespeare, as a writer of beautiful analogies he comes fairly far down, as a stylist he is an altogether obscure name – and as a tapestry-maker, I have to say that I do not know how high he comes in this respect. (*BA*, p.139)

The essential differences between a genius and an apostle are clear and simple. A genius is bounded by the limits of immanence. He cannot produce anything radically or decisively or qualitatively new; his 'new' work is 'new' only in relative terms and 'vanishes again in the race's universal assimilation'. (*BA*, p.139) An apostle on the other hand is marked forever by the transcendent origin of his calling: 'he has, paradoxically, something new to bring, whose newness . . . remains constantly'. (*BA*, p.139) A genius is what he is through his own gifts and abilities, but an apostle has divine authority: 'by this paradoxical fact an apostle is for all eternity made paradoxically different from all other men. The "new thing" which he has to proclaim is that which is essentially paradoxical.' (*BA*, p.141) Basically the issue is this: do we judge his message *aesthetically* or in the light of his claims to a divinely-bestowed authority? But such claims can never be guaranteed objectively. *Aesthetically* all we have to ask is whether the idea is being expressed in an appropriate manner. But what sort of manner might be appropriate to a communication from God?

> . . . look, God cannot help his emissary in such a sensuous manner as a King can, who gives him an escort of soldiers or police, or his ring, or his signature which all know: in short, God cannot help men by giving them a sensuous certainty that an apostle is an apostle. . . . Even the miraculous . . . is an object of faith. (*BA*, p.143)

For even a miracle can, after all, be explained (or explained away) in a thousand different ways. But an apostle has nothing more nor less to lean on than his assertion that he is sent by God or that his message is from God.

The whole question of the paradox has been dealt with many times in Kierkegaard commentaries. Usually, however, such discussions are concerned with the paradox as an epistemological issue, that is, as relating to the nature of our knowledge of God. Here, on the other hand, we are not concerned primarily with the issue of knowledge but the issue of communication. This does not mean that we thereby escape all the problems which arise from attempts to deploy the paradox as a solution to questions of religious knowledge but we find ourselves confronted by a quite different set of questions, questions like: What kind of communicational methods could be used to communicate an absolute paradox? What implications do our methods of communication have for coming to terms with the paradox?

The Book on Adler is, I would suggest, principally concerned with such questions as these and it moves forward Kierkegaard's discussion of the relationship between direct and indirect communication. If the *Lectures on Communication* seemed to imply that this relationship was such that the direct communication ('the God lived in time') was simply a direct factual statement which any child could learn by rote as an item of knowledge, while the indirect communication concerned the way in which the ethical and religious implications of this fact might be activated in the individual's life, it now appears that the relationship between the two is far more intimate. For the apostolic communication operates simultaneously at two different levels. At one level it involves the direct assertion of a fact – 'My message comes from God' – but, at the same time, this assertion itself is curiously indirect in the sense that the apostle is unable to offer any supporting evidence (no troops, no police, no seal, no signature) to prove that what he says is true. Just as in Socratic indirect communication (and in Kierkegaard's own pseudonymous works) the communicator vanishes behind the communication and the recipient of the communication is left to judge for himself as to the truth of the message, so, once more, the apostolic message invites a response and an interpretation which no one but the recipient can supply. There is nothing in the message to *compel* the response of faith – and the response of offence is equally plausible, for the truth-value of the message cannot be secured within any system of human understanding or calculation. The Kierkegaardian apostle, then, despite the vocabulary of 'authority' which encompasses him, does not occupy a safe house, immune from the complex and problematic dialectics of communication. This situation is, on the contrary, extremely complex and dialectical and his message is disturbingly direct–indirect. Its directness (its claim to divine authority) means that we cannot comfortably dismiss it as a literary game, a thought-experiment (and, in this respect, it is quite distinct from the altogether indirect communication offered by the pseudonyms). On the other hand, its indirectness (its 'failure' to substantiate its knowledge-element) means that we cannot evade our responsibility for interpreting it the way we interpret it. The authority of the apostle does not therefore overrule the freedom of the recipient of the message. The communication of the paradox expects and requires the full activation of the freedom and interpretative responsibility of the recipient (as is also the case with the indirect communication contained in the pseudonymous authorship).

A further point now arises. I have taken pains to emphasise the contextualisation of Kierkegaard's views on communication in the situation of early modernism. There is little doubt that that situation, both in general terms and, more specifically, in terms of the contemporary intellectual scene in Denmark, gives his views the flavour of a particular time and place. But was it ever otherwise? Was there ever a time when authority could stand up and command? When faith could be commended in simple, plain, direct speech without any kind of indirectness? The discussion of levelling and unrecognisability might well suggest that indirect communication is very much a requirement forced on to Christianity by the exigencies of the present age. But we are now seeing that the dialectics of communication go all the way back to the nature of the paradox itself. After all, in Kierkegaard's own terms, if the paradox is really to be the paradox then it must be equally paradoxical at all times. It cannot just become paradoxical at some point in the late eighteenth/ early nineteenth century! For all ages are equally confronted, challenged and, if they choose, saved by the message of the paradox, that God appeared in time as an individual human being. The essential paradox is the same yesterday, today and forever. For a tentmaker in the first century to say, 'I am sent by God' is no more and no less paradoxical than for a country parson in the nineteenth (or even twentieth) century to say, 'I am sent by God.' The relationship of one age to another is a relative matter: but the relation of time to eternity is not. Kierkegaard's requirement of an appropriate fusion of direct and indirect communication is not therefore simply an apologetic ploy framed for a specific set of cultural circumstances. Such a requirement springs from the paradox itself.

We have been looking at the issue of the paradox so far chiefly in connection with the claim, the paradoxical claim, to apostolic authority, but everything that has been said about the apostle is rooted in and is eminently true in the case of Christ himself. This is made clear in *The Book on Adler* when Kierkegaard asks us to consider whether the statement 'There is an eternal life' is the *same* statement when we hear it from the lips of a theological student as when we hear it from the lips of Christ. Logically, of course, it is the same statement, but, for Kierkegaard, the authority presupposed by the student and the Saviour respectively makes it quite different in each case. And yet even the 'authority' of Christ has no independent guarantees outside our willingness to accept it.

But it is not with the message *of* Christ but the message *about* Christ, the *person* of Christ, the God-man, as Kierkegaard calls him, that the whole issue of the paradox and, with the paradox, of Christian communication comes to a head. Kierkegaard's view of communication and his final judgement on the relationship between the aesthetic and the religious are Christologically determined. Using *Training in Christianity* I should now like to explore this further, seeing how his interpretation of Christ informs his recommendation that we approach dogmatics from the standpoint of rhetoric (as a system of communication) rather than from the standpoint of most previous (and especially, Kierkegaard says, most recent) dogmatics (that is, dogmatics understood as a system of knowledge).

THE SIGN OF CONTRADICTION

In *Training in Christianity* we find that the themes of Christology and communication are inseparable, Christ being regarded precisely in his communication character as a 'sign', and, more specifically, as a 'sign of contradiction'.

The book begins with a series of reflections on Christ's words

'Come unto me all ye that travail and are heavy laden and I will refresh you.' There is something in these words, Kierkegaard says, that is easily overlooked – the character of the inviter himself. This raises straightaway the possibility of offence, no matter how beautiful the message itself might appear to be. For the inviter is one who also, though living in the humiliated state of a human being, claimed to be God. About him we can 'know' nothing: 'he is the paradox, the object of faith, only there for faith'. (*SV* 16, p.36) As such, as we have seen, he is the same in every age, touching every moment of time but not finally identifiable with any: 'For in relation to the absolute there is only one time: the present; the absolute just doesn't exist for the one who is not contemporary with it.' (*SV* 16, p.70) But, as should by now be familiar, the paradox brings with it the equally contemporary possibility of offence. In a series of meditations on the invitation 'Come unto me . . .' Kierkegaard imagines the responses which might have been made to the inviter's claim to be God by a series of figures representing different facets of worldly life. We hear from the wise and the prudent, the clergyman, the philosopher, the statesman, the solid citizen and the mocker – all, in their differing ways, situated within the boundaries of 'normality'. It is clear that he regards these types and their responses as equally representative of both the first and the nineteenth centuries. In the second part of the book, 'Blessed is he who is not offended in me', the same issue, the possibility of offence, is dealt with more systematically. Firstly, it is examined simply in terms of the conflict between the individual and the established order, though here the judgement on this order is harsher than that given in *The Book on Adler* where it was identified with the universally human. For now the established order is seen as self-deifying, an attempt by the human collectivity to arrogate to itself that control over the individual human conscience which properly speaking belongs to God alone. When the individual then protests against this order in the name of conscience it looks as if he is setting himself above the commonality of humankind – whereas he is in fact doing only what every individual ought to do. When the establishment charges such an individual with blasphemy this is what Kierkegaard calls 'an acoustic illusion', a projection of its own self-deification on to the person who actually witnesses to the truth. But this is only one aspect of the possibility of offence. Kierkegaard next moves on to the more strictly theological aspects of this possibility. The first of these has to do with what he calls 'exaltation': 'that an individual human being speaks and acts as though he were God'. (*SV* 16, p.96) Here we have the element of direct communication in the paradox: that this man says that he is (or acts as if he is) God – a simple, direct statement taking the form of a knowledge-communication. But, as we have tried to show and as Kierkegaard here emphasises, in *this* individual man, in his words and actions, 'there is not anything to see *directly* . . .'. (*SV* 16, p.98) There is no supporting evidence such as we might expect in the case of a normal knowledge-communication. Even when Christ speaks and acts most directly the possibility of offence is present because he who speaks and acts is also 'an individual human being, a lowly human being'. (*SV* 16, p.98) And how can such a one claim to be God? Conversely, there is the possibility of offence which has to do with Christ's *humiliation*: that the one who claims to be God 'shows himself to be the lowly, poor, suffering and, finally, the powerless one'. (*SV* 16, p.104) The whole passion narrative, for instance, invites the possibility of an offence of this kind, since it portrays a figure who stands in such stark contrast to what is normally understood as divine (power, majesty, beauty, etc.). A corollary of this form of offence lies in the stipulation that the pupil is not above the master, that Christ's suffering is not merely a passing moment which won (at some point in the past) an eternal salvation for his followers, who are thereby spared the necessity of undergoing a similar suffering themselves. For though Christ is now in glory we cannot come to him otherwise than as to one who is forever the humiliated one, the paradox who offends all egocentric human expectations. We shall shortly return to the theme of suffering discipleship, but first we come to a section of *Training in Christianity* in which Christology and communication are brought into the closest possible connection, as Kierkegaard reflects on the sign-character of the God-man.

The God-man, he says, is a 'sign of contradiction' – but what does this mean? A sign, as such, 'is the negation of immediacy'. (*SV* 16, p.124) A nautical marker, for instance, 'is not the immediate thing it is': in itself it is simply a post or a light, but as a *sign* it has a distinct function and meaning. This sign-character, however, exists only for reflection and is, in principle, separable from the thing itself. A 'sign of contradiction', however, is something else again. 'There is no contradiction in its being immediately this or this and, in addition, a sign. . . . A sign of contradiction, on the other hand, is a sign composed in such a way as to contain within itself a contradiction.' (*SV* 16, p.122) Such a sign can never be part of a direct communication since it is internally self-negating. As an example Kierkegaard speaks of 'a communication which is the unity of jest and earnest', a communication, that is, which, like his own pseudonymous works, gives the reader no assurances as to how it is meant – it is serious, or is it just a thought-experiment? The concept of the God-man is likewise a 'sign of contradiction' – but in what way?

There is no *a priori* contradiction in the speculative notion of the unity of God and humanity, as propounded by the Hegelians, if this means that the totality of the history of the world and of humanity is conceived as the divine self-manifestation in and through time, the Odyssey of the spirit. What is contradictory about the Christian concept is that an *individual* man says that he is also God (or, is said by his apostles to be God). The apparent directness of this claim is deceptive: 'What he says can be quite direct, but the fact that he, the sign of contradiction, says it, makes it indirect communication.' (*SV* 16, p.131) This is, indeed, something we have already argued in the case of the apostle: similarly, even the God-man himself can offer no final objective criteria of decidability regarding his claims. Here, however, the situation is even more complex than was the case with the apostle. For when Christ says this, he *is* the paradoxical and offensive unity of the divine and the human which reason cannot think and language cannot state directly. The message of the paradox is, in Kierkegaard's phrase, *reduplicated* in the existence of the communicator *who is who he says he is.*

At this point, in this most decisive of all religious communications, the communicator emerges from behind the veil of maieutic self-effacement. But precisely because he is in himself the paradox of which his message speaks his life does not in any way guarantee or explain his message. We cannot say he proves himself to be the God-man because he was better or more knowledgeable or more honoured by his contemporaries than any other individual in history. Life and message alike frustrate knowledge, explanation and understanding. Both can only be the proper objects of faith – or offence. The reduplication of the message in the existence of the communicator does not therefore release the recipient of the communication from the burden of decision. The truth of the message can in no way be proved to or forced on the recipient. This terrible freedom of response, the impenetrable unrecognisableness in which not only Christ but every Christian communicator must go about his task is, for Kierkegaard, the true secret of Christ's suffering:

> He is love; and yet in every moment he exists he must, as it were, crucify all human sympathy and caring – because he can only be the object of faith, but everything which comes under the rubric of human sympathy relates to direct recognisability. . . . For the sake of love he will do everything for human beings, he puts his life on the line for them, he suffers for them the shameful death – and he suffers for them this life in which he must, in divine love, sympathy and mercifulness . . . be (humanly speaking) so hard. (*SV* 16, pp.133f.)

And, in the sufferings of betrayal, torture and death 'he goes through the suffering, the heaviest of sufferings, of the second order in his concern and care over the fact that his suffering may give offence'. (*SV* 16, p.134) For 'the God-man must require faith and must refuse direct communication in order to require faith'. (*SV* 16, p.138)

> In the relationship between one human being and another, each must and shall be satisfied with the other's assurance that he believes him; no human being has the right to make himself the object of another's faith. If the one uses dialectical redoubling in relation to the other, then he must use it in a quite inverse manner, maieutically, precisely in order to avoid becoming the object of faith or anything approximating to it for any other human being. . . . But only the God-man can do no other and must, as qualitatively different from humanity, require that he be the object of faith. If he does not become this, then he becomes an idol – and therefore he must refuse direct communication, because he must require faith. (*SV* 16, p.138)

Nonetheless, it is arguable that this provision extends to all essentially Christian communication. As we have already seen, the apostle too is a paradoxical phenomenon. He too must refuse the guarantees which would win a ready audience for his message. The same applies to ordination:

a priest is essentially what he is through ordination, and ordination is a teacher's paradoxical transformation in time, by which
though still in time, he becomes something other than what he
would become through the immanent development of genius,
talents, gifts, etc. . . . ordination is a *character indelibilis*. . . . By
ordination the Christian *nota bene* is once again affirmed. (*SV* 9,
p.229)

It is against this background that Kierkegaard could polemicise
so bitterly against the displays of worldly power which accompany
the preaching of Christianity in established Christendom. The
medium falsifies the message – or, rather, the real message shows
through all too plainly in such displays: that aesthetics has overpowered and neutralised the Christian message, robbing the paradox of its force and making it a sign among signs.

But what of the author of pseudonymous books in all this, the
writer who writes without the authority of an apostolic call or of
ordination? Kierkegaard himself was anxious that his own role as a
practitioner of Christian maieutics might lead him to neglect the
essential direct element in Christian communication and the concomitant requirement of existential reduplication. At one point, for
instance, he wrote: 'The thing to do now is to take over unambiguously the maieutic structure of the past, to step forth definitely
and directly in character, as one who has wanted and wants to
serve the cause of Christianity.' (*JP*,6231/IX A 218) Yet, conversely,
if even the most direct statement of the Christian message, uttered
by an apostle or by the Christ himself, has nonetheless something
essentially *indirect* about it, an indirectness springing directly from
the paradoxicality of the content of the message, then might it not
be that the practice of indirect communication, even if penned or
uttered by one without authority, has a place within the actual
communication of Christian truth, and not merely in the preamble
to such communication? In other words, despite the sharp distinction which Kierkegaard makes between his own practice as an
indirect communicator 'without authority' and the authoritative
communication of a priest, an apostle or the Christ, there is
nonetheless a significant continuity running through all forms of
Christian communication, and this continuity is implied in the
whole discussion of indirect communication. For Kierkegaard's
indirect approach was not simply a tactical ploy, determined by the
cultural situation of the modern world or by his own combination

of lay status and literary ability – it was rather an instantiation of an essential element in *all* Christian communication.

What is it then that such communication uniquely offers in all its forms? It is, as I have suggested at several points, that it honours, affirms and in the process of communication itself ensures and nurtures the freedom of the recipient of the message, or, more precisely, the mutual freedom of all the participants in the process. In this respect it is decisively Christian communication, communication in which the coincidence of ends and means is continuously sustained. At one level this might bear comparison with Paulo Freire's *Pedagogy of the Oppressed*, which attempts to cure education in economically dependent countries from what Freire calls 'narration sickness' or 'the banking concept of education'. In such a system of education, 'The teacher is the subject of the learning process, while the pupils are mere objects.'[20] The teacher simply narrates to the pupil what he or she is to learn, or deposits information which the pupils simply receive, file and store. Freire's argument is that if the poor are to break out of their economic dependence then this can only be as and when they start to become participants, subjects, in the learning process, contributing to it and bringing to it their own insights and experiences. Kierkegaard would possibly not have shared Freire's political priorities, but the comparison brings out what is perhaps for us the most accessible point of entry into Kierkegaard's understanding of the dialectics of communication. They are fundamentally inseparable from the dialectics of freedom, the process by which the self comes to be and to affirm itself in its own true being. Yet, as has also already been indicated, precisely because the dialectics of communication are made central to this process it should not be conceived in over-individualistic terms. The appropriation of freedom and the grounding of that freedom in absolute truth is a task within the communication process and therefore also a task within and only within the community of communicating persons. The Christian community in particular, as the community which God, as the supremely free person, seeks to bring about through the communication of the forgiveness of sins, is and must be a community of reciprocal freedom. This situation inheres in the whole structure of Christian communication in all its forms.

As we turn now to Kierkegaard's aesthetic works (and, later, to his ethical and religious works) let us bear the theoretical explanation which he offers of his practice as a communicator in mind. Let us not, however, allow it to constrain our reading unduly. For such theoretical reflections might tempt us to see ourselves as somehow outside the process of communication, looking in on it from outside. As readers of Kierkegaard, however, we are participants in that direct–indirect exchange in which we ourselves have so much responsibility for what takes place. Following a number of clues thrown up in this and in previous chapters we shall pursue our reading not by going from book to book but by picking out the key literary forms: the drama, the novel and the religious discourse. To some extent this will involve recapitulating the movement which we have already followed from the discussions of aesthetics in the early journals through to the commentary on 'the sign of contradiction' and we shall see how each of these forms in turn moves us closer to the dynamics of the Christian paradox, the call to faith in the God-in-time. Yet, if the argument of this chapter is true then that paradox in fact plays a constitutive role across the whole spectrum of Kierkegaard's writing, the aesthetic as well as the religious, and even the brightest and most luminous of Kierkegaard's aesthetic images will bear both the shadow and the illumination of the cross. We do not, however, see in this the evidence of an authorial master-plan, for, on Kierkegaard's own understanding of indirect communication, he is, with us, a reader and learner – and not the controller of the communication.

4

Life in the Magic Theatre

KIERKEGAARD'S CONCEPT OF DRAMA

There is ample biographical evidence relating to Kierkegaard's lifelong enthusiasm for the theatre and his frequent, sometimes daily, attendance at it. It is not surprising therefore that the world of the theatre pervades his authorship, providing him with a constant supply of illustrative material drawn from classical, Shakespearian, German and Danish sources. More importantly, it provided him with a paradigm of the aesthetic consciousness, a paradigm which relates equally to aesthetics (as the sphere of artistic practices) and 'the aesthetic' (as an existential category). This was in no way a personal idiosyncrasy, a mere reflection of his own predeliction for theatrical entertainment, since, as we have already observed, drama was widely regarded in contemporary aesthetics as constituting the supreme summit of the scale of aesthetic forms. Hegel and Heiberg were both examples of this tendency, Heiberg even going so far (quite illegitimately in Kierkegaard's view) as to ascribe speculative and apocalyptic powers to this particular art-form. If in this way the theatre was already being conceived within the system of absolute idealism itself as the maximum of aesthetic achievement, then it is easy to see how the critique of drama becomes the critique of art as such – as well as having important ramifications in respect of the wider critique of idealism in general which we find in Kierkegaard's writings. Kierkegaard's choice of the theatre as the paradigm of the aesthetic consciousness therefore has far-reaching systematic significance and some examination of the part played by the theatre in his authorship is an indispensable element in any interpretation of his understanding of aesthetics. In addition, such an examination offers valuable insights into how his own aesthetic writings are to be read. For the 'dramatic' aspects of his authorship should not be overlooked. This point was forcefully made in an earlier generation of Kierkegaard scholarship by Martin Thust, who described

Kierkegaard's aesthetic works as his 'Marionette Theatre'.[1] Before applying the dramatic model to our own reading of Kierkegaard, however, let us begin by exploring further the concept of drama which he himself held.

The first thing to be said is that this concept was largely framed within the horizons of dialectical idealism itself, although he also drew on earlier sources (notably Lessing) in support of his own position. The idealistic nature of his theory of drama stands out particularly sharply in his many discussions of dramatic character, and, as we shall see, dramatic character holds an especially privileged place within his writings on drama in general. I shall illustrate this by looking at four of the roles which he discusses at length: Don Giovanni (in Mozart's opera), Emmeline (in Scribe's *The First Love*), Juliet (in *Romeo and Juliet*) and Captain Scipio (a character in the long-forgotten musical play *Ludovico* by J.H. Vernoy de St Georges).

The brilliant essay on *Don Giovanni*, 'The Immediate Stages of the Erotic, or The Musical Erotic', is one of the best-known and most accessible of Kierkegaard's works. Following the aphoristic 'Diapsalmata' which open the 'Papers of "A"' (the aesthetic persona of the first part of *Either/Or*) the piece on *Don Giovanni* may be taken as the first full-scale exposition of the theme of what it is to live aesthetically. 'Living aesthetically', however, is not merely something which the Don, as an aesthetic personality, or Mozart, as a creative artist, do: it is also something which their commentator 'A' himself represents by the way in which he experiences and interprets both character and work.

The Don is seen, in accordance with the early papers on the three great representative figures, as the incarnation of the idea of sensuous passion. As the book develops it becomes clear that this is only one form of living aesthetically – again something which had been brought out in the notes discussing the relationship between Don Juan, Faust and the Wandering Jew. This idea is, in the language of Heibergian aesthetics, the 'immediate' pole of aesthetic life, and *Either/Or* will go on from here to lead the reader through a whole gamut of aesthetic figures, culminating in Johannes the Seducer, the absolutely reflective counterpart to Don Giovanni.

The argument of the Mozart essay is that *Don Giovanni* is unsurpassable as a musical work of art, because in it we can find an absolute congruence between form and content. The amorous Don himself is seen as constituting the essential content of the work, which centres on the presentation of his character. But what is this character? It is misleading to describe him as a seducer, since this already implies an element of artifice and deliberation. Rather, he is the incarnation of sensuous passion, he is desire itself: 'Therefore he does not seduce, he desires . . .'. (*SV* 2, p.93) If such desire is to be portrayed aesthetically then, Kierkegaard (or 'A') argues, it *must* be in the medium of music. 'This force of Don Giovanni, this sheer power, this life-force, can only be expressed by music, and I know no other predicate for it than this: that it is *joie de vivre* and cheerfulness.' (*SV* 2, p.96) Both music (form) and the sensuous passion of the Don (the content) are, moreover, to be defined in terms of immediacy, determined by but excluded from the sphere of authentic spiritual existence – in other words: as acquiring their specific historical and ideal significance from the stance taken by Christianity (Spirit) towards paganism and the life of the flesh (immediacy). Thus, that which in nature, in childhood and in the pagan world is experienced as innocent and thoughtless immediacy comes to be regarded as 'demonic' when the Christian revelation establishes the goal of a 'higher' self-conscious and ultimately self-responsible life as the true *telos* of human existence.

A key element in Kierkegaard's development of this argument is the relationship between Christianity, understood as the religion of the Word made flesh, and language. Christianity makes language into *the* absolutely appropriate mode of spiritual communication while, conversely, that which lies outside (or, in Christian parlance, *below* the threshold of) language is thereby stripped of any claim it might have had to ultimate ethical and religious seriousness. This, the essay argues, again applies both to music and to the character of Don Giovanni himself. The persona of the Don is not, in the last resort a *speaking* person but a *musical* person and, like music, he is essentially speechless. For language, according to Kierkegaard, presupposes reflection or difference,[2] and the essayist is very attentive to the way in which the Don's desire relates itself to difference. For example, he 'has' many women – but what is it he desires in each of them? It is, we are told, that which is universal or common to every woman. 'For Don Giovanni every girl is universal girlhood . . . it is not the exceptional which Don Giovanni desires but the universal, that which she has in common with every other woman'. (*SV* 2, p.92) What he desires, like his desire itself, cannot therefore be expressed in that realm of differentiation which belongs to language. Recognising the problem

which this situation poses for someone who wants to write about
Don Giovanni (man and opera) the essayist seeks, as far as possible, to bring the reader to the very frontiers of language, from
where, as it were, he might look over into the realm of music: '. . .
and when I have brought the reader to be so musically receptive
that he seems to hear the music, although he hears nothing, then I
have completed my task, then I will be quiet, then I will say to the
reader as to myself: listen'. (*SV* 2, p.83) There are indeed moments
(as in the stunning description of the overture) where the essayist's
language itself becomes lyrical to the point of making music with
words – and yet it remains language, not the desire of the great
lover, not the music of the opera, but the words of a commentator.

The exclusion of both music and the sensuous energy represented by the Don from language has a further important corollary: that both are thereby also excluded from the realm of the
ethical. In considering the other (by definition flawed, because
they are literary, not musical) attempts to portray Don Juan by
Molière and Byron, Kierkegaard notes that it is often said 'that
Molière's Don Juan is more moral than Mozart's'. (*SV* 2, p.108)
But, he suggests, this is as it should be, since the opera, as an
essentially musical work, stands outside the scope of moral or
ethical judgements. We must simply give ourselves over to be
seduced, to be carried away, by the sheer energy of the music, as if
we ourselves were the objects of the Don's attentions. The last
thing we must do is to obtrude inappropriate moral or ethical
categories. This does not mean that the critic may not speak at all,
but simply that his task is primarily to attune his reader to the spirit
of music that *is* the meaning of the work.[3]

In May 1845 (two years after the publication of *Either/Or*) *Don
Giovanni* was revived at Copenhagen's Theatre Royal in a production which prompted Kierkegaard to write a brief review article
criticising what he called 'a single point' (*SV* 18, p.51) in the opera.
This review underlines the account of *Don Giovanni* given in
Either/Or by putting the critical approach taken there to work. The
single point in question concerns the scene in which Don Giovanni
sets about seducing the peasant girl Zerlina. In Kierkegaard's view
the key aria was sung too reflectively by the male lead, Hr Hansen.
Instead of addressing himself commandingly *to* her, he sings as if
he were singing *for* her, aiming to arouse her passion by the song
instead of by the energetic desire of his very being, of which the
song is simply an expressive outpouring. No excellence of delivery

can make amends for the total misconception of the whole opera which occurs if a single note of reflection is allowed to creep into the portrayal of the Don. This is not a drama of significant words but of emotive, primitive powers.

Despite the fervent lyricism of the *Either/Or* essay, we find in these writings on *Don Giovanni* a clear application of Heiberg's critical requirement that there should be a perfect congruence between form and content. In the opera itself, we find just such congruence – in the 1845 production, however, we miss it. Less Heibergian is the way in which Kierkegaard makes the central character, the Don himself, bear the weight of meaning of the work as a whole and, more specifically, doing so by being the representative of a highly specific principle or idea. This tactic, as we shall see, is typical of Kierkegaard's general approach to dramatic art.

Either/Or I also contains an extraordinary analysis of Scribe's comedy, *The First Love*. It was dismissed by Heiberg himself, who wrote of the (at that point unknown) author of *Either/Or* that 'He has made a masterpiece out of a pretty little bagatelle and ascribes to it a tendency which is virtually the opposite of that which Scribe admits to.'[4] We are, fortunately, not concerned here with the correctness of the interpretation of *The First Love* offered in *Either/Or*, but only with the light it throws on Kierkegaard's view of dramatic art.

In contrast to *Don Giovanni* the reviewer of Scribe's play argues that the essential quality in comedy is not immediacy but reflection, not character but situation – principles perfectly in accordance with Heibergian dogma. Consequently, whereas the best approach to the opera is to 'hear, hear, hear Mozart's *Don Giovanni*', losing oneself in its musical immediacy, the effect of a comedy is actually enhanced by the reflective distance which one has from it. The contemplation of a truly comic situation is an incitement to the constant renewal of reflection: 'reflection is moving in it, and the more one discovers, the more infinite the comic situation becomes within itself, as it were, and the more one gets dizzy, and yet one cannot stop staring at it'. (*SV* 2, p.243) Nevertheless, because it is a comedy, what is at stake is essentially nothing, that is to say, the whole action of the play is a series of misunderstandings in which nothing serious ever happens. 'There must not be a single figure in it, not a single dramatic relationship, which could lay claim to survive the downfall which irony, right from the beginning, has been preparing for it.' (*SV* 2, p.252) The kind of reflective enjoyment which the connoisseur of comedy is able to make his own is thus likened to the enjoyment of a tobacco-smoker contemplating his smoke – that is, it is a vacuous contemplation of shapes and patterns utterly devoid of meaning. The reflective differences built in to language do have a place here: but they are not used to engender meaning and significance, only ironically manipulated in such a way as to bring about the total negation of meaning.

Although Kierkegaard asserts that the main interest in *The First Love*, as in all comedy, is the reflective interest afforded by situation and dialogue, rather than the more Romantic interest in character and monologue, he is particularly attentive to the character of Emmeline, the 'heroine'. 'The play must be aimed at Emmeline,' he says, 'of that there can be no doubt.' (*SV* 2, p.233)

> She has all possible qualities by which to become a heroine, yet not substantially, but in a negative sense. She is thus comic, and through her the play is a comedy. She is accustomed to rule, as becomes a heroine, but what she rules is a fool of a father, servants, and so on. She has pathos, but as its content is nonsense her pathos is essentially chatter; she has passion, but as its content is a phantom, her passion is essentially folly; she has enthusiasm, but as its content is nothing, her enthusiasm is essentially twaddle; she will make every sacrifice for her passion, that is, she will sacrifice everything for nothing. As a comic heroine she is incomparable. (*SV* 2, p.234)

Emmeline, we learn, is the daughter of a bourgeois household, brought up on romantic novels and convinced that she is in love with her cousin Charles, whom she has not seen since she was eight. She is wooed and, eventually, won, however, by Rinville, who masquerades as Charles in order to get her money, her status – as well as having a bit of fun. The real Charles, who is something of a cad, appears in the course of the play and, being unknown to the rest of the family, pretends to be Rinville. The unfolding of this situation is predictably complex and ludicrous, with everything being reduced to nothing by comic irony – at least, according to the reviewer in *Either/Or*. Always and everywhere it is Emmeline herself who is the vehicle for this annihilating irony: her whims, her fantasies, her choices. In this respect she is the perfect foil to the Don: whereas he is carried along by the powerful upsurge of primitive and overwhelming passion, she is lost in an empty world which exists only in her imagination. She is in herself the essence of comic irony and, in a very important sense, 'exists' only in the sympathetic imagination of the spectator who, in a Shakespearian sense, gives life to the nothing which she 'is' by making her the objective of aesthetic attention and reflection. Yet, despite the obvious differences, she, like the Don, is seen as embodying the spirit of the play as a whole and, indeed, of a very specific form of dramatic art, a highly characteristic aesthetic idea.

Another example of Kierkegaard's treatment of comic character is to be found in a review (not published in his lifetime) of the actor Hr Phister in the role of Captain Scipio.[5] Like Emmeline, Scipio is a self-negating character and is revealed as being trapped in a series of self-contradictions. He is a Captain of the Papal police, which means that he represents the dignity of a military uniform, but is also charged with the very unceremonious civic functions of looking after gutters and sewers. He is also perpetually tipsy, but this contains another contradiction: that he is both drunk and yet not drunk, for 'he has reached the maximum at which he cannot get drunk'. Any ham comedian can play a drunk – but not everyone has the reflection necessary to portray the ambiguity of a condition such as that of Captain Scipio in which 'the immediate is in a certain sense negated; it must never be immediately apparent that he is drunk, for he is not drunk in that way'. The drunkenness must be portrayed precisely in the way it is concealed. Furthermore, to be able to fully admire Phister's performance one must oneself have the reflective capacity to see the 'why' which determines its every detail. Again it is striking that Kierkegaard chooses to see the play through the lens of this single character, who, once again, is also chosen as the representative of a very specific aesthetic idea, the idea of the thoroughly reflective comic character.

The review of *Ludovico* (the play in which Captain Scipio appears) is as much concerned with a particular performance as with the play itself, and this is also the case with what was perhaps the most successful of Kierkegaard's theatrical reviews, the tribute he paid to Mme Heiberg's performance as Juliet when, in her thirties, she returned to the role in which she had first made her name as an 18-year-old discovery. Kierkegaard's contention in the review is that 'age has not withered her' but, on the contrary, she is now able to play the part even more successfully than before, since she brings to it an artistic maturity which has a firm grasp of the essential idea represented by Juliet: the idea of feminine youthfulness.

Kierkegaard draws a sharp distinction between what the public wants and what a serious critic will look for. The public want a young and good-looking female, 'a damned pretty and devilish smart lass of eighteen'. (*SV* 14, p.107) It wants nothing more than those qualities which might make a girl a 'hit' for a season in society. A genuine aesthetician, on the other hand, is in search of the *idea* of feminine youthfulness in a dramatic performance. What matters to such a one is what Kierkegaard calls the 'metamorphosis', the change to which the passing years themselves contribute by stripping away the merely external bloom of feminine youthfulness, thereby enabling the essential idea to stand out all the more clearly. He distinguishes two forms of this metamorphosis which he calls the 'metamorphosis of continuity' and the 'metamorphosis of potentiation'. The former is the process in which 'the actress gradually, as she grows older, changes her field, takes older roles, again with the same perfection with which she had performed her younger parts'. (*SV* 14, p.123) The metamorphosis of potentiation, on the other hand, is 'a more and more intensive return to the first', that is, the first role, the first idea – in this case feminine youthfulness itself. (*SV* 14, p.123f) It is for her triumphant accomplishing of just such a metamorphosis of potentiation that Kierkegaard acclaims Mme Heiberg. In such a return 'the pure, calming, rejuvenating recollection will irradiate the whole performance like an idealising light, and in this light the performance will be perfectly transparent'. (*SV* 14, p.123) That is to say, it will be transparent to the essential idea which it is the actress's (as it is any artist's) task to express.

This review brings out particularly sharply the way in which the theatrical role or character, in this case Juliet, is seen as representing a specific idea, and the actor's aim as being to manifest this idea in every detail of the performance.

Kierkegaard found support for this understanding of dramatic character in Lessing's *Hamburgische Dramaturgie*. In a long discussion centred on Voltaire's criticism of Corneille's characterisation of the Earl of Essex (Voltaire accusing Corneille of historical inaccuracy), Lessing makes it clear that in his view the task of drama is to present ideal types or situations, not to give details of a character in all of his or her particularity, but to evoke the universal element represented by the individual. The dramatist is not a historian and is therefore not concerned with repeating 'what really happened' but rather with showing what we can conceive as happening. History, the complex web of facticity, has no more than an external relation to the dramatic enterprise. 'In the theatre we ought not to learn what this or that individual has done, but what anyone of a certain character placed in certain circumstances would do. The aim of tragedy is far more philosophical than the aim of history.'[6] The tragedian chooses historical names simply because they are already associated (in the minds of his audience) with the sort of character which he wishes to portray on the stage: 'history is nothing for tragedy but a repository of names, with which we are accustomed to connect certain characters'.[7]

Dramatic character in this sense is therefore a means of representing an ideal type. This holds good for comedy as well as for tragedy. Although the names of comic characters are not customarily the names of actual historical figures (as are those of tragic characters) they are not merely arbitrary. In this respect Lessing chastises both the French and the German translators of Aristotle for obscuring the key point of Aristotle's discussion of comic names. This point, according to Lessing, is not that comic writers give their comic characters whatever names they please, but that 'The comedy gives names to its *personae* which, by virtue of their grammatical derivation and construction or also other meaning, would express the characteristics of these *personae* . . . it gave them eloquent names, names which one needed only to hear in order to know straightaway what type of person it would be who bore such a name.'[8] Returning to tragedy he reiterates that 'it is only the concept of the characters which we are accustomed to associate with the names Regulus, Cato and Brutus which provides the reason why the tragic poet gives these names to his *personae*'.[9] In tragedy and comedy alike, then, the ultimate interest of dramatic art is ideal, the poet removing from the character 'what merely belongs to and distinguishes the individual . . . and [his concept] raises itself as far as possible to the divine image [Ger. *Urbild*] in order to become an immediate likeness [*Nachbild*] of the truth'.[10] Each dramatic persona is in this way the representative of an actual and distinct idea, a type, an image of a universal truth of human action or suffering. The task of the dramatist and of the actor is to ensure that the character on stage correctly illuminates this idea, or, to use the term used so frequently by the idealists in relation to art, is transparent to it, with nothing to disturb the audience's immediate perception and enjoyment of it. We may note that this concept of dramatic art is profoundly visual, for what the actor represents is precisely the *image* of an ideal truth. Such an understanding lies ready to hand in the Danish language, since the term for actor, *skuespiller* (Cf. Ger. *Schauspieler*), effectively comprises a metaphor of visualisation. Nor, as in the English/Latin 'audience' do theatre goers go to *hear*: they are instead *tilskuer*, spectators. In this way the theatre is readily conceived as the place where time, action, feelings and relationships are sculpted into the plasticity of the image. The continuing currency of such an understanding of drama is often exemplified in contemporary drama criticism. This, for instance, is what the critic Michael Kustow has to say about the director Peter Brook: 'He has always claimed for drama the power to etch ineradicable images into the mind.'[11] This is not far from Kierkegaard's own view of dramatic art.

As he sees it the ideal nature of the *dramatis personae* applies very much to drama as a whole. Just as each individual character expresses a representative idea, so the play as a whole is a vehicle for an ideal communication. In this respect it is noteworthy, as has been stressed at several points, that Kierkegaard's reviews of various works of dramatic art tend to be dominated by one particular character in such a way that the idea represented by the character coincides with the idea of the work. Thus, in *Don Giovanni*

> Just as in a solar system the dark bodies which receive their light from the central sun are perpetually only half in light, light, that is, on the side which is turned towards the sun, so is it the case with the characters in this piece that only the moment in their lives, the side which is turned towards Don Giovanni is illuminated, while for the rest they are dark and opaque. (*SV* 2, p.116)

In this way, he remarks, to say that Don Giovanni resounds (*gjenlyde*) in Elvira is no mere figure of speech. But what is eminently true of *Don Giovanni* is true of drama in general. 'The chief interest in a drama is naturally altogether focused on the one who is called the hero of the play; in relation to him the other characters are assigned only a subordinate and relative meaning.' (*SV* 2, p.110) Even though he concedes that when the drama is more reflective, with action and situation taking the place of a simple evocation of mood, while the subsidiary characters acquire what he calls a 'relative absoluteness', he still maintains that the dominant idea of the play is supplied chiefly by the central character. Thus in the (by definition reflective) comedy, *The First Love*, the discussion quickly comes to centre on the so-called heroine, Emmeline.

Although this emphasis on the centrality of character is out of step with Heibergian orthodoxy, Kierkegaard does concur with Heiberg in holding that the idea to which both character and play correspond must be appropriate to the specific genre of the play: 'only where the idea has been brought to repose and self-transparency in a determinate form, can there be talk of a classical work . . . this unity, this reciprocal indwelling, belongs to every classical work'. (*SV* 2, p.53) The classical status which he bestows on Mozart's opera is not just a tribute to the splendour of the music but is much more a judgement on the absolute appropriateness of the content of the opera to its musical form. In just the same way the formal qualities of both tragedy and comedy will constrain the possible ideas which might be expressed in them.

This restraint on the expressibility of the dramatic idea has also (and importantly) a historical dimension. We have already taken note of how, in the early journals, the historical and cultural milieu played a key part in moulding the three 'representative figures' of Don Juan, Faust and the Wandering Jew in such a way that Don Juan belongs to the Middle Ages, Faust to the Reformation and the Jew to modernity. A similar point is made more extensively in *Either/Or* I when Kierkegaard discusses the difference there would have to be if a modern dramatist were to create a new Antigone, in the essay 'The Reflection of Ancient Tragedy in Modern Tragedy'.[12] This essay starts by acknowledging that there must be some common element in all tragedy if the word is to have any meaning at all, but there is still 'an essential difference between ancient and modern tragedy'. (*SV* 2, p.129) This difference is said to consist chiefly in the differing conceptions of character among the Greeks and the moderns respectively – the discussion of this point provides further insight into the peculiar prominence of character in Kierkegaard's understanding of drama.

For the Greeks, we are told, the tragic character was both actor and victim. On the one hand it is his own action which is the cause of his downfall, and yet this action is also seen as the result of a decree of fate or destiny – Oedipus did not know that the man he killed was his father nor that the woman he married was his mother. Modernity, however, has a more reflected understanding of character. *Our* heroes and heroines act more deliberately, more self-consciously, more responsibly, as the agents of their own destinies. One sign of this difference is the diminution of the role of the chorus, the epic background, as Kierkegaard calls it, in modern drama. Because of this absence the characters stand out all the more clearly in their assertion of responsible individuality. At the same time, he notes, some element of fatality, of suffering, must remain in the tragic hero's action, since otherwise his offence will be no more than the expression of simple badness and his downfall simple punishment. Thus the elements of fatality and of free action are present in both ancient and modern tragedy – but the balance between them has shifted drastically. This shift can be expressed by saying that while the destiny of the ancient tragic hero arouses sorrow, that of his modern counterpart arouses pain; also the modern hero will be able to reflect on the part his own guilt has played in his tragic destiny, thereby coming to the very frontiers of remorse and repentance. This frontier, however, cannot (according to Kierkegaard) be crossed so long as we remain within the field of aesthetics.

These differences also indicate why Kierkegaard, in company once more with Heiberg, believes that modern drama is essentially orientated towards comedy, since, beyond a certain point, the development of reflection undermines the element of fatality which is essential to all true tragedy. The reflective personality of modern times cannot assume the mantle of tragedy: he must either be pointed in the direction of ethics (that is, repentance) or be made the subject of comedy. In the former case he is driven to a serious and mature recognition and acceptance of his own nothingness; in the latter he is left to make much ado about the nothingness, the total absence of substance, which characterises his life.

All of this does not mean that the great tragedies of the Greeks have become irrelevant to us. We can come to understand them, though we must work hard to do so: 'in order rightly to understand the deep sorrow in Greek tragedy I must live myself into the Greek consciousness'. (*SV* 2, p.137) And yet it will never be *our own* tragedy we see there.

THE LIMITS OF DRAMA

The discussion of the difference between the ancient and the modern forms of tragedy touches on the further point of the limits of drama as such, especially as this is thrown into relief by the reflective character of the modern world. This issue engaged Kierkegaard at several points and in several ways. The discussion of the limits of the various spheres of human knowledge and action was one he found particularly engaging, as he acknowledged in this journal entry:

Some of the most difficult disputes are all the boundary disputes in the sciences. . . . Usually a single science is treated by itself; then one has much to say and gives no thought to the possibility of everything suddenly being dissolved if the presuppositions must be altered.

This is especially true to esthetics, which has always been assiduously cultivated, but almost always in isolation. Many of the aestheticians are poets. Aristotle is an exception. He easily perceives that it has a relation to rhetoric, ethics and politics. (*JP*,143/IV C 104)

The relationship between aesthetics and ethics is then immediately taken up in the next entry:

The relation between esthetics and ethics – the transition – pathos-filled not dialectical – there a qualitatively different dialectic begins. To what extent are poetry and art reconcilable with life – something is true in esthetics – something else in ethics. (*JP*,808/IV C 105)

These thoughts are taken up again by Frater Taciturnus, 'The Quiet Brother', in his 'Letter to the Reader' as the end of *Stages on Life's Way*. This letter deals with the situation of the 'hero' of a lengthy diary, who has been brought to the brink of a religious decision in favour of repentance and away from aesthetics. We shall look at this diary at greater length and from a different perspective in the next chapter (see 'Kierkegaard as Novelist'). The Quiet Brother's letter, however, relates directly to the point at which we have now arrived, since he is concerned to see how the 'classical' dramatic concepts of tragedy and comedy and fear and pity might be brought to bear on the predicament of the diarist. This discussion reflects Kierkegaard's reading of both Aristotle and Lessing and is set quite firmly in relation to a consideration of the implications for aesthetics of the reflective and self-conscious character of the modern world.

The Quiet Brother asserts that while it is true that drama

involves the purification of our fear and pity (the Aristotelian catharsis) 'from all basely egoistic ingredients', (*SV* 8, p.253) such purification nonetheless calls on a kind of self-love, since it depends on the sympathetic participation of the spectator in the action of the play: 'The aesthetic healing consists in the individual gazing at the dizzy sight provided by the aesthetic and by so doing he loses himself, like an atom, like a particle of dust, which is thrown in with the common lot of everyman, of humanity . . .'. (*SV* 8, pp.254f.)

Lessing too observes that the working of fear and pity depend precisely on our perception of a universally human, the ideal, in the dramatic role. But can such a sympathetic identification occur in relation to a *religious* situation? This, for instance, is how Kierkegaard raises the question in the journals:

> 'All poetry is imitation' (Aristotle) – 'better or worse than we are.' Hence poetry points beyond itself to *actuality* and to metaphysical ideality. – Where does the poetic center lie – As soon as it is directed toward sympathy – Therefore we cannot say that we sympathize with Christ. Scripture also says the opposite. See Hebrews 4. (*JP*,144/IV C 109)

In other words, can the kind of ideal unity which we find in dramatic character and, more generally, in drama as such, deal with the sort of situations and contradictions which engage religion? Lessing, at least, was sceptical: 'However convinced we may be of the immediate workings of grace, how little they are nonetheless able to please us in the theatre, where everything which belongs to the character of the *personae* must spring from the most natural causes.'[13] Everything which happens on stage, that is to say, must be in harmony with the universal laws and ideals of human nature and reason. Thus, a contemporary audience is too psychologically aware to find many of the narratives of the religious heroes of the past convincing, since we can see that their behaviour might just as well be motivated by various pathological factors as by the promptings of the divinity. Religion, like history, can be no more for the dramatist than a repository of names and situations, whose suitability for use in the theatre must be decided on purely dramatic grounds. In Lessing's opinion a genuinely Christian tragedy is, however, still awaited, a tragedy, that is, in which the Christian character would interest us precisely as a Christian – but is such a play even possible?

Is the character of the true Christian not somehow completely untheatrical? Don't [the qualities of] still resignation, the unalterable sweetness of temper, which are its most essential characteristics, come into conflict with the whole business of tragedy, which seeks to purify passion by means of passion?[14]

The Quiet Brother approaches this same question via an analysis of the various permutations of tragic and comic situation. Although he quotes Lessing frequently he does not seem to quite understand him, since he calls on him to support his own view that tragedy and comedy take very different attitudes in relation to history. Comedy, he says, has 'a metaphysical lack of concern . . . tragedy is interested in the actual, comedy has the disinterestedness of metaphysics'. (*SV* 8, p.240)[15] But what they do have in common is a reliance on contradiction. Thus, if the theme is love, then tragedy will find a hindrance to love's consummation in some external force or situation (as in *Romeo and Juliet*). Comedy, on the other hand, treats the love itself as being based on a misunderstanding (as in *The First Love*). But, he adds, there are also cases involving both tragic and comic elements. Perhaps the lovers are truly in love but due to some misunderstanding are unable to relate to each other in that love. Such dialectical cases are divided into the tragi-comic and the comi-tragic. The former type involves no essential passion and therefore neither the tragic nor the comic are genuinely present. As an example of such tragi-comic misunderstanding or contradiction the Quiet Brother imagines the following situation:

A deaf man enters a meeting-hall during a meeting; he does not want to disturb it and therefore opens the big folding-doors very slowly. Unluckily the doors have the property of creaking. He cannot hear this, he believes he is doing so well, but a protracted creak is being produced by the lengthy opening. The people become impatient; one turns round and hisses at him, he believes that he has possibly moved the door too suddenly, and the creaking continues. (*SV* 8, p.218)

In the comi-tragic situation, on the other hand, both the tragic and the comic are essentially present. This, the Quiet Brother believes, is the case with the love story narrated in the diary: 'both of them love, and love each other, but nevertheless it is a misunderstanding'. (*SV* 8, p.219) Religion, he adds, 'begins in the higher passion which out of this unity chooses the tragic'. (*SV* 8, p.220) A religious tragic hero, that is, *chooses* to be tragic, *chooses* suffering. In this way he is, perhaps, quintessentially modern, since, as the contrast between the ancient and the modern forms of tragedy showed, modern tragedy depends in a high degree on the hero's choosing the situation which brings about his own downfall.[16] But how can such a character interest us *dramatically*? Is it not too reflective, too interiorised to be susceptible to representation in any kind of image? And is it possible for us to have any degree of sympathy with such a character? As with any other dramatic character the possibility of sympathy depends on being able to understand the reasons why such and such a choice is made, such and such a deed performed – but in the case of the religious hero this is rendered problematic because, by *choosing* suffering, when under no external constraint to do so and with no foreseeable prudential advantage accruing either to himself or to the heroine as a result of this choice, he goes against the grain of universal human nature. For the natural man is motivated to avoid suffering and to seek pleasure. On this basis poetry and art are well able to represent the universally human because they are committed to showing the discords of life resolved in a final harmony. The unforced choice of inconsolable suffering, however, is simply uninteresting aesthetically (a problem both Kierkegaard and Lessing discuss in relation to Terence's play *Heautontimorumenos*, 'The Self-Tormentor') – or, at best, comic. We certainly cannot find in it the stuff of tragedy. This discussion, we might add, illuminates the problem which some commentators have with the kind of self-immolating religious gesture we find in a figure such as Simone Weil.[17] More importantly, it points back to the statement that we cannot, in the aesthetic sense, *sympathise* with Christ, the pre-eminent example of someone whose suffering was completely self-chosen and avoidable. A narrative concerned with such *religious* suffering does not invite sympathy. It is rather, as the Quiet Brother makes clear, a call to self-reflection. The 'pity and fear' which a religious address seeks to arouse is not the sympathetic 'pity and fear' for the characters in the drama being played out on stage: it is rather the fear which the listener should have for himself. For the religious address – by way of contrast with dramatic art – aims precisely to arouse fear, not to cleanse us of it; it seeks to confront us with, not distract us from, ourselves. 'What matters therefore is that one is not happy in the wrong place – and where is the right place? It is: in danger. With seventy thousand fathoms of water beneath and many, many miles from help, to be happy: yes, that is great.' (*SV* 8, p.261)

THE MAGIC THEATRE

We may, with the help of a different pseudonym, Constantin Constantius, approach this same question as to the ultimate limits of drama (particularly as regards the boundary between dramatic art and religious communication) from a quite different and considerably less systematic perspective, from a perspective, in fact, which has about it something of the magic and the mystery of the theatre itself. This approach will also throw further light on the way in which Kierkegaard's own 'aesthetic' authorship may be read as a kind of indirect communication relating to the project of acquiring a religious faith.

Constantin Constantius, the pseudonymous author of *Repetition*, has returned to Berlin after an absence, and has plans to enjoy a thoroughly good evening out at the Königstädter Theatre, a theatre specialising in farce. As he prepares for this treat he delivers an enthusiastic encomium on the magic of the theatre. 'There is surely,' he says,

> no young man of any imagination who has not at some time felt himself caught up by the magic of the theatre and desired himself to be transported into that fictitious reality, so that like a *Doppelgänger* he can see and hear himself, to split himself up into all manner of possible differentiations of himself from himself, so that each differentiation is in turn a single self. (*SV* 5, p.135)

What does this mean?

It is, as Constantin soon makes clear, to be understood in the context of a developmental view of the human self, and, in particular, the transition from childhood to adult life. This is the moment when the self acquires a definite character and becomes a 'self' in a decisive sense, moving from the immediate, natural and essentially passive spontaneity of childhood to the reflective ethical resolve of adulthood. Until this moment arrives – remember Nero – the child lacks real *self*-consciousness in the strict sense of the term, and cannot be held responsible for its words and deeds.

Prior to this moment of maturation, then, the life of the child is profoundly hidden, for it has no public role or identity – or, as Constantin puts it, it is 'cryptic'. Now it is precisely at this point, when the cryptic life of the child comes to the threshold of a new level of existence, when its life ripens and begins to flower, that the magic of the theatre is experienced most powerfully.

The child is to acquire a self, an adult identity – but where is it to acquire it from? Simply to repeat or to carry forward the thoughts, values and habits which it has received from its parents and through its upbringing is not enough, since the challenge of growing up is the challenge to *choose* for oneself, to acquire autonomy. The most that the factical circumstances of one's background can do is to provide the context in which the choice is made – they cannot in any way predetermine either the content or the timing of that choice, or if it takes place at all. What the theatre offers (and, it hardly needs to be said, in our culture this may easily be extended to include the cinema, rock music, television, sport, etc.) is a manifold of roles and possibilities with which the young person can play in imaginative, anticipatory deliberation, free from the not-yet-assumed burden of moral responsibility, able to try on or cast off the various roles at will. The mechanism by which this occurs is a kind of projective sympathetic fantasy, such that the spectator who intuits the dramatic ideas represented by the various *personae* of the stage actually comes to see himself in them, to see their idea as his idea. Constantin, alluding to a long tradition of thinking about drama, calls this the shadow-play (*Schattenspiel*) of the hidden individual. Thus, for instance,

> Among the shadows in whom he discovers himself, whose voice is his voice, there is perhaps a brigand chief. He may recognise himself in this mirror-image; in the brigand's manly figure, his rapid yet piercing glance, the marks of passion on his furrowed brow, all may be found there. He may lie in wait on the mountain pass, he may listen for the movement of the travellers, he may give the signal, his band charges down; his voice may drown out the noise, he may be cruel, letting all [the victims] be cut down, and turning indifferently away, [yet] he may be chivalrous towards the anxious girl, etc., etc. (*SV* 5, p.137)

Of course, the spectator whose fantasy is caught up in this way would not dream of behaving like that 'in real life' – and that is precisely the freedom of the theatre. If he does not wish to be such a brigand chief (a Robin Hood, perhaps?) he might try his hand at a Don Giovanni, a Faust, an Emmeline, an Antigone, and so on. It is in this way that he splits himself up 'into all manner of possible differentiations of himself from himself', finding in the theatre an almost limitless store of role-models, a vehicle for the mirroring in an external form of the myriad possibilities latent in his own (emergent) self-consciousness.

Constantin is clear in his own mind that despite the tangible objectivity of actors, stages and sets, the real action of the theatre takes place in the medium of the imagination. The 'shadows' of the theatre exist only in the consciousness of those who behold them and opt to entertain them. For it is really only himself that the young person wishes to see and hear. The 'shadows' on the stage are essentially cast by the imagination of the audience.

Constantin is also clear that just as there is a time when it is right to give oneself over to the spell of the theatre in this way, so there is also a time to leave it behind for other, more serious concerns.

> It is naturally only at a very young age that such a desire expresses itself. Only the fantasy is awake in this dream of personality, every other faculty is still sound asleep. In such a fantastic self-contemplation the individual has no actual form, but is only a shadow, or rather, the actual form is invisibly present, and is therefore not content with casting one shadow, but the individual has a multiplicity of shadows, which all resemble him, and for each moment have an equal claim to be himself. This personality is not yet discovered, its energy announces itself only in the passion of possibility. (*SV* 5, pp.135f.)

But what is fitting for the unrepeatable moment of spiritual adolescence becomes a perversion if it continues beyond the point at which moral and religious factors come into play – again we may recall Nero. For there comes a point when the self must choose itself, when it must commit itself with total seriousness to its own actual future and to the claims and obligations which its being with others imposes on it. This is one sense of Constantin's favourite concept of repetition: the moment when the self becomes a self a second time (the first time having been its biological coming into existence). Now it is no longer sufficient to strike dramatic poses, to go on trying on one role after the other. Now the self must respond to the summons: become what you are! be what you will be!

> At the same moment the cock crows and the twilight figures flee away, the voices of the night fall silent. If they continue, then we are in a quite different domain, where all this goes on under the disquieting eye of responsibility, then we are at the border of the demonic. (*SV* 5, p.137)

The word translated here as 'disquieting' (*aengstende*) might also be translated as 'causing *angst*', a sign that we have once more come up against that border zone between the aesthetic and the religious which is under the sway of *angst*, the tension between the ideal and the actual, between the form of the aesthetic image, the shadow, and the inner, inexpressible freedom of the Spirit.

We are, then, urged to leave the artistically contrived half-light of the theatre for the harsher, but real, light of the newly-dawning day – literally, perhaps, but also (and more importantly) meta-phorically. For this process is (with Plato in mind) Kierkegaard's reworking of the parable of the cave, and the mechanism of self-projection which Constantin sees as vital to the magic of the theatre is a mechanism constantly at work in human situations and relationships of all kinds. So much so, indeed, that we may well ask whether there is a world outside the theatre at all – or whether all of life is no more than a constantly shifting shadow-play, devoid of seriousness and responsibility?

Such thoughts are particularly tempting for the citizen of the modern world who experiences the fragmentation of urban life, and the isolation of the individual from familial and other social bonds: such a person could, fairly easily, slip the net of account-ability and create a life-style which is almost entirely a concatena-tion of poses, assumed images and self-dramatisations. Having no essential obligation to the world about him, anything becomes possible. Kierkegaard epitomised the spirit of such a life in many places, but perhaps nowhere more brilliantly than in a journal entry, in a series entitled 'My Innocent Diversions' which he had planned to include in an unfinished humorous work called *Writing Sampler*:

> The special point about my diversions is that they are varied. Here are two principal variations. I regard the whole city of

Copenhagen as a great social function. But on one day I view myself as the host who walks around conversing with all the many cherished guests I have invited; then the next day I assume that a great man has given the party and I am a guest. Accordingly, I dress differently, greet people differently, etc. I am sure those who know me have frequently observed that my manner may be somewhat different, but they probably do not dream that this is the reason – If an elegant carriage goes by with four horses engaged for the day, I assume I am the host, give a friendly greeting and pretend it is I who has lent them this lovely carriage.

I also vary my diversions by sometimes regarding Copenhagen as a large city and sometimes as a little one. (*JP*,5763/VI B 225)

For such an individual – a nineteenth-century flâneur or a member of the modern leisure society – life itself has become theatre. This is the epitome of the aesthetic attitude portrayed in such a figure as Johannes the Seducer. In this aesthetic world there is no concrete, stable matrix of meaning and significance. Everything is only what it seems: perspective, point of view, image. The 'rotation method' is the aesthetic individual's ultimate resource against the terminal boredom which constantly threatens a life lacking any deep, cohesive interest. This method, we may recall, has realised the pointlessness of seeking external distractions and aims instead to manipulate the individual's point of view in relation to the external situation in such a way that life will always offer some new aspect to be enjoyed. Johannes the Seducer, for example, is not interested simply in slaking a physical passion for sexual enjoyment and is no Don Juan in this respect. His 'interest' is much more excited and engaged by the process and method of seduction itself: not the girl, but the way he goes about getting the girl. He has come to the brink of realising that aesthetic existence derives its power from the aesthete himself, that what happens in the external world is no more than a reflection of his own self-projection and self-dramatisation.

This is how 'A', himself an advocate of the aesthetic way, describes the Seducer:

Behind the world in which we live, far away in the background, lies another world, which stands in approximately the same relation to this world as the scene one sometimes sees in the background in the theatre stands in relation to the main stage. Through a thin gauze one sees, as it were, a world of gauze, lighter, more ethereal, of a different quality from the real world. Many people who are physically present in the real world do not actually belong to it but to this other world. (*SV* 2, pp.283f.)

The Seducer, whom Victor Eremita describes as moving 'like a shadow across my floor' (*SV* 2, p.15), is indeed a 'shadow', a creature of the shadow-world of the theatre – even when he is out and about in the parks and cafés of Copenhagen pursuing some assignation. This is what he himself says about himself on one such occasion: 'Everything is symbol, I myself am a myth about myself, for is it not like a myth that I hasten to this meeting? Who I am has nothing to do with it . . .'. (*SV* 2, p.409) What is frightening about the Seducer is not his erotic adventurousness but 'that a man can thus fade away, indeed almost vanish from reality . . .'. (*SV* 2, p.284)

But the question is whether the Seducer is unique otherwise than in the degree of self-consciousness with which he reflects on his situation and lives out the myth about himself that he himself has created. What is the real world, anyway? Are we not all of us trapped in a web of projections, never sure where interpretation ends and reality begins? Such thoughts, indeed, could well be taken as typical of those most identified with the spirit of modernity and, with a slight change of emphasis, post-modernity: a rootless, deliberately superficial, intelligently but capriciously eclectic spirit, without meaning or goal.[18] If there is no reality outside the magic world of the theatre – or if that magic is itself the sole reality – what then? The question acquires added urgency if we think through the implications of this situation at the level of social or communal life. For if the mutual relationships between the members of a community were unable to break through the manifold interplay of projected images, then that community could scarcely be one in which responsible freedom flourished. For such freedom presupposes the possibility of recognising, affirming and acting on perceived actual commitments. If we are unable *at any point* or *in any way* to trust in the reality of such commitments then we will soon find ourselves in the realm of non-speak, the non-community of collective schizophrenia.[19]

Constantin Constantius himself seems to reach the conclusion that this is, in fact, how things are. His trip to Berlin had been planned in order to bring about a repetition, a term which he describes as meaning the movement from possibility to actuality, such that through it life acquires continuity within flux together with seriousness and ethical pith. Repetition, in other words, is one avenue of escape from the magic of the theatre. But, he concludes, repetition is not, after all, possible. At the end of the day all there is is meaningless flux – 'you cannot step twice into the same stream'. His critical intellectuality is quite distinct from the immediate enthusiasm of adolescence which is so spontaneously entranced by the theatre's world of glittering images, yet his chosen *métier* of reflection and logic is also (as Hegel described his *Logic*) a realm of shadows. For Constantin too life contains many ideas, many possibilities – but no overarching, unifying idea or reality. Like (though in other respects unlike) the Seducer he is 'a vanishing person'. (*SV* 5, p.194) His life is no more 'real' than the theatre and all its illusions: a sequence of roles without rhyme or reason. This thought fills him with despair, as he claims as his symbol the coach horn (on which one can never be sure of playing the same note twice) – a reminder that 'one does not need to move from the spot in order to be convinced that there is no repetition. No, one sits quietly in one's room, when all is vanity and passes away, one nevertheless travels faster than a railway-train, although one is sitting still.' (*SV* 5, p.153) The individual is in this way seen as dissolved into a vortex of flux – with only the one certainty of death.

> Speed on, you drama of life, which no one calls a comedy, no one a tragedy, because no one ever saw the end! Speed on, you drama of existence, where life cannot be spent again any more than money! Why did no one ever return from the dead? Because life does not know how to trap one as death does, because life has no persuasive powers like those of death. (*SV* 5, p.154)

Is this not the 'wisdom' of T.S. Eliot's 'Marina' – that all the images of this life have only one meaning: death? The most that a Constantin can hope for is to trick a new image, a new angle, a new interest from this constantly shifting sea of change, until he must finally resign himself to death, the final nothingness to which all things return. Constantin's view of this, I have suggested, is deeply despairing, though he manages to give his pessimism a wry, ironic twist. But is this the only possible response to the recognition of the radically aesthetic and foundationless character of life, to the vision of life as nothing but the interplay of multiple projections and self-dramatisations?

Nietzsche, it is well known, distinguished two forms of nihilism.[20] The first he identified with the philosophy of Schopenhauer, the pessimistic appraisal of the meaninglessness of life and the abandonment of the self to the will to death and oblivion. This, I would suggest, is very much the position of Constantin Constantius. But Nietzsche also offered a second response to the same fundamental insight into the ultimate vacuity of the world: the yea-saying to life which requires no metaphysical underpinning because it is its own justification; an affirmation of existence in its very transitoriness without reference to God, ground or goal, without any unifying idea, reality or purpose. Those who opt for this second, life-affirming form of nihilism may dance joyously across the abyss, reckless of the 'fact' that the sustaining power of art, the supreme lure to life, is no more than an illusion.

A literary realisation of such a joyful wisdom, a realisation which provides the most striking contrast to the philosophy of Constantin Constantius, has been provided by Hermann Hesse in his novel *Steppenwolf*.[21] Its 'hero', Harry Haller, is approaching fifty and in the throes of a mid-life crisis, torn apart by the conflicting demands of his 'human' world of culture, literature and music and his 'animal' shadow, the steppenwolf, who inhabits 'a dark world of instincts, wildness, cruelty, raw, unsublimated nature'. (*S*, p.64) We are told in the course of the novel that the situation is, inevitably, more complicated than that, for 'Harry does not consist of two beings, but of hundreds, thousands. As with every human being his life does not merely oscillate between two poles such as instinct and spirit, or holiness and profanity, but oscillates between thousands, between innumerable pairs of opposites.' (*S*, p.65) But if Constantin consoles himself in the face of such an insight by calling up the thought of death and oblivion, Hesse has a different solution in store for Harry. The 'human' and 'wolf' *personae*, in terms of which Harry has rationalised his predicament, are both illusions, yes, but what Harry must learn is precisely to give himself over to the journey from illusion to illusion, and *living* the myriad new modulations and symbolisations through which alone he 'is' what he is.

At the end of the novel Harry is initiated into the Magic Theatre, a theatre which contains countless loges, each being the entrance to a different 'drama' – in which the spectator himself is a participant. Here Harry can learn to dance the tango, to be a general or to talk with Alexander the Great. In short, he can be whatever he wishes, for the moment, to be. Frightening, erotic, comic, the Magic Theatre is a world of appearances with no underlying reality, Nietzsche's non-metaphysical and amoral universe.

In order to be a worthy participant in the life of the Magic Theatre Harry has to leave behind both his 'human' and 'wolf' selves, while his mysterious mentor, Pablo (who periodically transmutes into Mozart), tells him that this is a school for humour and that 'all higher humour begins when one no longer takes one's own person seriously'. (*S*, p.193) This proves to be a hard lesson for Harry to learn. In the course of his many surreal adventures in the Magic Theatre, he encounters, for example, Pablo lying with Hermine, the woman he loves, and stabs her to death in a fit of jealousy. But soon he discovers that the whole scene was just one more illusion. He is put on trial – not for murder, but for having 'dirtied our lovely world of images with the dirt of reality.' (*S*, p.236) Harry is condemned to stay in the Magic Theatre until he is able to enjoy it with genuine humour, ridding himself of all vestiges of belief in a 'real' self.

What Nietzsche and Hesse both seem to be saying is that the mechanisms of self-projection and self-dramatisation constitute a *ne plus ultra* in human life, something behind, beyond or beneath which we cannot go. We live only in the myths and dramas we make of ourselves. The acceptance of such a view is the gateway to a joyful wisdom, a liberation from the deadweight of metaphysical uniformity and the futile quest for reality. Is this then the choice: *either* the world-weariness of Constantin and Schopenhauer *or* the yea-saying of Nietzsche and Hesse? To narrow our alternatives down to these, however, is to accept the premise which both sides share: that there is no reality outside the life of the Magic Theatre. But are we bound to accept that premise? And what of Kierkegaard's talk of a 'religious' point of view standing over against the bewitching images of dramatic existence?

We have seen that Kierkegaard is prepared to go along with Constantin's view of life in this at least: that the aesthetic universe has no ultimate grounding in reality. This is noticeably similar to his judgement on Hegelian idealism. For idealism, he believes, is as such, deeply sceptical. He cannot therefore see the relation between art and reality as being simply like the relation between two points on the same ontological scale, with art functioning as a lower, weaker or 'merely' external form of that same reality which (let us say) religion and philosophy represent more appropriately. Art and metaphysics – as from a quite different perspective, many of his contemporaries in the idealist camp also claimed – stand or fall together. Kierkegaard's religious alternative, then, will not be a repudiation of art in favour of a metaphysically conceived 'real' world. There are therefore hopeful signs that what he is going to put forward is a *tertium quid*, a third way, alongside the ways of Constantin/Schopenhauer and Nietzsche/Hesse. There are further signs that this is indeed what is on offer when we look at the way in which he poses his alternative to the aesthetic form of life. As was emphasised in the previous chapter his tactic is to proceed indirectly and, instead of describing the shortcomings of aesthetics from the outside, from some supposedly superior and unbiased position, he seeks instead to show the untenability of the aesthetic point of view in its own terms. This makes his critique of art and of aesthetics itself into an aesthetic event, as he criticises art in and through works of art.

His aesthetic works are complex and challenging, strewn with interpretative booby-traps, and further complicated by the interrelationship between them, with some of the 'authors' and 'editors' turning up as characters in other works, and one of them, Johannes Climacus, offering a series of reflections on the aesthetic authorship as a whole. At the moment, however, I wish only to highlight that characteristic of these writings in which their aesthetic quality is most evident: their theatricality.

Martin Thust has described Kierkegaard as being not just the 'poet of the religious' but also the 'dramatist of the religious', and wrote of the pseudonymous authorship as 'Søren Kierkegaard's Marionette Theatre'.[22] Why – and why, particularly, 'marionette' theatre? Because, Thust argued, the 'characters' who appear in these works do not have the fluidity or ambiguity which we might expect in a flesh-and-blood theatre. Instead, they are more like puppets constructed with absolute precision in order to represent particular spiritual attitudes and movements – 'ideas', we may say. But this, as we have repeatedly seen, is exactly the function of dramatic character (according to Kierkegaard, that is). The books themselves, Thust goes on to say, are so many stages, so many sets on which the interior drama of religious development is played out before the eyes of the discerning reader. This way of reading the pseudonyms is especially helpful in the context of our present task – though, as I shall suggest, it does not preclude other ways of reading them. For Thust's concept of the function which Kierkegaard gives the pseudonyms answers to Kierkegaard's own 'dramatic' project of creating 'sculptural pictures for the imagination'.

Yet these are dramatic characters of a peculiar kind. Whereas, for instance, Don Juan, Faust and the Wandering Jew all represent distinct ideas (passion, doubt and despair) *aesthetically*, the 'idea' running through Kierkegaard's aesthetic authorship is the problematic nature of aesthetic representation. He depicts the aesthetic imagination precisely at the point where it isolates itself from reality, choosing the world of ideas and dreams in place of the world of responsibility, claim and calling. His characters are creatures of the twilight zone, caught in their various aesthetic poses at that very moment when, as Constantin put it, the cock crows and a new phase of life is called for. Thus we may still choose to look on them aesthetically – or we may find ourselves jolted into seeing what such figures look like in broad daylight. In *Stages on Life's Way* some of the most eminent pseudonyms have spent the night carousing together, delivering witty and elegant speeches on the subject of women and love. Now the day has come, and they prepare to go their different ways. 'They made a fantastic impression on me', a mysterious narrator tells us,

> a nocturnal society, seen in the morning light in a pleasant natural surrounding, has an effect which is almost *unheimlich*. One might think of ghosts, surprised by the dawn; of subterranean beings, who cannot find the crack through which they must vanish, because they are only visible in the dark; of unhappy creatures, for whom the difference between day and night has vanished in the uniformity of suffering. (*SV* 7, p.76)

We can see the Seducer in his own terms as a subtle and amusing connoisseur of life's sweetest pleasures *and* one who knows how to enjoy them without getting caught – or, we can see him as a 'failed' one-dimensional perpetual adolescent. His 'failure', moreover, is not simply due to the pathological nature of his idiosyncratic idea: it is rather the failure, the emptiness, of all attempts to construct the personality around or on the basis of an idea, that is, the mechanism of dramatic self-projection. Once we see this we will not be tempted to carry on going endlessly round and round the Magic Theatre and trying on ever-new roles. Instead we will want to seek a way out. Not, however, that the pseudonymous works themselves directly offer such a way, but they can prompt us to ask what other options lie open before us.

This can be put even more graphically. Heiberg's play *Christmas Jest and New Year's Fun* centres on the conflict of interests between author, director, character and audience.[23] In the course of the play Harlequin, the clown, disillusioned with the author, decides to get his own back by putting on a play of his own in the middle of the main production. A 'second' audience assembles on stage and the play begins, a rather peculiar play which features such absurd characters as a boot, a hat, a bottle and a book. The author arrives in the midst of this 'second' play and is shocked at what he sees. In order to undermine the clown's rebellion he gets the theatre watchman to call out 'Fire!' A fire-chief happens to be among the members of the 'second' audience and stands up, wanting to know if there really is a fire, or if this is part of the play. The author tells him that yes, the fire is real, since he wants to get the audience of the clown's play off the stage so that he can get on with his own play. But now another fire-chief stands up in the main auditorium, also wanting to know if the fire is real. No, no, the author, says, not wanting *his* 'real' audience to rush off after an imaginary fire. After much confusion authorial control is re-established and the play resumes. In the play-off between reality and illusion Heiberg demonstrates how authorial irony, the firm grasp of the dramatic idea, can bring about an ultimately harmonious synthesis in which each finds its proper place.

Kierkegaard, alluding, it seems, to an actual incident,[24] portrays a not-dissimilar situation in one of the 'Diapsalmata' in *Either/Or*. He reminds his readers of the clown who rushed on to the stage to warn the audience of a (real) fire – but 'They believed it was jest and applauded; he repeated it; they enjoyed it even more . . .'. (*SV* 2, p.33) I suggest that the tension between these two stories mirrors precisely the tension which is aroused through Kierkegaard's 'dramatic' depiction of the various aesthetic *personae* and situations. It is the tension between reality and imagination (obviously) but also the tension between trusting in authorial guidance and assuming our own responsibility for the meaning we find in the text – where authorial guidance also means the 'idea' of the work or performance. Do we carry on living the life of the Magic Theatre, passing from one image to another – and risk being annihilated in the final conflagration of some aesthetic *ragnarok*? Or do we look for a way out – and risk being made to look ridiculous, if, after all, there is no fire and no reality, only the endless play of appearances? Commenting on the parable of the clown and the fire Don Cupitt has written

> The image of the stage, the question of whether one is a spectator of existence or an actor, the still-hidden but fast-spreading fire, the problem of communication and the difficulty of awakening frivolous mankind to the seriousness of existence, and the plight of the original Teacher who cannot but appear to be a fool speaking folly – with astonishing (and perhaps even unconscious) economy Kierkegaard evokes a whole religious tradition and sets out the programme for his own life's work, all in a few brief sentences.[25]

In the light of what we have been reading of Kierkegaard's understanding of drama we may well suspect that the rich associations of the text are by no means unconscious, a suspicion which our further reading of other aspects of his authorship and the continuing use he makes of similes and metaphors drawn from the theatre will strengthen.

One more parable, which strikes a similar note and which brings us back to the relation between Kierkegaard's critique of the aesthetic and his analysis of the nihilism of the present age.

In the context of his later attack on established Christianity, Kierkegaard tells the following story: imagine a vast ocean liner. There is a great festivity on board and the Captain is in the ballroom, enjoying himself with the guests, for the sea seems quiet. One passenger goes on deck, however, and spots a white speck on the horizon which signals the imminent advent of a storm. He rushes down to warn the Captain – only to be ignored. After all, he is only a passenger. (*JP*,3069/XI[3] B 109) The aesthetic authorship is 'without authority', both at the aesthetic and at the religious levels: it contains no direct communication, no authorial testimony, as to its 'real' meaning. And yet, if we choose, we may read it as a warning, albeit the messenger comes dressed like a clown or seems to be just another passenger like ourselves. And we may then decide to take it seriously, to turn our gaze away from the aesthetic shadow-world and seek a reality – a reality to which these works allude, but of which they tell us nothing. What then might this reality be? And how might we learn of it? Are there media which can show us, without distortion, what life outside the Magic Theatre is like?

5

Nihilism and the Novel

KIERKEGAARD'S VIEW OF THE NOVEL

If, at one level, Kierkegaard's aesthetic authorship may be seen as a kind of auto-destructive theatre of the imagination, that does not mean that all further possibilities of interpretation are forthwith exhausted. There are other modes of reading, equally well-grounded in Kierkegaard's own understanding of literature and aesthetics, which we can use to bring into prominence further aspects or dimensions of that authorship. In particular it is possible to read certain works *ethically*, and to do so precisely by reading them *as novels* and, as I hope to show, this correlation between ethical interest and novelistic form is in accordance with Kierkegaard's own literary theory. My argument will, in part, involve shifting our attention to a different set of texts, but, on the other hand, several of the same texts we have already called on will now appear again in a different light. The point is that the different genres within Kierkegaard's authorship are not invariably demarcated with absolute rigidity but that the same works can, on occasion, operate simultaneously on a number of different levels, and that the different methods of reading are necessary in order to realise the full complexity of the authorship. I shall therefore seek to show, first, that Kierkegaard's view of the novel did indeed require the application of ethical criteria; secondly, that this is directly relevant to his own literary productivity; and thirdly, how this relates to a further, *religious*, reading of the authorship.

It is quite striking that Kierkegaard's work as a critic of the arts falls neatly into two categories. This has been carefully analysed by Merete Jørgensen in her monograph *Kierkegaard as Critic*.[1] Here she describes these two categories of criticism as 'aesthetic' and 'ethical', according to whether Kierkegaard confines himself to solely aesthetic criteria (for example, the congruence of form and content) or whether he brings ethical criteria into play. But such a twofold division of his critical writings coincides exactly with a division in the nature of the works he discusses. The aesthetic criticism is concerned exclusively with dramatic art, examples of which we have already examined (*Don Giovanni*, *The First Love*, Mme Heiberg as Juliet and Hr Phister as Captain Scipio). Here the only thing that counts is the internal relation within the work itself (or the performance of the work) between content and form. What Ms Jørgensen refers to as the ethical reviews, however, are just as exclusively concerned with works of novelistic literature. This already raises a strong presupposition in favour of the view that Kierkegaard regarded the novel as being ethically concerned in a way in which dramatic art is not.[2] Thus, in the same way that the theatre provided us with a paradigm of the aesthetic consciousness it might seem appropriate to look to the novel to find a paradigm of what Kierkegaard meant by ethical concern.

The concept of 'life-' or 'world-view' played a key role in Kierkegaard's writings on the novel. These concepts had been in circulation in German and Scandinavian literature and philosophy for a generation and more, but particular importance attaches to Poul Martin Møller's use of the notion of 'world-view' as a literary category. Møller's views have already been discussed and it is only necessary at this point to recall that he did not regard the adoption of a certain 'world-view' as being merely the intellectual acceptation of a particular set of philosophical propositions but depends on the conjunction of three elements: 'The Christian tradition, empirical experience as well as the higher experience in which the supersensuous encounters us in a real form at particular times and places, give the discrete points which must have their place in a proper world-view. . . .'[3] At the same time, as has been emphasised, he was highly doubtful as to whether such a world-view *could* be sustained by members of a generation which had been exposed to the kind of Romantic nihilism which he saw exemplified in a thinker like Schopenhauer. If then, as he also believed, the possession of such a world-view was a part of the essential equipment of the novelist, then the stage is set for particularly painful literary confrontations.

Kierkegaard's first book, *From the Papers of One Still Living* (the title of which may well contain an allusion to Møller's recent death) was concerned with the problems of contemporary novelistic literature in Denmark, the main subject (or, one might say, victim) being Hans Christian Andersen and his novel *Only a Fiddler*. Before closing on his prey Kierkegaard surveys a number of other contemporary novelists, singling out Mme Gyllembourg for singular praise. Mme Gyllembourg, apart from being Heiberg's mother, was the author of a series of anonymous novels, published as the works of 'The Author of *An Everyday Story*', the first novel of the series. The ground of Kierkegaard's commendation is precisely that she possesses a 'life-view' of a kind which the younger generation so signally lack. This life-view is described as essentially optimistic, always prepared to see a hopeful aspect in events and circumstances at a personal, individual level; it is positive in its attitude to people and ready to recognise the 'divine spark' glowing under even the most trivial forms of personal life; though not unacquainted with sorrow and disappointment it does not on that account succumb to pessimism or despair. Whereas the present generation are more likely to remark on what is wrong with the world, the possessor of a 'life-view' of the kind exemplified by this author will have an eye for what is right with the world. It is, in short, the outlook of 'the individual who has run the race and kept the faith'.[4]

The theological basis of the life-view is clear:

A life-view, namely, is more than . . . a sum of statements maintained in their abstract neutrality; it is more than experience, which as such is always atomistic, it is in fact the transubstantiation of experience, it is an unshakeable confidence in oneself, won in the teeth of the empirical manifold; whether it has merely orientated itself with regard to all worldly relationships (a purely human standpoint, e.g. Stoicism), which thereby keeps itself back from contact with a deeper empiricism, or whether it has by being directed towards heaven (the religious) therein found the central point, both for the heavenly and the earthly existence, has won the true Christian assurance 'that neither death nor life, no angel, no prince, no power, nothing that exists, nothing still to come, or height or depth, or anything else in all creation, can separate us from the love of God in Christ Jesus our Lord.' (*SV* 1, pp.34f.)

The echoes of Møller's account of the three elements of the 'world-view' are unmistakable, in particular the combination of a commitment to the reality of the empirical world with the experience of a higher power which no empirical analysis can ever adequately explain.

Kierkegaard was to return to Mme Gyllembourg at the close of his aesthetic authorship, when he wrote a substantial review of her novel, *Two Ages*, a review which was to become the platform for his most sustained critique of 'the present age'. Again he praised her for her possession of a life-view which imbued her work with 'a quiet joy over life' and he amplified the relationship between such a life-view and the work of the novel-writer.

The life-view . . . must have ripened in the author before he produces. His productivity is not a moment in his development, but when this development has ripened, then it brings forth as its fruit a work of inwardness. It is not geniality, not talent, not virtuosity which constitutes the work . . . The possibility of being able to write such works is rather the reward which God has bestowed on the author, as he, twice-matured, won in his life-view something eternal. (*SV* 14, p.18)

(Incidentally it does not seem that the thematic correspondence between *From the Papers of One Still Living* and the review of *Two Ages*, the correspondence, that is, regarding the twinning of the themes of *Zeitkritik* and the nature of literary art, has ever been adequately commented on in Kierkegaard literature. Although both works stand outside what he himself called his 'aesthetic authorship' in the strict sense, taken together they provide a frame for that authorship which invites a far-reaching reflection on the essential interest at stake in it.)

To return to *From the Papers of One Still Living*. Having delivered due homage to Mme Gyllembourg, Kierkegaard moves at last to his main subject: Hans Christian Andersen, or, more precisely, as he puts it, 'What is Andersen's character as a novelist?' Using the terminology of Heibergian criticism he finds that Andersen cannot be said to be a lyrical genius, since he lacks the naive self-assurance of one marked out by 'nature's imprimatur'. The hapless Andersen is, on the contrary, described as 'a mere possibility of a personality, caught in a . . . web of accidental moods'. (*SV* 1, p.29) If he were to qualify as an epic writer – and whatever else may be required of him, the novelist must be able to incorporate an epic element into his work – he would have to engage in 'a deep and serious embracing of the given reality . . . a life-strengthening abiding in it and admiration for it'. (*SV* 1, pp.29–30) But this he has not done. Instead, as Kierkegaard says, 'Andersen has leapt over his *epos*.'

(*SV* 1, p.29) However, this is not entirely Andersen's own fault but has much to do with the character of the age as a whole, since neither in society nor in art was there any great substantial movement afoot in the time of Andersen's youth. Lacking the possibility of acquiring epic extension through identification with such a great movement Andersen was 'continually pushed back down the funnel of his own personality' in such a way that his poetic powers became 'self-corroding', producing 'a kind of disaffection and bitterness towards the world'. (*SV* 1, p.31) The conclusion is that Andersen altogether lacks the life-view which is nonetheless 'the *condition sine qua non* for a novelist of the type to which Andersen belongs'. (*SV* 1, p.35) Without such a life-view Andersen's novels lack a centre of gravity; they have a 'too finite and accidental relation to the author's flesh and blood' – so much so that they are 'not so much to be regarded as a production but as an amputation of a part of himself'. (*SV* 1, p.39) Andersen's inability to make of himself a firm and rounded character is consequently transposed directly into the situation of the central character of the novel *Only a Fiddler*, a musician whose genius is unrecognised and, lacking the opportunity to become a great artist, becomes 'only a fiddler'. Kierkegaard, however, has little time for the view that genius requires appreciation and good fortune to come to fruition. True genius, he says, is like Athena, springing fully-armed from the head of Zeus: true genius itself sets the agenda for the world and commands attention.[5]

Lack of a life-view will always result either in the kind of self-indulgent self-expression which Kierkegaard finds in Andersen or in what he calls the 'dogmatic, doctrinaire novel'. (*SV* 1, p.39) Such a novel sacrifices the tough complexity of life to the overriding *diktat* of an ideological position which either has not been or cannot be practised in reality. As an example of such a novel Kierkegaard picks on Friedrich Schlegel's *Lucinde*, a novel which engaged his attention not merely on account of Schlegel's historical significance as one of the key figures of Early Romanticism but also because it had become topical in the context of Karl Gutzkow's republication in 1835 of Schleiermacher's *Confidential Letters on Lucinde*. In his preface, Gutzkow paid tribute to Schleiermacher, recently deceased, and claimed him as a forerunner of the radical 'gospel of the flesh' proclaimed by the 'Young Germany' movement – rather than as a member of the bourgeois establishment (and, indeed, its most distinguished theologian).

With Gutzkow and 'Young Germany' very much in mind Kierke-gaard argued that *Lucinde* made up for its lack of an essential life-view by reducing literature to propaganda, making of it a vehicle for an ultimately *im*personal idea.

What idea is this? Kierkegaard's discussion of *Lucinde* is to be found in the context of his Master's dissertation *On the Concept of Irony*, and the 'idea' of the novel turns out to be irony itself. We have already seen how Kierkegaard regarded Romantic irony as an illegitimate extension of Fichte's concept of the self-productive absolute 'I', since, by ascribing an absolute creative freedom to the individual self, the Romantics actually condemned the self to final meaninglessness (for, as the possessors of a life-view know, exis-tential meaning is the product of a confluence of elements of which individual experience is only one). Thus, Julius, the novel's 'hero', claims that the supreme expression of his artistic freedom is the 'unquestionable right to cause confusion,';[6] and he favourably compares the erotic freedom which the novel celebrates to the two-year-old Wilhelmine lying on her back and kicking her legs in the air. Anarchy, confusion and shamelessness are the recurrent motifs of this small but explosive book.[7] And what does it all *mean*? Simply – as far as Kierkegaard can see – whatever the artist cares to make it mean. And this, he believes, leads to the further contradic-tion that 'that which is remarkable about *Lucinde* and the whole tendency which is connected with it is that one, taking the freedom of the self and its constitutive authority as a point of departure, instead of reaching a still higher spiritual existence only arrives at sensuousness, and so to one's opposite . . .'. (*SV* 1, p.309) Like Andersen leaping over his *epos*, the ideologues of 'Young Ger-many' lack the experience of a deep and sustained engagement with reality in all its complexity and resistance to human willing, with the result that their 'idea' is 'acosmic' and 'docetic', the result of a cowardly refusal to face the task of becoming transparent to oneself in all one's factical contingency and yet in the self's 'absol-ute and eternal validity'. (*SV* 1, p.307)

When Kierkegaard returns to the novel in his review of *Two Ages* he wastes little time before reminding us of his view of the radical literary left. Their cult of the new, their rejection of established forms and conventions is 'literary parricide'. (*SV* 14, p.12) Over against such aesthetic iconoclasm he commends the 'sameness' which characterises the works of 'The Author of *An Everyday Story*'.

The life-view which creatively sustains these stories abides the same, while an ingenious inventiveness, the resources acquired from a rich experience, and a fruitful disposition's vegetative luxuriance all serve the production of change within the creative repetition. The turbulence is essentially the same, the pacifying of it essentially the same, the movement in all the stories is from the same and to the same; the tension which is posited has essentially the same elasticity, the peacefulness and relaxedness are also the same, i.e. the life-view is the same. (*SV* 14, pp.16–17)

If anyone wants to criticise such sameness he asks us to consider whether 'God, with whom the poet is likened when he is described as creative, is less admirable in sustaining than in creating the world?' (*SV* 14, p.17) Another reflection of this sameness is the loyalty which characterises the relationship between the author and her readers, a loyalty which has continued through a productivity lasting twenty years.

Kierkegaard makes an important distinction which Ms Jørgensen believes to be maintained throughout his critical writings between poetry and the poet (*poesi* and *digter*) on the one hand and authorship and the author (*forfatterskab* and *forfatter*) on the other. The standpoint of the poet is that of the purely aesthetic approach to art, in which the work of art is appraised purely and solely as a work of art. The 'author', however, calls on precisely those ethical principles which belong to the composition of a healthy 'life-view'. An authorship, such as that of Mme Gyllembourg starts, Kierkegaard says, where poetry stops, 'For poetry does not involve an essential reconciliation with *reality*, it reconciles through fantasy with the ideal world produced by fantasy, but this reconciliation is in the real individual precisely a new splitting away from reality.' (*SV* 14, p.17) Whereas poetry is said to 'inspire' or 'transport' or 'enchant' the reader (as theatre bewitches the spectator who has fallen under its spell) the author who is a real *author*, *persuades* the reader (*overtale*). Such persuasion requires the reader's 'relaxed compliance' as 'the condition for persuasion being able to win a new harmony in place of discord.' (*SV* 14, pp.21–2) It is, in fact, 'the way of the life-view' (*SV* 14, p.22) and as such unites author and reader in ethical seriousness – seriousness, however, which is not in any way 'heavy' but has just that kind of easy and relaxed atmosphere which Kierkegaard finds in these novels. It is a seriousness which is comfortable in its assurance that all will be well and which therefore communicates just such comfortable assurance to the reader.

Again, however – and this is the theme of the lengthy closing section of Kierkegaard's review – this is precisely what the present age rejects. For the present age is one in which envy has replaced enthusiasm, levelling has undermined nobility and greatness, and an anonymous public, manipulated by the daily press, has taken over from the serious and loyal circle of readers of the previous generation. It is an age of idle chatter and of impersonal, depersonalised communication. Such an age simply does not know how to respond to the kind of persuasive good will represented in Mme Gyllembourg's work – though it will follow blindly the latest literary, artistic or political cult, no matter how trivial or absurd, if this is endorsed by the press. An ethically concerned literature, therefore, must, in the present age, find itself taking a controversial position *vis-à-vis* the contemporary world, a fact which raises the further question as to whether the calm assurance of a Mme Gyllembourg will ever again be possible. Once society has plunged into a critical phase, once the sting of aesthetic nihilism has infected the cultural situation, is it possible to sustain the life-view which, in turn, is to sustain the ethically serious novel? We have already noted this problem in connection with Hans Christian Andersen, and the problems raised for his development by the absence of any great serious contemporary movement. For if, as Møller insisted, the Christian tradition was itself a part of the synthesis comprised in the life-view, how was it possible to maintain that synthesis in a period when that tradition was called into question, or when the publicly validated language of faith appeared increasingly bankrupt? Such questions broach the possibility of a crisis in religion and in literature which the easy confidence of the life-view and the kind of novel which is the fruit of the life-view are unable to resolve. But more of this later. . . .

TAKING THE ARTIST TO COURT

The philosophy enshrined in Kierkegaard's literary reviews is very close to the position of that most prolix of all of Kierkegaard's pseudonyms, the Assessor William. The Assessor, a legal official, features both in *Either/Or* and in *Stages on Life's Way* as the representative of the best of bourgeois Christianity, pedantic and patriarchal, but a by no means inconsiderable philosopher and psychologist as well. He also appears to be an exponent of the philosophy of the life-view and a firm believer in the possibility of integrating aesthetic values into a socially responsible and re-ligiously grounded view of the world.[8]

We first hear from him in two extremely lengthy letters ad-dressed to the young aesthete whose life-view (or, rather, lack of a life-view) he is seeking to correct. In terms similar to those of the early journals and *On the Concept of Irony* he attacks the poetic egoism of the Romantics, and their reluctance to undertake the travail of a serious commitment to the real world, without which there can be no talk of a vigorous and envigorating life-view. It is not that he wants to ban the poets from the city altogether, for the point is that the life-view itself requires the integration of the poetic into a synthetic whole. As he sees it, ethical resolve, a resolve rooted in a fundamental act of self-commitment, does not at all undermine art but rather sets the aesthetic in a true perspective. While insisting that true beauty is to be found in life, not art, he is equally insistent that it is precisely a narrowly aesthetic point of view which separates the two, thereby vitiating art itself. Those who have a genuine life-view will be all the more sensitive to the beauty which is to be found in even the most humble everyday situations – situations which the over-refined sensibility of an aesthete might well find ugly or depressing. Art should not dis-tract us from life, still less set itself in competition with life, but, instead, should *transfigure* life, enabling us to see the ideal truth in, with and under the actual forms of the real world. 'Or does it disturb you', he asks his young friend, 'that I still pronounce the word: aesthetic; do you think that it is almost a type of childishness in me, to want to seek this quality among the poor and suffering?' (*SV* 3, p.118)

Let us look at three aspects of the Assessor's philosophy which serve to distinguish his outlook from that of an exclusively aes-thetic position: the nature of self-choice; the responsibility towards others; and, lastly, selfhood and temporality.

Self-choice is a key element in his thought and is expounded at length in the second of his two letters in *Either/Or*. Recognising the force of the idealist position that the self is not merely a passive epiphenomenon of material processes, but itself contributes to its own formation, he nonetheless draws back from the Fichtean and

Romantic position that the self is, in effect, its own creator. The self does not *create* itself – it *chooses* itself, and, as such, must choose itself along with the very specific factical conditions under which it exists: history, family circumstances, social position, etc. . . . Thus, on the one hand, this act of self-choice is *absolute*, the absolutely essential basis for all talk of selfhood in a real or decisive sense. 'But what is it then I choose, is it this thing or that thing? No . . . I choose the absolute, and what is the absolute? It is myself in my eternal validity.' (*SV* 3, p.199) On the other hand, he is insistent that this is no act of self-creation: 'that which is chosen, does not exist and comes to exist only by means of the act of choice; that which is chosen does exist, otherwise it would not be an act of choice. For if that which I chose did not exist, but came into existence in an absolute sense by means of the choice, then I would not be choosing – I would be creating; but I do not create myself, I choose myself.' (*SV* 3, p.200) Through these careful dialectical manoeuvrings the Assessor clearly hopes to reconcile two super-ficially opposed principles: the sovereignty of God and the inalien-able freedom of the human subject. His concept of self-choice is thus theological all the way down. It means affirming ourselves in our solidarity with the concrete totality of that history which stretches back through the individual, through the family to the race, to Adam, and, in Adam, to God. Moreover, because this history is the history of a fallen humanity, a history of alienation from God and from what we ourselves ought to be, the act of self-choice is at the same time an act of repentance. In such repentant self-choice, then, we acknowledge both our dependence on the providentially ordered world which God has set as the stage of our existence and our own failure to be what He has called us to be – but, by our repentance, we re-establish ourselves in a right relation both to the world and to God: we choose ourselves 'from the hand of the eternal God'. (*SV* 3, p.201) In this way, by con-forming ourselves to His will for us, we show a proper love of God: 'there are many types of love . . . and every one of these various types of love has various names, but there is also a love by which I love God, and this has only one expression in language, which is: repentance'. (*SV* 3, p.201)

By insisting on the exclusive freedom of the self in the act of self-creation Romantic philosophy excludes itself from the fulness of a life which is able to take the totality of its factical, material existence into the God-relationship and to let all of that fulness be illuminated by the light of the divine idea, the true 'transfiguration' of life which the 'transfiguration' of matter in aesthetic experience merely echoes or reflects. The aesthetic personality conceives of himself and lives his life as if it were simply a dramatic idea, a role, a part he has thought up for himself, or, as in Hesse's Magic Theatre, a succession of such roles, having only that degree of reality which he himself is prepared to concede to them. If there is to be a question of life basing itself on a foundational projective act, the true source of such an act must be God – and not the individual's self-dramatisation, which can produce no more than a shadow-world. The Assessor himself is prepared to call on the imagery of the theatre – but he does so in a significantly different way from anything we have seen previously:

> And in truth, he who has humility and courage enough to here let himself be aesthetically transfigured, he who is in sympathy with himself as if he were a character in a play written by God, where the poet and the prompter are not separate persons, where the individual, like an experienced actor, who has lived himself into his part and his lines, is not disturbed by the prompter, but feels that what is whispered to him is just what he himself would say, so that it is almost doubtful whether he puts words in the prompter's mouth or the prompter in his, he who in the deepest sense feels himself to be at one and the same time, creating and created . . . he and only he has realised what is highest in the aesthetic. (*SV* 3, p.130)

The stage, demoted from its status as the supreme symbol of aesthetic self-creation is, as it were, reinstated as a metaphor for the divine *modus operandi* and for the paradox of self-choice. We must, henceforth, take the roles in which we find ourselves cast with absolute seriousness; for they are not the arbitrary projections of our own individual fantasies but the parts assigned to us by the divine dramatist himself. If life itself is the play, then to refuse our part is to refuse life; to accept it, on the other hand, is to realise that true transfiguration which takes place, not on the stage or in art, but where life itself becomes transparent to its divine ground. But, to come down from the metaphorical heights, what might this involve, concretely?

First, it is clear that it will involve us in becoming fundamentally open to others, to admitting that dimension of mutual responsibility into our lives which the aesthetic personality stead-fastly resisted. It is in this light that the theme of marriage in the Assessor's writings is to be approached. The aesthetic personality, culminating in the 'persona' of self-dramatisation, exists only within the field of the individual's self-projection. Taking pleasure solely in his spectating of his own role he is, in relation to others, no more than a voyeur, as the Assessor recognised. The Assessor has observed his young friend taking advantage of a casual en-counter in one of his café haunts:

> A pretty young girl, beside whom you quite by chance . . . were sitting at table was too prim to bestow a glance on you . . . she sat opposite a mirror, in which you could see her. She cast a sly look at it, not foreseeing that your eye had already taken up its place there; she blushed when your eye met hers. Such things you register as accurately as a daguerrotype – and as quickly as one, which, as is known, needs only half-a-minute, even in the worst weather. (*SV* 3, p.13)

It is the reflection in the mirror, the image, and that alone, which interests the aesthetic individual.

Over against such narcissism the Assessor commends the mutual trust and responsibility which lies at the basis of the marriage relationship. He denounces the aesthete's self-indulgent 'mystery-system' in relationships with women, a 'system' which involves the man, and only the man, in controlling and directing the course of the relationship. Again he is ready with an example of this, which he also refers to as the 'system of silence':[9]

> For a certain period I used to visit a house where I had the opportunity of observing a more artistic and refined execution of the system of silence. The man was young, exceptionally gifted, a fine mind, a poetic nature, too indolent to care to produce anything, but, on the contrary, with an unusual tact and sense for making daily life poetic. His wife was young, not without spirit, but with an exceptional character. This tempted him. It was quite astonishing how he knew in so many ways to awaken and nurture all her youthful enthusiasm. Her whole existence, their whole marital life together, was interwoven with a poetic magic. His eye was everywhere, but when she looked around, it was turned away; his hand was in everything, but, in a figurat-

ive and in a finite sense, invisible, as God's hand is present in history. Her thought might bend where it will, he was already there, with everything ready. . . . His domestic life was a little creation story, and just as man is that towards which everything tends in the great creation, so was she the centre in a magic circle, in which she nevertheless enjoyed her full freedom, for the circle moved with her, and had no limits which proclaimed: thus far and no further. . . . She moved as in a toddling-basket, but it was not woven of wickerwork, but braided out of her hopes, dreams, longings, wishes, anxieties – in short, it was made out of the whole content of her soul. He himself moved in this dream-world with the greatest confidence, he surrendered none of his dignity, claimed and asserted his authority as Man and Master. (*SV* 3, pp.109–10)

This does not please the Assessor. 'No, my friend,' he says, 'uprightness, open-heartedness, openness, understanding – these are the life-principle of marriage . . .'. (*SV* 3, p.111) But the aesthete is from the beginning confined to the magic circle of his own self-projection – even within the context of what might appear to the world as a marriage relationship. He knows no relationship, no 'Thou', no real 'Other', divine or human.

His world is also a world without time. Throughout the metaphysical tradition time has been understood as the chief cause of the dispersal, fragmentation and corrosion of human existence, the decay of Being and of the human subject alike. Art, however, has, as idealist aesthetics maintained, a unique power to take us out of time, to suspend its corroding effects. The dramatic *persona* is just who he is, just the 'idea' he is, forever, suffering no change or alteration of the passing years. The peculiar stance of the aesthetic individual, who sees himself as just such a character, seeks to avoid such dissolution no less energetically than he seeks to avoid the threat of the Other to his self-created autonomy.

The work of self-choice, then, will require not only the reorientation of the self in relation to its factical givenness and to the co-presence of others in its world, but an acceptance of its essential temporality. The Assessor calls this the task of acquiring an 'inner history'. Reminding his readers of the distinction between the plastic and musical elements of art, and of the progression in art itself towards ever more musical, that is, ever more temporal forms, he says that nonetheless even poetry as the most temporal

of all arts, is 'compelled . . . to concentrate itself in the moment.
It has therefore its limit, and cannot show that (as was previously
shown) whose reality is precisely the reality of temporal succession.' (*SV* 3, p.130) All art, even poetry, involves a foreshorten-
ing of the temporal movement, concentrating into a single moment
of vision, an image, that whose existence is actually spread
through time. If the poet is telling a tale in which external actions
are predominant (tales of knights slaying dragons, etc.,) then there
is a sense in which such actions, actions with very little essential
interiority, can be represented in the moment, in the image of the
hero achieving his goal. But if the history is internal, if, for instance, it is a story not of one who conquers but of one who keeps
and preserves that which he has conquered, then the atemporal
bias of art will invalidate all artistic attempts to represent it.

> Romantic love can very well be represented in the moment,
> marital love not, because an idealised husband is not one who is
> that for one moment in his life, but who is that every day . . . a
> cross-bearer who every day takes up his cross cannot be rep-
> resented in either poetry or art, because the point is that he does
> it every day . . . long-suffering cannot be represented artisti-
> cally. . . . (*SV* 3, pp.128–9)

The point (I hope) is not that all husbands are cross-bearers or
long-suffering but that being a husband, being a cross-bearer,
being long-suffering are all examples of life-situations in which the
element of time is central and which, precisely on account of this
essential temporality, cannot be encompassed or represented by
the aesthetic imagination. 'If I were to think of a hero who gave up
his life, then that could be superbly concentrated in the moment,
not, however, if he had to die every day, because the point would
be that it happened every day.' (*SV* 3, p.130) Thus, courage can be
shown artistically since courage is commensurable with the great
deed, the heroic moment, but patience cannot be dealt with in this
way, since patience does not fight against any external foes, but
against time itself.

The poetic flight from time is unable to achieve final security in
the face of time's inexorable and omnivorous universality, an
awareness which even the poets themselves possess: deep down
they know that the 'eternity' they offer is a pseudo-eternity:

The poetic ideal is always an untrue ideal, for the true ideal is always the actual. So when the spirit is not allowed to rise up into the eternal world of spirit, it stops half-way and rejoices in the images which mirror themselves in the clouds, and he weeps at their transitoriness. A poetic existence is, as such, an unhappy existence, which is higher than finitude and yet is not infinite. (*SV* 3, p.196)

Or, more humorously (for the Assessor is not without humour), William reminds his young aesthetic friend of the story of the Englishmen who went to Arabia to buy horses (Englishmen featuring regularly in Kierkegaard's work as epitomising the attitude of aesthetic *ennui*). They took with them some horses of their own and proposed racing them against their Arab hosts. The horses are chosen, forty days are set aside at the Englishmen's request for training and the prize money is fixed.

. . . the horses are saddled, and now the Arabs ask how long they should ride. One hour, was the answer. This astonished the Arab and he answered laconically: 'I thought we should ride three days.' Now look, that is how it is with you. If one would race against you for an hour, 'Satan himself couldn't keep up with you' – but in three days you would fall short.(*SV* 3, p.185)

This, then, is the challenge which the Assessor makes to the novelist: Can you, by virtue of your life-view, show us in your work that you have in your life repentantly humbled yourself under the sovereign creativity of God, that you accept as a condition of your work as of your life, that 'It is He who has made us and not we ourselves', that, because of this, you have essential obligations to others as to yourself, and that you do not shrink from the changes and chances to which all temporal existence is subject? Beware: we shall be on the lookout for the slightest sign that you are a defector from the real world or that you are using the world only as an occasion by which to display your artistic virtuosity. If you pass the test, however, we shall be faithful readers, open to your persuasion.

However, as we have repeatedly seen, Kierkegaard's writings raise the question as to whether the kind of life-view which the Assessor here commends, and which Mme Gyllembourg and Poul

Møller also represent in their different ways, is in fact sustainable in the context of modernity. For such a life-view presupposes a deep grounding in communally-shared ethical and religious values and the recognition of a common religious vocabulary. But such objectively 'given' cultural and linguistic resources are no longer available – or not available in any direct way – in an 'age of reflection'. Whither, then, the novel?

The way to answer this question in the context of Kierkegaard's authorship is, I would suggest to attempt a reading of that authorship (or parts of it) in the light of the principles he himself regarded as the *sine qua non* of the novel. We turn, then, to examine 'Kierkegaard as novelist'.

KIERKEGAARD AS NOVELIST

To approach Kierkegaard 'as novelist' will surprise only those readers who think of Kierkegaard as some kind of philosopher or theologian. Students of literature, however, will easily recognise a number of works as belonging to well-established literary forms. This is particularly true of *Either/Or*, *Repetition* and *Stages on Life's Way*. F. Billeskov Jansen refers to these as 'the great novelistic works'[10] and sees them as belonging to the tradition of the *Bildungsroman* exemplified in such 'classics' as Goethe's *Wilhelm Meister*, Schlegel's *Lucinde* and Novalis's *Heinrich von Ofterdingen*. In his study of *Kierkegaard and Goethe*, Carl Roos draws particular attention to Goethe's *The Sorrows of Young Werther* as a model for Kierkegaard's 'unhappy love' stories.[11] Writing of Kierkegaard's 'broken engagement' stories (*The Seducer's Diary* in *Either/Or*, *Repetition* and *Guilty?–Not Guilty?* in *Stages on Life's Way*) Aage Henriksen (in a book called, simply, *Kierkegaard's Novels*) says that 'They are novels in a traditional sense: fictional prose accounts in which circumstances and reflection form the links in a coherent action which takes place in a determinate space and which has a certain extension in time . . .'.[12] There are also, it is true, differences between these works of Kierkegaard and the classic works of the *Bildungsroman* genre. There is, for instance, relatively little development in the action or characterisation, a point to which Louis Mackey alludes when he comments that in *Either/Or* 'There is no resolution of the stretto among A, Judge Wilhelm, the priest from Jutland and all the real or putative others. Each is stuck fast in his own categories . . . the novel in which they live is a *Bildungsroman*, but without *Bildung*.'[13] (A point which relates to what I have argued above about Kierkegaard's conception of dramatic character as exemplifying a clear and distinct spiritual 'idea'.) Henriksen too speaks of the larger works (*Either/Or* and *Stages on Life's Way*) as containing a 'timeless dialogue . . . carried on between typified representatives of forms of existence, who talk to each other without influencing each other'.[14]

What are the characteristic features which, despite such reservations, allow us to speak of 'Kierkegaard as novelist'? They are, in general, precisely those features which strike philosophically and theologically interested readers as a bit queer. The most obvious example is the use of pseudonymity itself. Anonymity or pseudonymity was a well-established device among the Romantic novel-writers, as in Wackenroder's seminal *Outpourings from the Heart of an Art-Loving Monastic Brother* or (perhaps the best-known example of all) Friedrich von Hardenberg's use of the pseudonym 'Novalis'. As with Wackenroder's book, Kierkegaard's pseudonyms often have a 'monastic' reference: Victor Eremita, Johannes Climacus, Frater Taciturnus, and Johannes de Silentio. He had also at one time considered using Simon Stylites. (*JP*,5659/IV B 78) Such an allusion to the world of the cloister may be taken as a clue to the religious intention of the work (as in his comment that *Either/Or* was 'written in a monastery') or as an echo of the Romantic image of the monastery as a place for the timeless cultivation of beauty and art. (A double significance, we may add, which highlights the complex ambiguity of the authorship, poised between the aesthetic and the religious.) The role of the pseudonym as 'editor' of a collection of papers is similarly well-precedented.

A further prominent device is that of the text-within-the-text. We have had occasion to comment on Heiberg's virtuoso staging of a play-within-a-play involving characters 'planted' in both the actual audience and the second audience on stage, but many examples of more or less autonomous texts-within-texts can be culled from the Romantic literature with which Kierkegaard was familiar.[15] This device plays a prominent part in all of the three 'great novels' and, it might be argued, something similar is afoot in the 'Interlude' in the *Philosophical Fragments*.[16] As we shall be concentrating the discussion of 'Kierkegaard as novelist' on a part of *Stages on Life's Way*, however, let us look at the way Kierkegaard uses the device in that work, which is in any case interesting as possibly the most bizarre and complex use of the text-within-a-text by any author.

The work as a whole comprises two main sections, probably being originally conceived as two separate books.[17] These two sections are said to have been 'collected, forwarded to the printer and published by Hilarius Bookbinder.' (*SV* 7, p.5) Hilarius, in a prefatory letter to the reader, describes how the papers had been sent to him by a literary gentleman – only to be overlooked and only rediscovered too long after their despatch to make it worthwhile attempting to return them. He himself does not read them, but his son's tutor persuades him to have them published. This, however, is only the beginning, for each of the two parts again falls into two parts. The first main division is made up of *In Vino Veritas* and a further lengthy letter from the Assessor on the subject of marriage. *In Vino Veritas* is the account of a banquet involving a number of familiar faces from *Either/Or* and *Repetition* – Johannes the Seducer, Victor Eremita and Constantin Constantius – narrated by a new pseudonym, William Afham. After a night's carousing in which the banqueters deliver speeches on the subject of woman they find themselves in the vicinity of the Assessor's country house, from where the elusive William Afham steals the *Observations on Marriage*. The second main division of the book is entitled *Guilty?–Not Guilty?* and this, in turn, falls into two parts. Its pseudonymous editor (who hints later that he might be the author) describes how he had by chance fished up a rosewood box from the bottom of Søborg Lake. This box turned out to be locked from the inside. On opening it he found a manuscript of a diary, telling the story of an unhappy love-affair. The diary itself contains further surprises. It is made up of three kinds of entries. First, there are 'morning' entries, telling the story of events a year previously, relating the main events of the hapless love-affair in which the diarist (known only as Quidam, 'a certain one') was involved; then, secondly, there is a series of 'midnight' entries, which describe the diarist's current state of mind, detailing his inner anguish and torment; and, lastly, there are six separate midnight entries which, by means of a variety of literary pastiches, illuminate the theme of guilt which emerges as the main 'subject' of the diary. We then return, finally to Frater Taciturnus, who, in an extended 'Letter to the Reader' gives his view of the problem dealt with in the diary.

Although it is a matter of judgement whether Kierkegaard might not have over-laboured his game of literary hide-and-seek, the method itself, described by Georg Brandes as like a 'cabinet of mirrors with its duplication of reflection',[18] is well within the *Bildungsroman* tradition. Moreover, it enables the novel to reflect on itself, to make itself its own subject (as in Frater Taciturnus' 'Letter to the Reader'), though this does not in any way make it 'philosophical' or 'theoretical' rather than literary. We can find similar examples in *Lucinde*, Hoffman's *Kater Murr* and elsewhere, where art itself becomes the subject of literary reflection. In Kierkegaard's case there is, though, the further complication – that in this work he reflects precisely on the impossibility of art, on that border region which aesthetic categories are unable to cross and which aesthetic forms are unable to express. If idealism saw art as the unity of idea and appearance, a unity which even the most complicatedly structured novel was still able to sustain, the 'idea' of this novel is in raging discord with the aesthetic means of the work itself. We thus find ourselves confronted with a work of literature which makes the ultimate failure of literature itself a literary event. Not quite a paradox perhaps, but a multiply-reflected strategy which generates many possibilities of interpretation.

Let us now concentrate on the diary itself which, I believe, brings together many of the themes and problems which run through Kierkegaard's 'novels'.

The story which the diary tells is soon told. In the January of an unspecified year Quidam (the narrator) becomes engaged to the girl on whom he has set his heart. Almost immediately he discovers that they are psychologically incompatible. They live on different levels of reality and cannot begin to understand each other. This situation provokes in him a crisis with distinctly religious dimensions as he reflects on his responsibility towards her – a crisis of which she in her blithe sweet innocence has no inkling. His understanding of marriage requires that the partners meet as equals before God, with the kind of candour and open-heartedness which the Assessor was so anxious to commend. But because, at a very deep level, she is quite incapable of understanding him, they lurch backwards and forwards between domination and submission now on one side and now on the other, but unable to achieve a genuinely mutual understanding. After seven months he decides to end the engagement, an action which sends shock waves through the social circle to which they belong. Nor is this the end. She becomes ill. Perhaps she has gone into a decline and will die (after all such things happen in nineteenth-century

literature)? If this happens will he be her murderer? Was he really
justified in rejecting her, he asks himself, or were his religious
scruples demonic obsessions? When it becomes clear that she is
not in any physical danger he nonetheless continues to torment
himself with questions: Will she go insane? Or commit suicide?
However, a chance meeting in Church convinces him that she is
now quite happy, and when on another occasion he sees her
chatting merrily with a friend he knows she is over it. But now the
full absurdity of his own situation comes home to him and he sinks
deeper and deeper into a feeling of utter meaninglessness. He has
staked the whole meaning of his life on a relationship which
turned out, on her part, to be non-existent, something one gets
over in a few months! He has thrown away his life for nothing,
and, as he ends the diary he comments bitterly that 'It contains
nothing, but if, as Cicero says, the easiest letter is one which is
concerned with nothing, it is sometimes the hardest life which is
concerned with nothing.' (*SV* 8, p.198)

With these words Quidam points to the more serious theme
which lurks below the narrative surface of the diary and which the
constant disruption of the narrative cohesion by means of the
different kinds of entry itself helps to bring to light. This theme is
the nothingness which permeates Quidam's existence, the void
through which he journeys on his solitary path through life. The
real 'action' of the diary is his gradual collapse into this void, so
that as the diary progresses we hear less and less of what is
happening in the external world and more and more of Quidam's
monotonous and obsessive broodings on his own nothingness.

This theme is introduced early on in the story, in a wry comment
which Quidam makes about the relationship of the engaged
couple. 'Lovers should have nothing between them. Alas! Alas!
We have been together too short a time to have anything between
us – we have nothing between us . . .'. (*SV* 8, p.37) At first he
treats this nothing as nothing, imagining himself to be its master
and nonetheless able to shape his own destiny by means of the
will-power on which he prides himself. But instead the 'nothing'
becomes *his* master, humbling his pride and establishing itself as
the total environment of his existence. 'There is nothing new
under the sun, says Solomon. Well, that may be so, but it is worse
when nothing at all happens . . . I am still continually about the
exposition of this nothing and the scene is unalterably the same.'
(*SV* 8, p.154)

Quidam calls this condition his melancholy, and sees it as being closely connected with his religiousness, a religiousness, however, which has no positive content and which consists primarily in the readiness to contemplate the annihilation of all finite aims. 'How is eternity portrayed?' Quidam asks himself, and answers: 'As the wide horizon where one sees nothing. That is how it is portrayed in the picture of a grave: the bereaved sits in the foreground and says, "He departed hence, into the beyond." But in the wide horizon I see nothing at all.' (*SV* 8, p.192) If this is religion it is the religion of Schopenhauer, the final renunciation of the will-to-life, or we might say, looking back on Kierkegaard from a twentieth-century perspective, the apophatic theology of extreme modernism.[19] In one of the six midnight 'insets' in the diary, 'Nebuchadnezzar', Kierkegaard uses the story of the mythical emperor's humiliation to portray this mood of final renunciation, in what is a brilliant parody of Biblical style.

38. For my days are soon told, and my reign is passed like a watch in the night, and I do not know whither I am bound.
39. Whether I shall come to the unknown distant place where dwells the Mighty One, that I may find grace before his eyes;
40. Whether it is He who takes the breath of life from me, so that I become like a cast-off garment, like my predecessors, that He might find pleasure in me.

(SV 8, p.168)

If there is here a hint of a possible reversal of fortune, a restitution corresponding to and compensating for the preliminary renunciation, it is not substantiated. Quidam's journey, like Nebuchadnezzar's, is a journey into a wide and empty horizon, an unknown land. Yet the dramatic action of the Biblical legend and the talk of a journey are only metaphors for what engages Quidam. His 'journey' is to the unknown self within, a self wrapped in the incognito of the void. 'And when the eye has gazed after nothing for a long time it sees at last itself or its own seeing: thus the emptiness around me again forces my thoughts back into myself.' (*SV* 8, p.163)

Quidam's melancholy – located in the imagination and nourished by possibility, we are told (*SV* 8, p.193) – seems endless. The very infinity of possibilities on which the artist draws to dazzle and surprise his audience is for him an infinite quagmire from which he cannot escape. His mind is constantly in pursuit of fresh possibilities of interpretation, new angles on his situation – but he cannot connect with his reality at all. Another of the 'insets', called 'A Possibility' and this time taking the form of a short story stylistically reminiscent of Poe's *Tales of Mystery and Imagination*, highlights this theme. It tells the story of a shy book-keeper who is led astray by some office friends. They get him drunk and take him to a brothel. He subsequently becomes obsessed with the idea that there might somewhere be a child which owes its life to him. He looks anxiously into the faces of the children he sees on the street as this remote 'possibility' becomes his *idée fixe* and, eventually, drives him insane. Only in death does this preoccupation end, when 'he had to tread the dreadful bridge of eternity in earnest'. (*SV* 8, p.101) For 'eternity takes possibility away'. (*SV* 8, p.193) But, for Quidam, eternity is – as we have seen – an empty horizon.

There is a curious congruence between Quidam and an aesthetic personality like the Seducer. Both are poised on the line separating external reality and inner fantasy. Quidam fits well the description Kierkegaard gives of the hero of a story called *Unhappy Love* which he omitted to include in *Either/Or*:

> It was to form a contrast to the Seducer. The hero in the story acted in exactly the same way as the Seducer, but behind it was melancholy. He was not unhappy because he could not get the girl he loved. . . . He won her . . . he was loved with all the enthusiasm a young girl has – then he became unhappy, went into a depression, pulled back; he could struggle with the whole world but not with himself. . . . (*JP*,5628/IV A 215)

Like such an aesthetic persona, Quidam, if he is to become 'real', must negotiate the Assessor's favoured category of choice: he must repent. But, he says, 'My existence is nothing but useless effort: I cannot return to myself.' (*SV* 8, p.190)

Quidam's problem with self-choice is taken up in Frater Taciturnus's 'Letter to the Reader'. Here the Quiet Brother sets out the threefold schema of the aesthetic, the ethical and the religious, the three 'existence-spheres', and asks where Quidam stands on this existential scale. It is soon clear that although Quidam's life has, as we have seen, a certain dark religiosity about it, it is not *decisively* religious. For religion presupposes the ethical act of choice, that is, repentance. But Quidam does not choose, does not repent. He is caught in the endless web of possibility, endlessly questioning himself, endlessly saying 'perhaps' instead of 'it is'. The Quiet Brother himself defines repentance as the highest expression of the ethical sphere, a negative action by which the ethical is able to pass over into the religious. Quidam's problem, in relation to the girl, is that since he is unable to decide what the truth about their relationship was, 'it is as if it is still not decided what he is to repent of'. (*SV* 8, p.245) On the other hand he is said to be essentially sympathetic towards the girl (and in this respect, of course, quite different from the cold egotism of the Seducer) so that he is equally unable to withdraw into the defiant attitude of indifference. Wounded by the relationship he must bear its pain with him in his wanderings through the desert, like a mussel which has been prodded with a stick by a child, and which retains a deeply-lodged splinter even when it shuts its shell again. (June 30th. Midnight) Yet his sympathy is not enough to bring him to the point of marriage – for he and the girl cannot, he believes, understand each other, and understanding (as the Assessor said) is essential for marriage.

Repentance is said to be the most dialectical situation of all, the constantly-to-be-repeated transition from the ethical to the religious, but Quidam's situation is so dialectical that he cannot come to repentance. He stands on a 'dialectical razor's edge', as the Quiet Brother puts it. (*SV* 8, p.199) He cannot now return to the innocence of the aesthetic and his youthful poetic dreams, that magical moment of spiritual adolescence when the aesthetic imagination dramatises itself in a myriad transient forms, nor is he capable of pressing through to the radical freedom of the religious which is able 'to lie over seventy thousand fathoms of water and still be joyful'. (*SV* 8, p.193) He, and his diary, express the absolute borderline between the aesthetic and the religious. They articulate the nothingness in which the aesthetic is annihilated but in which the religious has not yet come to birth. This borderline is, as we have seen previously, describable in psychological terms as the place of *angst*, for '*Angst* and nothing correspond at all times to one another.' (*SV* 6, p.183) But what are the implications of all this for the way in which we read the diary: can we read it as a novel? Is it in any sense a work of literature?

Clearly Quidam cannot claim for himself the 'life-view' which we have seen to be the prime *desideratum* of the novelist, for this life-view presupposes precisely those acts of self-choice and repentance which he is unable to make. We are then in a dilemma: the text, by virtue of its form, invites a 'literary' reading – and yet such a reading cannot (on Kierkegaard's own principles) satisfy us, since we cannot find in the work the traces of that life-view which alone can harmonise aesthetic ideality with lived experience: its 'content' resists the formal finality inherent in all artistic productivity. This disruption of the relationship between content and form makes a purely aesthetic reading unsatisfactory – but, conversely, how can we read the work 'religiously' if the key religious concepts are unable to come to expression in it?

There are two points here which need to be particularly stressed.

The first is that the ambiguity of Quidam and his diary in relation to aesthetic and religious categories is closely correlated to the ambiguity inherent in the whole situation of modern society. In both instances we are able to speak of a crisis of reflection acting as the focus of a whole series of artistic, moral and religious problems. Let us, then, read what the Quiet Brother has to say about this, before going on to see how this crisis is worked into the matter of the diary itself.

Like Kierkegaard himself, the Quiet Brother sees the modern world as being permeated in its entirety by the spirit of reflection. Love, for instance, 'like all passion, has become dialectical for the existing generation. One cannot grasp such an immediate passion, and in our age even a grocer's boy could tell Romeo and Juliet astonishing truths'. (*SV* 8, p.207) It is the same with regard to politics and every other sphere of life. It is especially significant for our enquiry that the triumph of reflection and the evaporation of immediacy mean that the age of poetry too is past, for poetry can only thrive where there is immediacy and passion. This has serious implications for the philosophy of the life-view which, though composed of a number of elements and to that extent hardly categorisable as belonging to simple immediacy, has about it something of the aura of immediacy, stressing as it does experiential appropriation and quiet enthusiasm.

Again like Kierkegaard himself, the Quiet Brother is sceptical about the possibility of there ever being any return to a Romantic golden age of poetry and art. Instead, he offers a different tactic by which to escape the debilitating effects of reflection: the infinitisation of reflection in the individual life in such a way that it brings about a kind of reversal in which the individual is once again brought to immediate self-presence – only this time it is a 'second' or 'higher' immediacy that is involved.

> In relation to every finite reflection, immediacy is essentially higher. . . . But an infinite reflection is infinitely higher than immediacy, and in it immediacy relates itself to itself in the idea. But this expression 'in the idea' indicates a God-relationship on the widest sense. (*SV* 8, p.213)

The second or higher immediacy in which the self, after exhausting every possibility of reflection, becomes 'transparent' to itself is a state of freedom or, simply, faith. 'If it is true that the time of immediacy is past, then what matters is to gain the religious, nothing in between can help.' (*SV* 8, p.214)

This, again, is precisely the situation of Quidam, who thereby represents in himself the fate of art and of the artist in the modern world. For although the Quiet Brother takes pains to distribute the logical polarities of immediacy and reflection between the girl and Quidam in such a way that she is all immediacy and he is all reflection, this is not a totally accurate representation of the situation in the diary (nor, indeed, does it quite fit with other comments by the Quiet Brother). On the one hand Quidam is, as has been described, paralysed by possibility, by his power of excessive reflection. Yet he is also said by the Quiet Brother to be an 'anachronism in the nineteenth century' (*SV* 8, p.201) because he is, despite everything, an enthusiast in an age of reflection, a knight seeking a decisive and unambiguous truth by which to give meaning and value to his life and, also, by which to 'do right' by his beloved. Quidam himself thus embodies the meeting and mutually annihilating conflict between immediacy and reflection which characterises the age in general and the fate of poetry and art within modernity in particular. Although an enthusiast and, as such, essentially immediate, he cannot live in his immediacy, but conceals his enthusiasm and passion from others, both in his behaviour and in the duplicitous revealing-concealing literary labyrinth through which we follow his elusive trail. In the very first entry of the diary he recalls seeing a crippled child who could run as well on his crutches as any normal, healthy child. In the same way, he says, I am able to conceal my melancholy from the world and appear to be just like the others. Similarly, he is only able to express his love for the girl by driving her away from him, while his religious strivings and *attraits* are unable to find any positive expression.

If he is to resolve this situation in any way, as a man or as an artist, it would seem that he must break the spell of reflection and return to the wholesome primitivity of immediacy – and the same applies by extension to any 'modern' who seeks poetic or religious authenticity. 'In the great cities both men and buildings are crowded much too closely together. If one who lives there is really to get a primitive impression, there must either be a dramatic happening or one must have another way . . .'. (*SV* 8, p.182) Must art and faith then opt for a new exodus from urban modernity if they are to find themselves anew?

Such an appeal to 'primitivity' has, without any doubt, had considerable appeal to a great many 'moderns'.[20] 'Why is it,' asks Quidam,

> that in isolated places, where there are a couple of miles between each little hut, there is more fear of God than in the noisy towns . . . if not because they experience something, and experience it in such a way that there is no escape. When the night-storm rages and the hunger-cry of the wolf is ominously heard inside . . . then one learns to entrust one's soul to something other than nightwatchmen and gendarmes. . . . (*SV* 8, p.182)

But Quidam is no apostle of the 'noble savage'. He (like Kierkegaard) is a thoroughly urban individual, who never leaves the city except in a carriage. He certainly cannot himself claim to be familiar with the hunger-cry of the wolf. It would seem, then, that the 'call of the wild' is, in this case, metaphorical. What Quidam is stating is the requirement of a primitivity which is like, but not identical with, the primitivity of those who live in the earth's lonely places, the barren heaths and isolated fjords where the writ of the 'nightwatchmen and gendarmes' has little force. In other words, it is not the 'first' immediacy of natural life to which Quidam is calling us back, but the 'second' or 'higher' immediacy which lies on the far side of reflection's maximal intensification, 'beyond the wasteland'.

He says of himself that he has quite 'another way' of living primitively from that practised by the frontiersman, a way which has to do with his 'melancholy' – that is, his enduring of the mutual annihilation of enthusiasm (immediacy, passion) and reflection, while refusing to surrender to the half-solutions of comfort and compromise. It is in the fact that although his life is reduced to a meaningless vacuum by the dialectical conflict within his breast, he nonetheless continues to live it with absolute seriousness – within this fact, that he has a key by which to open the door leading to an authentically primitive religious existence.

Yet, since such primitivity presupposes the relativisation of the sphere of immediacy in its totality, and since poetic and all other artistic representation avails itself of the figurative potentialities inherent in (and only in) immediacy, it is no wonder if the diary turns out to be aesthetically unsatisfactory. What this unsatisfactoriness confronts us with, however, is not the poetic ineptitude of its author but the question as to whether any work of literature can claim the kind of ultimately serious attention which religious communication demands when once the aura of immediacy has been desecrated and human life is enmeshed in an inexhaustibly complex network of reflection running through both the objective (social) world and subjective (individual) life. But such questions have also repeatedly engaged artists and critics themselves over the last one hundred and fifty years: Quidam, this so-called 'anachronism in the nineteenth century' is perhaps not quite so strange to either the nineteenth or the twentieth centuries as he had at first appeared.

The second point about the ambiguity of the diary with regard to the relationship between the aesthetic and the religious has to do with the nature of religious communication itself. It has already been remarked that the Quiet Brother's closing 'Letter to the Reader' refers at several points to Aristotle's *Poetics*. One of the issues discussed by Aristotle which concerns the Quiet Brother is the way in which fear and pity function to bring about that emotional catharsis in the spectator which is the aim of dramatic art. The Quiet Brother (and Kierkegaard too) is confident that such catharsis is achieved by means of the spectator being taken out of himself:

The aesthetic healing consists in the individual gazing at the dizzy sight provided by the aesthetic, and by doing so he loses himself, like an atom, like a particle of dust, which is thrown in with the common lot of everyman, of humanity; he loses himself

like an infinitely small element of sound in the spherical harmony of existence. (*SV* 8, pp.254ff.)

In this way the spectator's 'fear and pity are purified from all
basely egoistic ingredients'. (*SV* 8, p.253) This, as we saw at length
in the preceding chapter, hinges on the spectator's capacity for
identifying himself with the 'idea' represented in the dramatic
person on the stage – but how can we lose ourselves in a figure
such as Quidam with whom it is so almost impossibly difficult to
sympathise? Aren't we more likely to be just downright annoyed
by the way in which he creates problems for himself by his
neverending crises of conscience, his purposeless self-dramatisation
and his restless reflection? That was certainly how it struck P.L.
Møller, a contemporary critic (not to be confused with Poul M.
Møller):

> Here one meets a masculine individual who has lost everything
> that constitutes personality. Feeling, understanding, will, resol-
> ution, action, backbone, nerve and muscle power – all are
> dissolved in dialectic, in a barren dialectic that swirls around an
> indefinite centre, uncertain as to whether it proceeds as a result
> of centrifugal or centripetal force, until it eventually slowly
> vanishes.[21]

But are we intended to see Quidam in this way, that is, sym-
pathetically or dramatically?

Kierkegaard discusses at some length the aesthetic quality of
someone, like Quidam, who seems to be the cause of his own
problems, a self-tormentor (a masochist, we might say). The extreme self-consciousness of Quidam, his essential modernity,
pushes the tendency analysed in the essay on ancient and modern
tragedy to the point at which any kind of aesthetic sympathy
breaks down. For, if Quidam suffers, it is his own fault. There is no
residual element of destiny or fate left in his story. If we try to look
at such a figure aesthetically, it can only be as a comic figure.
Terence's play *Heautontimorumenos* is used to illustrate this point
(though we might think of such better-known examples as
Molière's *Le Malade Imaginaire* or Dostoievsky's *Notes from Under-
ground*). Religiously considered, however, his situation or the
situation of any such figure is no laughing-matter. For such self-
inflicted suffering is a culpable abuse of the gifts and opportunities

given by God. What is religiously interesting about Quidam is simply whether he ever gets round to repenting; but repentance, like other religious categories, is not a matter for discussion in the third person: 'For Spirit asks these two things: (1) Is that which is said possible? (2) Can I do it? But it shows lack of Spirit to ask these two things: (1) Is it real? (2) Has my neighbour, Christophersen, done it . . .?. (*SV* 8, p.235) Quidam frustrates the reader's attempts at self-identification with him precisely to the extent that his situation is religiously significant. For, once repentance is the issue, it is no longer a question of whether Quidam repents or not – but whether you and I, the readers, are rightly situated in the God-relationship. Religious categories require religious communication; and religious communication goes about things in a very different way from artistic communication. 'The religious fear is precisely fear for oneself; the religious healing consists first and foremost in arousing this fear, and one easily sees from that that the matter is thereby made more difficult.' (*SV* 8, p.259) The motto for the communicator of religious issues is therefore '*de te narratur fabula*'. (*SV* 8, p.267) If Quidam is in danger of living a wasted life, then so are we all, according to the religious point of view.

The 'failure' of an aesthetic reading of the diary therefore points once again to the dictum that 'if it is true that the time of immediacy [that is, the time of poetry and art] is past, then what matters is to gain the religious, nothing in between can help'. (*SV* 8, p.214) But *if* we are to venture a religious reading of this text then we must be willing to put in play our own need for repentance. The magic circle of aesthetic harmony is broken as the religious matter bursts out of its aesthetic form – *if we wish it to*: and it is precisely in this, our response, that the issue lies. The implication of this, however, is that religion relativises all questions of aesthetic value and excellence and it follows that, to the extent that 'Quidam's Diary' seems to call for a religious reading, it undermines its own standing as a work of literary art – it is a novel whose theme is the death of the novel. But though it might be tempting to ascribe this death solely to the universal corrosion of reflection (thereby blaming it on the age), a closer examination shows that the ethically-motivated novel carries the seeds of its own dissolution. For by setting the values associated with repentance at the foundation of literary art, the philosophy of the life-view introduces an element which must *at least at one moment* confront both authors and readers with the relativity of all aesthetic form-giving. It may be the task of reflection to test out the mutual correlation of idea and form, but life is more than and prior to such questions, and, thus by virtue of its interest in *life*, the novel invites formal chaos. If the city of pure aesthetics, the magical theatre of illusion, had to perish because it was built on a deception, the realm of the literary life-view must perish precisely because of the element of more-than-literary truth it contains, as it points to a reality which imagination cannot encompass or limit. The educative journey of Kierkegaard's novels of *Bildung*, a journey from the aesthetic, through the ethical, to the religious, therefore brings us to a moment of decision: how are we going to read these books? Aesthetically? Or, religiously? It's really up to us. It really is – because if it isn't then it isn't a religious decision.

6

Reading, Repentance and the Crucifixion of the Image

THE RELIGIOUS DISCOURSES

In the course of the last two chapters I have attempted to show how drama and literature provide us with clearly defined paradigms of reading and interpretation which open up important dimensions of Kierkegaard's many-levelled work as an author. In doing so they also disclose a tension which runs through virtually every line of the authorship: the tension between the aesthetic and the religious. Yet though they allude to – perhaps, on occasion, even speak explicitly about – the religious situation which Kierkegaard claims is the determining element in every human life, they do not themselves depict that situation directly. To be sure, the need for repentance is clearly broached in Kierkegaard's 'novels', but this is only a preliminary to the religious point of view in the full sense. For, first, repentance is only an initial moment in religious existence. Although Kierkegaard does not regard repentance as something we do once-for-all in the emotional heat of a revival meeting but as an act which needs to be continuously repeated in the course of the Christian life, it is nonetheless essentially transitional only, and does not itself determine the final goal or content of faith. Secondly, the kind of literary reading of Kierkegaard which we have undertaken so far only illuminates one aspect of repentance; for such a reading can only show us the need for repentance as that is experienced within the context of aesthetic despair – whether that despair is figured in the defiant personality of the Seducer or in the *angst*-ridden nonentity of the Quidam. It cannot show us the other side, as it were, of repentance; that is, it does not show us how repentance is connected with the rest of the religious life.

To acquire a fuller understanding of repentance and of the religious requirement to which repentance is the necessary point of entry, we need to examine both a different stratum of Kierkegaard's authorship and a different way of reading from any we have yet seen. We need, that is, to turn to the explicitly religious writings which Kierkegaard produced throughout his career, and, just as importantly, we need to learn what it is to read *religiously*.

Kierkegaard wrote a great many 'religious discourses', mostly published under his own name, which together constitute a distinct group of writings within his overall production. I shall make two assumptions about these discourses. The first is simply that they do indeed form a homogenous group, if only by virtue of their literary form or genre. Kierkegaard himself was at pains to distinguish between (for instance) those he called 'upbuilding' (or 'edifying') and those which were decisively 'Christian'. This distinction corresponds to the kind of distinction he makes in the *Postscript* between a merely 'immanent' form of religiousness, a religiousness which is universally open to all human beings and which reaches a climax in the 'hidden inwardness' in which the religious person realises their own nothingness and in that recognition becomes altogether open to God, and a 'transcendent' faith, a faith which takes as its starting-point the paradox of the God-in-time, the incarnation of Jesus Christ.[1] The former of these positions is called 'immanent' because it is entirely circumscribed by the consciousness of the religious person and thus by the universal conditions of human consciousness. The latter position, paradox-religion, depends on faith in an event outside of the innate capacities of the human mind and is therefore said to be 'transcendent'. Only this 'transcendent' faith is said to be decisively Christian. This distinction, however, though it is in some ways applicable to Kierkegaard's religious discourses, is not entirely satisfactory, and there are certain respects in which it is more helpful to emphasise the continuity among them.[2] They share, for instance, a common 'discourse' form, a form which would be familiar to those of Kierkegaard's readers who regularly read devotional works. Then the early *Eighteen Upbuilding Discourses* (supposedly representative of the merely 'immanent' form of religiousness) already raise the question of the human need for redemption, for Grace, and appeal constantly to the Scriptures (that is, to divine revelation) as the ground and endorsement of their message, even though they themselves are 'without authority'.[3]

Conversely, even the later *Christian Discourses*, the discourses (or 'expositions') which form the final part of *Training in Christianity* or the Christological discourse 'Christ the Pattern' (in *Judge for Yourselves!*) all retain (and not merely marginally) the requirement of repentance, edification and existential appropriation which is already present in the earlier, supposedly 'immanent' discourses. Finally, all the discourses (except, arguably, those which appear under the name of the 'higher' pseudonym, Anti-Climacus) are examples of 'direct' communication; that is, they are examples of a quite different kind of communication from the 'dramatic' and 'literary' forms we have examined so far.

The case for the unity of the religious discourses is well stated by Anders Kingo – despite the present author's reservations regarding the general thrust of his argument – in his assertion that 'the "upbuilding discourse" is a category and *qua* category the common name for all of Kierkegaard's discourses, irrespective of the fact that he calls them by various names . . .'[4] As examples of these 'various names' we may note that *Works of Love* is described on the title page as 'Some Christian reflections (Dan: *Overveielser*) in the form of discourses', which would seem to put it under the rubric 'Christian', yet in the text itself Kierkegaard insists on the 'upbuilding' nature of the work. No less confusingly, the third division of the *Upbuilding Discourses in Various Spirits* ('The Gospel of Sufferings') is subtitled *Christian Discourses*. In any case, a formal-literary approach allows us attend to the unity of literary form that overrides the subtle conceptual distinctions Kierkegaard seeks to maintain.

The chief qualification I would want to add to this is regarding one very particular group of discourses, those designated for the service of Friday Communion. These, as I shall show below, are in several respects distinctive – not so much in terms of content, however, but in the kind of communication they are intended to be.

The second assumption I am making is that although the discourses were offered by Kierkegaard with his 'right hand', as *direct* communication, it does not follow that we should treat them as instances of 'knowledge-communication'. In terms of the distinction between WHAT and HOW, these discourses are no less governed by the logic of the HOW than are the pseudonymous 'indirect' works. I have suggested that Kierkegaard was concerned to redirect the task of Christian dogmatics by giving the kind of foundational role to rhetoric which had previously been given to metaphysics (or, sometimes, history). But if rhetoric, in Thomas Hobbes's rendering of Aristotle, 'is that faculty by which we understand what will serve our turn, concerning any subject, to win belief in the hearer',[5] then it should not be hard to see that the discourses are eminently suitable subjects for the application of rhetorical principles, since they are aimed precisely at winning belief in the hearer (in Kierkegaard's specific sense of belief). It is thus not quite right to see the discourses as *explaining* the real meaning of the indirect communication offered in the pseudonymous works. Louis Mackey, for instance, writes that 'The direct writings provide the ultimate *what* and the ultimate *why* of the pseudonymous books, while these latter supply the *how*. The edifying discourse and the Christian witness define the religious end to which the aesthetic and philosophical works are the means.'[6] What I am suggesting instead is that the HOW factor is just as important here, in the edifying works, as it is in the pseudonymous writings. If there is any 'explanation', *what* or *why*, to be found in Kierkegaard's work it is rather in the theoretical reflections on the nature of Christian communication than in the religious writings themselves. Thus, the upbuilding discourses are not *about* repentance; they are not dogmatic treatises (examples of knowledge-communication); they are, rather, attempts to lure, provoke or otherwise persuade the reader to make the act of repentance. They are literary works in which content and form, WHAT and HOW, are so inextricably interwoven that there is a sense in which (to stay with the particular but by no means arbitrary example) reading is repentance.

To show how this is so, and how Kierkegaard seeks to guide the reader along the path of repentance, away from the aesthetic and toward the religious in such a way that the reading itself becomes an act of repentance, I shall start by examining the themes of temporality and figuration in the religious discourses. These two categories correspond closely to the aesthetic categories of musicality and plasticity, but, as we shall see, Kierkegaard uses them here in a thoroughly non-aesthetic way. So, whereas idealist aesthetics saw the peculiar excellence of drama as being closely related to the way in which it combined these two elements, Kierkegaard's discourses display a startling reversal of this synthesis, and make quite different demands on the reader from those works which invite a 'dramatic' reading.

TEMPORALITY AND FIGURATION IN THE RELIGIOUS DISCOURSES

One way of explaining the work of repentance might be to say that it is to live with the expectation of an eternal happiness as the measure and the goal of life on earth. To repent comprises both the action of coming to one's self and living for God (the Eternal). Selfhood and eternity are entirely correlative. In the discourse 'The Expectation of an Eternal Happiness' we read that 'if a man has expectation in his soul then he has a goal which is always valid and valid in itself; by means of this goal and this measure he will always understand himself in temporal existence.' (*SV* 4, p.234) In the discourse 'The Expectation of Faith' Kierkegaard makes the same point more graphically by comparing the situation of the human being existing in time to that of a sailor navigating his ship through a wild and chartless ocean. How does the sailor know where he is? Not by looking around him at the constantly changing sea, but by looking up at the stars which do not change. (*SV* 4, p.26) Orientating itself by the unchanging standard of eternity while it still lives in time the self thus acquires continuity, identity and unity in the midst of temporal flux, decay and death.

This is all familiar pietistic stuff, implying as it does a sharp and final dualism between time and eternity, with the world of change and decay on one side and the world of timeless self-identical truth on the other. That certainly enters into Kierkegaard's equation but it is not the whole story. For in order to appropriate the standard of eternity existentially it is necessary to make a complete and unreserved acceptance of temporality as the ineluctable and universal condition of human selfhood. The discourses present the self as being temporal all the way down. The human self is the point of contact between eternity and time, the meeting of which generates a form of life (human existence) which is more than momentary but which can sustain itself through time. (*SV* 11, p.179)[7] This is what distinguishes *human* life from that of the non-human creation. (*SV* 4, p.24)

Human temporality is, for instance, disclosed in that kind of relation to the future which we call wishing or willing. The concern which characterises the attitude of wishing and willing may make us vulnerable to anxieties from which unconscious life is free, but it may also be deepened into a total concern for our future state in its entirety. When this occurs then we are no longer concerned merely to wish for or to will into existence this or that imagined event 'in' the future: what we will is the future as absolute meaning, 'the incognito of the eternal'. (*SV* 6, p.177) However – and this is one of the very distinctive themes of Kierkegaard's many discussions of temporality – we cannot hope to attain the absolute future by leaping over the extension of temporal existence which separates us from it. Time determined as the expectation of an eternal happiness is also time determined as patience. If we are to make the journey *from* the merely momentary consciousness of a less-than-human life *through* the future and *to* eternity we can only do so in and through time itself. But this throws a fresh light on the image, for the 'truth' which can be expressed in an image is only the kind of truth commensurable with a single moment of time. As an attempt to stabilise the voracious onrush of time, the image is thus, very precisely, the poet's tribute to the terror of time, a prophylactic by which to ward off the universal dissolution that is time's sole certainty. But it is always a vain attempt, since the image shares the transiency of those it would redeem from futility and meaninglessness: it can never satisfy the insatiable appetite of time, and time's servant, death. The way of repentance is therefore very different from the way of the image; it is to come to the eternal through time, by learning to become 'older than the moment' (*SV* 4, p.83), a practitioner of patience. For God himself, in his un-changeableness (*SV* 19, pp.249ff.)[8] is a 'God of patience' (*SV* 14, p.154), a title which, Kierkegaard says, uniquely describes his relation to human beings: 'In relation to the lilies and the birds, God is the fatherly Creator and Sustainer, only in relation to human beings is he the God of patience.' (*SV* 14, p.154) This point again emphasises the way in which temporality is a specifically human attribute.

It is easy to understand why several of the discourses advertise the theme of patience in their titles: 'To Acquire One's Soul in Patience', 'To Preserve One's Soul in Patience' and 'Patience in Expectation' – although the subject itself is by no means confined to these. As the first of these two titles clearly indicates, patience (that is, a right relation to time) is intimately bound up with the task of becoming and of continuing to be who we really are: the task, that is, of 'acquiring' and 'preserving' one's soul or self. In the first of these discourses it is stated that patience is not simply a *means* to the end of acquiring a self, not just one condition of selfhood among others, but that it is precisely in and by becoming patient that we also 'acquire' a self. Kierkegaard cites the counter-examples of the farmer who must wait patiently for his crop to mature, the trader who must wait for his customers, the fowler and the fisherman who wait patiently by their nets and a mother who patiently attends to the needs of her children. In all these cases, no matter how necessary patience may be at a practical level, it is essentially extrinsic to the end pursued – an argument which the development of technology might well be taken as vindicating, since it enables us to perform these same tasks in less, or even minimal time. But with regard to selfhood the means are insepar-able from the end. The HOW determines the WHAT. Thus, once we have 'in patience' 'acquired' a 'soul', we cannot just leave patience behind but must 'in patience' 'preserve' the 'soul' we have in this way 'acquired'. This argument importantly parallels the discussion of ends and means in the discourse 'On the Oc-casion of a Confession' (better known as *Purity of Heart*) and it has a significant bearing on the literary or rhetorical structure of the discourses, as we shall see.

To be patient is to humble oneself under the conditions of temporality, to accept and to affirm – not notionally but existen-tially – that human life, the life of a psycho-somatic entity, is permeated by temporality through and through, subject to flux and destined for final dissolution. Nonetheless patience does not mean simply abandoning oneself to the wisdom of imperma-nence.[9] It is rather, within the context of utter impermanence, at the same time to affirm the hope or expectation of an eternal happiness: to believe that we are what we are only in relation to the eternal. In this way patience and expectation are essentially complementary. In the discourse 'Patience in Expectation', Kierke-gaard takes the prophetess Anna as an icon of the attitude which exemplifies the fundamental reciprocity of these two qualities: the person who imitates in their own life the values to be seen in the scriptural picture of Anna will have a concern which 'is every day the same, because his inner life is equally important to him in every moment. Yet he does not consume his soul in impatience but in patience brings forth his expectation, in patience offers it up, by submitting it to God.' (*SV* 4, p.199)

On the other hand, the human mind has a deep-seated antag-onism to recognising its own impermanence. Instead of patiently enduring the burden of time we are all-too-prone to break off waiting and assert the presence of unambiguous meaning in one or other aspect of what must sooner or later be delivered over to decay. This tendency is the temptation of impatience, a temptation which accompanies us at every moment of our journey through time and which, in its extreme form, can lead to a wild rage against human helplessness in the face of time. Thus impatience is said to be restless, defiant, a child, a prolix liar, 'who, hardened in lying, finally believes his own poetic invention'. (*SV* 4, p.178) Sceptical of the possibility of attaining an eternal happiness, impatience leads us to seek various substitutes for such ultimate fulfilment, substitutes which range from sensuality and the pursuit of fame through business and respectability to outright atheism and the despair of defiance.[10] Impatience can even assume a pious disguise and argue its case in the form of a religious or moral appeal. In the discourse 'Against Cowardice' Kierkegaard gives us a caricature of a religious address which has allowed itself to be infected by the spirit of impatience:

> simply be resolute; dare, like a bold swimmer, to plunge into the sea, dare to believe that a human being is lighter than all sufferings, that the swimmer's way passes through all currents and foaming waves right to the goal. See him, the undaunted swimmer: he mounts a high place, his eye delights in danger, his figure is gladdened by the tremor of fear – intrepid, he plunges into the waves; he disappears as if swallowed by the sea, but soon rises to the surface. He has won! Won in single moment! Thus resolution takes its stand upon the mountain of transfiguration, delights in danger, plunges down into the sea, and in the same moment rises up in triumph. (*SV* 4, pp.307f.)

This is, of course, of its time: but we can readily recognise the jargon of 'resolve' – from the political arena, if not from the revival meeting. But what is the deception involved in such speechifying?

In answering this question we are reminded again of the rhetorical strategy which shapes the religious discourses, for the question concerns the very kind of communication which a religious discourse sets out to be. A genuinely edifying discourse will go about its task in a very different way from such appeals to boldness and resolution. These appeals may well make an impression – but what sort of impression? 'Give unto the theatre that which belongs to the theatre and to stage heroes' (*SV* 4, p.308) is Kierkegaard's response to the intrepid swimmer. True edification does not seek any such 'sudden effect' (*SV* 4, p.269) and avoids feeding the impatience which is gratified by such histrionics. 'No, one crawls before one learns to walk, and to fly must always be questionable.' (*SV* 4, p.308) The genuine religious discourse is in this sense an exercise in crawling; as such it not only commends patience – it also requires it. Just as the relationship between patience and selfhood points to the unity of ends and means, so too the discourse which promotes patience must initiate the reader into that relation to time which it seeks to commend. The discourses are not 'about' patience in the sense that a historical report is 'about' an event or a traveller's tale is 'about' a faraway place: the discourse can only deal with patience in an appropriate manner if it does so patiently and if patience emerges as the fruit of the process of reading. This has important implications both for the style of the text itself and for the work of the reader.

The pace of the discourses is slow and repetitive to the point of turgidity; it eschews novelty and stimulation in favour of developing ideas with which the reader is assumed to be already familiar. (*JP*,641/VIII[1] A 293) The discourse turns each issue, theme or text over very slowly, examining the subject from a variety of angles, considering objections and pursuing their implications. In this way it invites us to take part in a process of weighing up the balance between time and eternity, this figure of 'weighing up' (*Overveielse*) being said to 'show what is essential in human nature'. (*SV* 11, p.283) Referring to the pietistic writer Johann Arndt's image of God pursuing the human soul like a cunning hunter who, having exhausted his quarry in the chase, allows it to rest for a while so that it can recover, the hunt begin again and the thrill of the chase be prolonged, Kierkegaard concedes that the method of edifying literature is not dissimilar. (Arndt, we may note, was one of his own favourite devotional writers.) This chase, moreover, or (to use a different figure) the 'school' which the religious individual attends, must, since it is to fit us for eternity, last as long as life itself. (*SV* 11, pp.231ff.) The discourse cannot, of course, be expected to last as long as that, but its time, its way of relating to the reader in time, attempts to break out of the confines of a purely literary, purely aesthetic time, into the time of life, of existence itself.

The aesthetic attitude, we may recall, is governed by the logic of the image. The image, however, is, as such, essentially impatient, seeking to charge a single moment with unambiguous and absolute meaning. Such an attitude is not only characteristic of art but (among other things) of the kind of religious address which we have seen Kierkegaard satirising as no more and no less than religious theatricals. Yet his own discourses are themselves often intensely plastic, making use of vivid pictorialisations of people and situations. We are, for instance, invited to 'talk pictorially for a moment . . .' (*SV* 4, p.241) or to 'see' or to 'behold' such edifying examples as Job, Anna and Paul.[11] Virtues such as patience (and their opposing vices) are boldly personified. The divided self of the person caught in the throes of a religious crisis is portrayed under the figure of two powerful wrestlers. (*SV* 4, p.275) Christ himself is said to have translated 'the woman who was a sinner' into a picture for the edification of his hearers and of succeeding generations. (*SV* 14, p.197) Do his own discourses themselves, then, fall victim to his strictures on the aesthetic and the image? Does he himself slyly offer us a feast of figuration in exchange for the simple but sustaining bread of God's word?

He himself often noted that there was something a little bit 'poetic' about his discourses, and this is nowhere more true than in the many discourses he wrote on the lilies and the birds. These discourses repeatedly ask the reader (in terms which echo the biblical text itself – Matt. 6, 24–end) to 'consider' or to 'behold' these creatures which are given to be our 'teachers'. On a first reading there is indeed something almost idyllic about these discourses. They strike a note of pastoral lyricism which is rare in Kierkegaard's writings. He himself acknowledges that they are a reminder that the upbuilding discourse (*nota bene* the personification) does not forget how to smile in the midst of its serious struggle for the victory of the eternal in human life. The discourses invite us, like weekend sightseers, to go out from our towns and cities into the great empty spaces under the heavens, out into nature, into 'the great fellowship of existence' (*SV* 11, p.168) and to gaze upon these simple, unreflecting creatures of field and sky. Like aesthetic experience itself, the sheer visuality of nature distracts us from ourselves – but it does so in an entirely wholesome way. What nature provides us with is a 'divine distraction' which does not serve the evil of impatience, but which 'distracts, quietens, persuades'. (*SV* 11, p.169) Man-made distractions (Kierkegaard's example is fireworks, but we could all think of others: how about narcotics, those 'artificial paradises'?) have an immediate, momentary impact, but soon bore us. A divine distraction, on the other hand, is hard to get into, but is increasingly effective –

and 'so it is with everything in nature.' (*SV* 11, p.170) We are safe, then, in beholding the beautiful array of the lily and the soaring, inspiring flight of the bird. Though these creatures are not like God (God, after all, is invisible), they are marked by a vestige, a memento of God's creative activity, and they are given to us by God to be our teachers.

For all this, however, there remains a difference between nature, with its spontaneous obedience to divine law, and the kind of God-relationship which the discourses are seeking for their readers. There is an analogy between the way of nature and the way of repentance, but the two are essentially quite distinct. For the way of repentance presupposes humanity's whole history of alienation from God, as well as our capacity for thought and will. Thus, the bird is indeed a divinely-appointed teacher 'but sometimes a teacher also shows in himself the defect against which he will warn'. (*SV* 11, p.163) For instance, nature expresses a visible glory, the representability of which is entirely commensurable with the capacities of the image: but God's glory is an invisible glory, and it is precisely this invisible glory which is reflected in that 'image of God' in which human beings were made and to which they are to be restored. Or again: the lilies and the birds are obedient, they do not serve two masters but fulfil God's design for them and are, thus far, a pattern for human learning; but human beings have *choice*, our task is repentantly to choose ourselves and in this way (and only in this way) to become ourselves. This is a reflection of our first disobedience, but it is also an aspect of the privilege of being human. If we (unlike the lilies and the birds) are anxious about food and drink, poverty and abundance, highness and lowness, presumption, self-torment and irresolution, it is because we have consciousness and, with consciousness, a whole realm of possibilities which nature simply does not have. Thus, the bird is said to be only a 'bird of passage', it does not know what it means to deliberately seek for something, but we are commanded to *seek* the Kingdom of God and, in the light of this Kingdom 'all nature's beauty and peace pales and vanishes'. (*SV* 11, pp.190f.) Likewise, time is 'a dangerous enemy which the bird does not know' (*SV* 11, p.179) but it is also, as we have seen, a factor in the specifically human God-relationship which takes its characteristic form from the patient endurance of temporality. Again, the bird simply lives on its daily bread, but human beings have the dignity of being able to *pray* for their daily bread (*SV* 13, pp.20f.) and, with that prayer, they find a blessing and a satisfaction which the bird does not have.

A truly edifying attentiveness to the lilies and the birds, then, is quite distinct from the poetic attempt to lose oneself in nature, sloughing off the consciousness of time and self in favour of an intense but momentary and therefore illusory aesthetic image. What we learn when we go out into nature is not the universal cosmic sympathy beloved of Romanticism, but the specific *difference* which characterises human life. In this way the discourse's indulgent smile turns out to be the kind of smile which Arndt's cunning hunter might permit himself, for Kierkegaard allows us to rest in the contemplation of natural innocence only long enough to gather our energies for a further venturing of the road to consciously-chosen selfhood, selfhood of a kind which has no parallel in nature and which no image can communicate.

There is another element in the discourses on the lilies and the birds which has important implications for Kierkegaard's understanding and use of imagery throughout the discourses, namely, the silence of the image. The image is without language. In this respect the correspondence between nature and figuration is once again affirmed, since nature as a whole is said to be silent, speechless. 'The forest is silent; even when it whispers it is nevertheless silent. . . . The sea is silent; even when it rages noisily it is nevertheless silent.' (*SV* 14, p.137) So too the lilies and the birds are silent. But the silence of nature is nothing to do with the absence of noise. As the references to the sound of the wind in the forest or the raging of the sea make clear, nature can make a great deal of noise. What nature does not have, however, is speech, language. This is particularly important for an age when language is reduced to 'idle chatter' in such a way that the more that is said the less gets communicated.[12] 'No, only by being silent does one catch the moment; if one talks, even if one only says a single word, one misses the moment; the moment only *is* in silence.' (*SV* 14, p.138) (The 'moment' here, it should be said, is not meant in the sense of the abstract, aesthetic moment but of the moment of time-fulfilled-by-eternity, the *kairos*.)[13] Thus, true prayer is not 'talking to God' but silence, though 'not as if . . . prayer always began with silence, but because when prayer truly becomes prayer, it has become silence.' (*SV* 14, p.136) Nonetheless it is not the case that the silence of nature is immediately identical with the silence of prayer, any more than the images generated by the visual plenitude of nature were able to mirror the invisible image of God in which human beings are made. It is rather that the silence of nature might just enable us to break the habit of language long enough to allow prayer to begin, in the spirit of a 'divine distraction'. In an analogous manner the function of figuration in the discourses is to draw the reader into a figural space, arrived at through but essentially outside of language, in which the conventions of worldly discourse fall away to permit the maturing of that meditative silence which may be for us the beginning of prayer.

This is further illuminated by a curious passage in the discourse 'The Woman who was a Sinner', based on the story of Jesus at the house of Simon the Pharisee. An unnamed woman bursts in, throws herself at his feet, weeping, kissing them and wiping them with her hair, then anointing them with oil.

> She says nothing, and is thus not what she says; but she is what she does not say, or what she does not say, that she is; she *is* a characterisation, like a picture: she has forgotten speech and language and the restlessness of thought and, what is even more restless, forgotten this self, forgotten herself, she, the lost one, who is now lost in her Saviour, lost in him as she rests at his feet – like a picture. And it is almost as if the Saviour himself, for a moment, regarded her and the situation thus, as if she was not an actual person, but a picture . . . he does not speak *to* her . . . he speaks *about* her . . . it is almost as if he turned her into a picture, a parable . . . and yet the same thing was happening in that place at that very moment. (*SV* 14, p.197)

This scene, and Kierkegaard's commentary on it, suggest how the translation of reality into pictorial space may enable us to elude both the judgement and the confusion of language. It is almost implied that the woman escapes the judgement due to her on account of her many sins, because of her essential silence. In regarding her as a picture, and in talking about her as such (not only to Simon the Pharisee but also, through him, to us) Christ brings this essential silence into view. If we are to speak about her at all we must therefore do so figurally, to let her be the icon she is.

This scene thus provides Kierkegaard with a model for his own figuring practices in the religious discourses.[14]

Yet it would be premature to conclude from this that Kierkegaard is attempting to privilege figuration over language or to offer the immediacy of iconic representation as a 'resolution' of the dialectics of religious communication. The 'smile' on the face of the discourse does not dispel the underlying seriousness of its task. Neither figuration nor language are able to sustain any kind of claim to be a uniquely privileged medium of communicating godliness. The relationship between them is rather that of mutual annihilation. Thus, whereas language can serve to undo the illusion of an instantaneously-given plenitude of meaning which indwells aesthetic figuration, we now see figuration being used to put language in its place, or, more precisely to show that language is only *a* place and not *the* place of truthful communication. In this negative dialectic of image and language there thus occurs a reversal of the equation which underpins all aesthetic communication. For aesthetic communication requires the mutual transparency of form and content, a requirement which is preeminently fulfilled in drama's profound integration of plastic and musical, figural and linguistic elements. In the religious discourse, by way of contrast, the formal elements of the communication resist such integration, thereby preventing the establishing of any final resting-place for meaning within the textual body of the discourses themselves. Again, perhaps, the spirit of Arndt's cunning hunter may be sensed, as image and word bring each other to the point of exhaustion – at which point the reader must, if she is to make any sense of the discourse at all, realise her own responsibility in relation to the text.

The 'truth' which the religious discourse is concerned to communicate is coming to seem increasingly 'extra-' textual and, in this respect it is significant that the relationship between image and language which has just been described duplicates the situation of the human self, as that is depicted in the discourses. For the self is consistently portrayed as a double-self, a divided self, a self in conflict with itself, a situation which recalls the 'unhappy consciousness' of Romanticism. For the person whose feet are set on the religious way, however, this split is not merely a fate to be suffered but a conflict to be faced. The religious individual seeks unity and integration, but to achieve this he must overcome: himself. Yet, 'no man is stronger than himself.' (*SV* 4, p.25) In this strife, this holy war, then, the self must wrestle itself to a standstill and, in doing so, discover its actual inability to be itself: 'This is the human being's annihilation and this annihilation is his truth . . . to grasp this annihilation is the highest to which a human being can attain.' (*SV* 4, p.275) For in this annihilation we learn that, since we cannot bring about the unification of the self by our own efforts, the achievement of authentic selfhood depends utterly and solely on divine grace. The annihilation of the individual is his transfiguration in God.

> Only when he himself becomes nothing, only then can God shine through him, so that he comes to be like God. . . . God can only impress himself on him when he himself has become nothing. It is precisely when the sea exercises all its might that it cannot reflect the image of the heavens above, and even the smallest movement means that it does not reflect it quite properly; but when it becomes still and deep then heaven's image sinks down into this nothingness. (*SV* 4, pp.350f.)

This, in the language of the discourses themselves, is what it is for God to triumph in the strife of prayer or for the individual to be satisfied with God's grace. In all this, we may note, we are never far from the situation elsewhere described as the crisis of the aesthetic consciousness, the experience of nothingness and meaninglessness which haunts even the most brilliant of poetry's glittering images. Here, however (can we say: in true Lutheran fashion?),[15] the trial of doubt and despair is precisely the occasion of the self's winning through to authentic existence.

Since the reader must in this way undergo a process of self-annihilation in order to gain his true life, it follows that the reader *in his immediate existence* can no more be regarded as a repository of assured meaningfulness than the text of the discourse itself. Both the text and the human subject whose situation it addresses point to a ground of meaning beyond themselves: the text points to the human subject whilst the human subject in turn points to God. Outside God there is no 'real presence' of meaning in the process of communication – but God in turn is said by Kierkegaard to be essentially and inalienably transcendent: sublime, hidden, inaccessible, beyond all systems of communication, conceptualisation and representation, whether linguistic or figurative. It would seem to follow that the only sure ground of meaning is itself shrouded forever in ineffable mystery. This would, however, seem to be unsatisfactory, since it appears to 'answer' the 'question' of human existence with a still more impenetrable question. Yet what is the alternative? If Kierkegaard were to allow the transcendent ground of meaning to be spoken of as a presence within either the text or the reader, then it would open the door to a metaphysical, aesthetic or naturalistic objectification of that presence, re-enclosing the work of edification within the sphere of knowledge – exactly what his proposed rewriting of the ground rules of dogmatics in terms of rhetoric sought to avoid. Are these, then, the two alternatives: *either* to submit to the hegemony of objective knowledge, *or* to surrender to the abyss, thus abandoning the quest for a sustainable meaning in human life? As far as the religious discourses are concerned we can best address this question by looking at the role of the reader, before going on to consider the specific contribution of Kierkegaard's directly Christological discourses. If in doing so, however, we seem to separate what has been said so far about the methods of the religious discourses, the role of the reader and the contribution of Christology, this is due to the exigencies of presentation. Essentially they belong together as three interlocking dimensions of the one problematic: the communication of Christianity in a situation of epistemological, cultural and personal nihilism.

THE ROLE OF THE READER

If the theatre provided us with the supreme paradigm of aesthetic communication in its purest form, where the imaginative sympathy between actor and spectator etched 'ineradicable images' into the mind of the spectator, Kierkegaard now returns us to the theatre – but it is a theatre with a difference, a rather alarming difference.

> In the theatre the play is acted out before the people who are present and are called spectators; but at the devotional address it is God himself who is present, he is in the most serious sense the spectator who judges, who observes how the word is spoken and how it is heard; precisely for that reason there are no spectators. The speaker is then the prompter, and the hearer, he stands open before God, he is, if I may dare say it, the actor who in a true sense acts before God. (*SV* 11, p.115)

Thus, instead of losing himself in the contemplation of the imaged idea represented by the actor, the reader too becomes himself an actor, precipitated as he is into that maelstrom of self-annihilation in which he discovers his nothingness before God and his dependence on grace. His reading becomes a matter of absolute seriousness, because, as he reads, he is the object of God's absolute attention, an attention which bestows meaning, reality and coherence to the communication. This is not only quite different from what happens in aesthetic communication, it is also different from the Assessor's image of the ethical individual as an actor in a drama written by God, since there God functions as a prior and assured ground of meaning. Nor is God here regarded as himself an object of possible knowledge.

Yet it could easily be argued that the implications of Kierkegaard's analogy remain distinctly transcendental, suggesting that the truth of the human situation cannot be found apart from its relation to a stable, permanent and objectively 'there' presence of absolute being. In his monumental study of Pascal and Racine, *The Hidden God*, Lucien Goldmann asserted that the portrayal of the human situation as 'a play in which God is the spectator' is the key to the continuity of what he calls 'classical thought' from the Greeks to the present.[16] For, he says, it contains 'a doctrine which explains the paradoxical nature of human reality, and a hope in the essential creation of values which endows this contradiction with meaning and which transforms ambiguity into a necessary element of a significant whole'.[17] Is Kierkegaard then – perhaps unwittingly – transforming the ambiguity, paradoxicality and, indeed, downright voidness of the human situation into 'a necessary element of a significant whole' by means of this analogy of the divine spectator? And does this in turn reopen the door for knowledge to enter into and stake its claim on the God-relationship? Before rushing to the conclusion suggested by these questions, however, I should like to offer three reflections which point towards the ambiguity – the fruitful ambiguity – of this analogy, both in its own terms and in the specific context of reading Kierkegaard's religious discourses.

Firstly, Goldmann's study emphasises that the context of the analogy is that of tragic thought, and that it posits a requirement for human life to be lived at a level of seriousness and self-commitment which does not find any ready-made justification in any existing state of affairs. As a result 'the permanent demand for the unambiguous and the unequivocal' (which is to be found in the analogy) 'is only a "wager" and a "permanently unproveable possibility"'.[18] The tragic requirement, in a quotation from Lukàcs which Goldmann takes as his constant point of reference, is that 'value creates reality and does not have to be dreamed or imagined as reality'.[19] It is thus precisely subjectively posited values which are to endow the contradictions of the human situation with meaning and transform the paradox into an element in a significant whole. But in no way is the person who wagers on the triumph of such values insured against the possibility that the world might rise up and crush him or, perhaps, subject him to a 'martyrdom of laughter'.[20] On the contrary, the description of the analogy as 'tragic' implies that it involves an affirmation of values which the world (reality) does not endorse. This tragic implication holds, I believe, for Kierkegaard's concept of repentance which, I have suggested, plays a key role in our reading of the religious discourses. The link between tragedy and repentance is firmly stated by the Quiet Brother in his 'Letter to the Reader' which concludes *Stages on Life's Way*. Here he says that 'Religiousness begins in the higher passion which out of the unity [of the tragic and the comic] chooses the tragic.' (*SV* 8, p.220) Quidam, to whose diary the Quiet Brother is contributing a commentary, doesn't actually get round to repenting, to becoming religious in a decisive sense. Thus he fails to sustain an evaluation of his own existence which would give it meaning and coherence – even if it is only the meaning and coherence of a tragic hero.

Secondly, the God of the analogy is (as the title of Goldmann's book indicates) the *hidden* God. In his *Christian Discourses* Kierkegaard makes the same point by giving the analogy a further twist. He is speaking of the difference between the paganism, old and new, which is weighed down by anxious care for the morrow, and the Christian attitude which has the expectation of an eternal happiness but does not turn away from the present, the time that now is, in favour of a purely fantasised future. The situation of the Christian is said to be like that of a rower who is always turned away from the direction in which he is going (that is to say, he is heading for an eternal happiness but in doing so keeps his eyes fixed on the present) – or, he is like an actor:

> It is well known that in front of the actor, blinded as he is by the stage lights, lies the deepest darkness, the blackest night. One might well think that this would disturb him, make him nervous. But no, ask him, and you will hear (he says it himself) that

it is precisely this which supports him, makes him calm, sustains him in the magical spell of the illusion. On the contrary it would disturb him if he could see a single person, make out a single spectator. So with 'the morrow'. . . . When a person, with the help of the eternal, lives deeply in 'this very day', he turns his back on 'the morrow'. (*SV* 13, p.74)

To be sure, there is no direct mention here of God being the spectator of this performance. Instead it would seem to be 'the morrow', the future, which lies before us, hidden in the darkness of the auditorium. But, as we have already seen, the future, viewed from the standpoint of the work of edification, is precisely the 'incognito of the eternal'. (*SV* 6, p.177) It is through his relation to the future that the believer lives eschatologically for and before God. The hiddenness of the future in Kierkegaard's parable is thus itself a mode of the divine incognito. The point of the parable being that it is essential that this hiddenness, this incognito, is not broken, it follows that all the actor can ever get to see (the actor being the human subject) is the illuminated field of action which constitutes his present. Thus, our concern with an eternal happiness must never be allowed to tear itself loose from the patient attention to the exigencies of a life in time which is lived always in the present. Therefore the only 'presence' of God which can be spoken of in this situation is a kind of presence totally conformed to the present of lived time. Kierkegaard is not abashed in affirming such a presence, and its character as the pure joy in which the crisis of the divided self is resolved. This joy is said to be 'the present time, with the whole emphasis on: the *present*. Therefore God is blessed, who eternally says: today . . .'. (*SV* 14, p.160) It is in this context, and only in this context, that we can make an unconditional predication of being: 'There is a today, which *is*, and there is an infinite emphasis on the *is* . . .'. (*SV* 14, p.160) The future is unknown, the God is unknown: the affirmation of presence implied in the analogy of the divine spectator is an affirmation which can only be made again and again each time in a new present as we bring to the living of our role the full seriousness and commitment of existential passion. It is not the 'presence' of an overarching universal ontology, but the sacrament of the present moment, the 'is' which invades the *now*, eliciting absolute attention, devotion and decision. Such a presence contains no guarantees which might serve to make the divine future an object of possible knowledge, for the God remains hidden even in his presence, his eternity concealed behind the incognito of the future.

Thirdly, let us recall that the context of this whole discussion is a reading of Kierkegaard's religious discourses. What has been said about tragedy and about the hidden God may now be restated within this more focused context, as a pointer to the HOW of reading the discourses. Thus, as she reads, it is the reader's responsibility to affirm (or to reject) the values which she finds represented in the discourses and to maintain that affirmation within the parameters of her actual present. When this is done then her reading *is* repentance, a religious act in which the patient reader acquires and preserves her soul. Like everything that belongs to patience and to the good, such an affirmation is an end in itself, a confession of faith and an act of worship which requires no other and no higher justification. It must be stressed that such a disclosure of meaning in the hidden presence of the future God is no sudden effect or dramatic event (like Sartre's 'lightning-flash' of freedom)[21] but comes as a patient continuation in present-ness through a right and sustained concentration. We do not win through to the meaning of the text by imitating the bold swimmer who plunges into the boiling sea in a moment of great daring and so gains the prize, but by becoming still as the ocean is still when it reflects without distortion the depth and clarity of the sky, and in that stillness (which could equally well be described as luminosity or as darkness) receiving the grace and the joy of divine communication.

THE CRUCIFIXION OF THE IMAGE

I have previously suggested that it is Christology which provides the decisive element in Kierkegaard's theory of communication, that it is the character of the Christ-event as 'paradox' and as 'sign of contradiction' which necessitates the reworking of Christian doctrine as a system of communication (a *Rhetoric*) as opposed to a system of knowledge (a *Dogmatics*). If we now turn to the actual presentation of Christ in the religious discourses we will similarly find many by-now familiar themes brought to a head, as the stage is set for the final confrontation between the aesthetic and the religious.

The characteristic word which Kierkegaard applies to Christ is

'pattern'. The Danish term *Forbillede* (cf. German: *Vorbild*), however, contains within itself the notion of an *image* (*-billede*; cf.
German: *Bild*), an allusion lost in English translation. For Kierkegaard, therefore, it is natural for talk of Christ as 'pattern' to
comprise the idea of Christ as 'image', so that to speak of Christ as
'pattern' leads on to speaking of Christ as the image of God
restored to a fallen humanity. As such he is the true image of that
spiritual reality which the visible, material world is unable to
express or to reflect. But what does it mean to talk of an image
which is incommensurable with visual form? Or, to put it another
way: if it is only in 'becoming as nothing' that human beings enter
into a right relation to God, then for Christ to be the true image of
God manifested in human form would seem to mean that he is
precisely the 'image' of that nothingness, that void, that abyss in
which all human self-interest and self-assertion disappear and
humanity becomes transparent to God – but what could it possibly
mean to talk of an image of nothingness?

Kierkegaard's answer to such questions is simply to point us to
the life of Christ: that is where we will *see* what a life lived in
continuous and complete self-annihilation is like. In the discourse
'Christ as the Pattern' (in *Judge for Yourselves*) Kierkegaard discusses the notion of Christ as pattern in relation to Matthew 6: 24,
'No man can serve two masters.' Christ's life, he argues, is a life
entirely devoted to showing what it is to serve one master and this
in turn means a life of absolute self-annihilation: 'He who only
serves one master, wills to be unconditionally: Nothing.' (*SV* 17,
p.196) This requirement can be seen to govern the whole structure
and narrative of Christ's life: his lowliness, obscurity and eventual
rejection. The circumstances of his birth, the flight into Egypt, his
'hidden' childhood are all determined by the overriding imperative
to be the image of a life of nothingness.

> Thus the life of him who is the pattern was from the beginning
> aimed at being able to express this: only to serve one master. He
> belonged to nothing and to nobody, stood under no obligation
> to anything or anyone, a stranger in this world, in poverty and
> lowliness, without a nest, without a lair, without a place
> whereon to lay his head. Like the straight line [that is, the
> tangent] which only touches the circle at one point: thus he was
> in the world and yet outside the world, only serving one master.
> (*SV* 17, p.191)

The further development of his life, however, brings into play another aspect of the concept of the pattern. For if Christ is to be *for us* the image or pattern then he must at some point reveal himself to others, 'and therefore he must step out, if I may put it like this, on to the stage of human history so that he might, if possible, fix the attention of all upon him'. (*SV* 17, p.191) This move, though, is highly ambivalent:

> To this thing of being nothing there corresponds quite reasonably an obscure life, not drawing any attention to itself. To this thing of being something corresponds drawing attention to oneself. . . . But here comes the madness: to be nothing – and to have the attention of all fixed upon one. It is just as mad as wanting, in the very midst of this world, to establish a Kingdom which is not of this world. (*SV* 17, p.198)

Yet this is just what Christ does; 'he uses the powers of omnipotence to ensure at all times – that he is nothing!' (*SV* 17, p.197)

Here, then, we may *see*, directly yet at the same time paradoxically, a life lived 'as nothing', the kind of life towards which the persuasive efforts of Kierkegaard's upbuilding writings sought to direct us. But Christ's 'stepping out' 'on to the stage of human history', his 'fixing the attention of all upon him' has further implications. For it is this 'stepping out' which provokes the conflict between him and his contemporaries. To live pietistically 'as nothing' in quiet obscurity is one thing – and the rulers of the world can very well afford to ignore such a life; but the 'madness' of wanting to establish a Kingdom not of this world in the midst of this world is something else – and it is not something that worldly powers and authorities can safely ignore. For this is 'an assault on the whole human race and on what it means to be human.' (*SV* 16, p.199) In this respect there is even a certain perverted justice in the fact that he ended up being crucified between two thieves, since

> He did not steal the rich man's money – no, but he took away the worth of having money. . . . Nor was he a slanderer, who slighted someone's honour or good standing, no, but he took away the worth of human honour and good standing. . . . If it is perhaps too harsh to impose the death penalty for robbery and theft, there can only be one sentence for the kind of robbery he has practised on us: the death sentence. (*SV* 16, p.200)

In *Training in Christianity* (from which these last quotations are taken) Kierkegaard reflects on the text of Matthew 11:28, 'Come unto me, all that travail and are heavy laden and I will give you rest,' and invites us to think about the one who offers this invitation, the inviter, Christ himself. How must the inviter have appeared to his contemporaries? Kierkegaard imagines the responses of Mr Worldly Prudence, the Cleric, the Philosopher, the Politician, the Burgher and the Mocker (figures who are all quite plainly Kierkegaard's own contemporaries just as much as they are Christ's) and through these responses shows how Christ's paradoxical combining of a life lived 'as nothing' with having 'the attention of all' fixed on him must provoke hostility and rejection. To be as nothing in the way that Christ exists as nothing is to be on a collision course with the human establishment. To serve only one master is to be on the way that becomes the way of the cross.

But there is a further dimension to the concept of the pattern to which we must now be attentive. 'The pattern' does not merely describe Christ's existence as the renewed image of God in human form (*-billede*): it is also the prototype (*for-billede*) of a renewed humanity. As 'image' alone, Christ would mean the *presence* of God to humanity; as 'prototype' this *presence* is brought into relation to the requirement of a future-directed ascesis which, by virtue of this futurity, decompresses the fulness of *presence* implied in the concept of 'image'. More plainly, to accept Christ as the pattern is to accept him as a model for imitation, to commit oneself to strive to be like him.

> Christ came into the world with the intention of redeeming the world, and, moreover, with the intention – which again is implicit in the first intention – of wanting to be the pattern, of wanting to leave behind a footprint for the one who would cleave to him, who must thus become a 'follower', which concept corresponds to 'footprint'. (*SV* 16, p.221)

Or, quite succinctly: 'Christ is the pattern, and to this corresponds "imitation".' (*SV* 16, p.226)

This emphasis is intended to correct what Kierkegaard describes as the misuse of Luther's doctrine of justification by faith by making it an excuse for dodging the authentically Christian 'obedience of faith'. (Romans 1:5) It means that the disciple must be prepared also to accept the same kind of rejection which Christ

himself endured. The way of the cross is normative for the follower, precisely because it was the way of the one who is the
follower's pattern.

But in what way can Christ as pattern, inclusive of the requirement of suffering discipleship, be communicated? Here, it would
seem, the 'image' element in the concept of the pattern is a
hindrance, since the way in which we respond to an image (the
aesthetic mode of communication *par excellence*) is precisely the
antithesis of the kind of response we must make if the pattern is to
be truly the pattern for us. It is, for instance, in this spirit that
Kierkegaard plots the aestheticising of the Christian sermon by
means of an analysis of the concept of reflection (*Betragtning*) in the
sense of 'Let us reflect on . . .', 'Consider . . .', 'Behold . . .' (*SV*
16, pp.217ff.) Such reflection regards its object as an image to be
contemplated rather than as direct speech requiring a personal
response. For to reflect on something in this way is to create a
distance between oneself and the object reflected on, as one stands
back to take a look, thereby ceasing to be subjective. The preacher
(the typical modern preacher, Kierkegaard believes) who offers
such reflections in place of the appeal of direct speech has actually
turned the pulpit into a stage, a place for displaying images, and
he sets up a distance between himself and his hearers which is
exactly comparable to the distance between an actor and his audience. We can see a sign of this in the way in which the preacher
avoids eye contact with his congregation, seeming to be looking
inwards, in on himself. This may appear to have to do with
modesty or humility, but such a preacher, Kierkegaard says, is 'not
so much like a human being as like a figure carved in stone who
has no eyes'. (*SV* 16, p.219)

Corresponding to all this is the way in which Christ has been
made into an object of admiration, as if he were an aesthetic object
or personality. But what he himself wanted was *followers, disciples*.

> Now it is well enough known that Christ constantly used the
> expression 'followers'; he never talks about requiring 'admirers,
> worshipping admirers, hangers-on'; and when he uses the ex-
> pression 'Disciple', he always interprets it in such a way that one
> sees that what is understood is 'followers', that it does not mean
> adherents of a doctrine but followers of a life. . . . (*SV* 16, p.221)

By way of contrast to the *distance* between preacher and hearer
and between preacher and hearer together and the object (or

subject) of the address, the words of Christ call us to the closest possible intimacy with him in a relationship which is supremely personal. How then are the elements of personal address and the requirement of discipleship to be restored to their proper place? The answer of reformers and revivalists would be that we need more faithful priests or more clear-cut biblical teaching. Such solutions, however, will not work in a pseudo-Christian society which has learnt how to absorb, defuse or marginalise such enthusiasm, either by labelling even the most sincere and impassioned Christian orator a fanatic, or by interpreting his teaching as a knowledge-communication which does not require a personal response. The problem is compounded by the character of the modern world, caught up in the process of levelling which negates all direct authority in such a way that there is no longer any one objectively validated court of appeal for the deciding of religious issues. In this situation it is essential to pay full attention to the HOW of the communication – a point which is lost on the reformers and revivalists who thereby condemn their well-meaning efforts to futility. How then can Christ be communicated as pattern (*Forbillede*) without being reduced to an aesthetic, idealised image (*Billede*)?

As one answer to this question consider the following passage from the 'Christian Expositions' which conclude *Training in Christianity*:[22]

Think then of a child, and now please this child by showing it some of those pictures one can buy in a bargain shop, pictures which are insignificant artistically but so valued by children. – This man here, on the snorting steed, with the waving feather in his hat, with an expression of command, at the head of thousands upon thousands you cannot see, his hand lifted as giving the order: 'Forward!', forward over the mountain peaks which you see stretched out before you, forward to victory: it is the Emperor, the one and only Napoleon; and now tell the child a little bit about Napoleon. . . .

Similarly with William Tell, the great nationalist hero and freedom-fighter.

And so you show the child various pictures to the child's unspeakable pleasure, till you come to the one which you had cunningly placed among them, which shows a man fastened to a cross. The child will not understand this picture straightaway, and will not understand it quite clearly. It will ask what it means, why he hangs on such a tree. Then you explain to the child that it is a cross, and that to hang on it means to be crucified, and that crucifixion was the most painful form of execution in that country, and, moreover, a dishonourable form of execution, only used on the worst law-breakers. How will this now affect the child? The child will be in a strange state of mind, it will in all likelihood be surprised that you could have thought of putting such an ugly picture in among all the other nice ones, this picture of a coarse criminal among all these heroic and noble figures. For just as [the title] 'King of the Jews' was put above his cross in defiance of the Jews, so this picture, which is brought out every year, is a defiant reminder to the race, which never can and never shall be rid of it: so must he always be portrayed, without alteration. And it shall be as if it were *this* generation which crucified him, each time *this* generation shows the child this picture for the first time, explaining for the first time how things go in this world; and the child shall, the first time it hears it, become anxious and afraid for its elders, for the world and for itself; and the other pictures must all surely turn away, as it says in the poem, because this picture is so different. (*SV* 16, pp.168f.)

But then the child will want to know *why* this man was put to death in this way. 'Then tell the child that this crucified one is the redeemer of the world . . . or . . . tell it therefore simply that this crucified one was the most loving person who ever lived.' (*SV* 16, p.169) Why then, the child will ask, even more persistently, did men do this to him? Now, Kierkegaard says, now tell the child the story of the incarnation, the life, the passion, the death, resurrection and ascension of Christ as if it was all as new to you as it is to him. What impression will it all make?

First, he suggests, the child will scarcely notice the conclusion of the story (the exaltation of Christ to 'on high') because it will be so gripped by the story of the passion. Next, the child may want to know why God did not intervene. At last, it will grow angry; it will want to become Christ's soldier and take up arms against those who could do such a thing. Finally, however, as it grows older and more experienced it will instead want to suffer with Christ, affirming its solidarity with him against the world. 'In this way the sight of this humiliation *can* move, can it not move you in the same way?' Kierkegaard asks. (*SV* 16, pp.171f.)

This exposition as to HOW to communicate Christ, and to communicate him precisely as the pattern, is striking in many ways, not least in its extraordinary simplicity and childlikeness. Not only is it *about* a child, but its narrative simplicity reflects something of the stylistic simplicity of a children's story. Everything in it is reduced to a minimum. This extreme simplification is further sharpened by the way in which a readily imaginable picture of the crucifixion is made the constant focus of the exposition, so that we are brought back again and again to a simple reflecting on, a 'beholding', of this picture – a picture which is in itself, as a picture, very much a child's picture. In this way the exposition seems to offer a kind of return to the directness and simplicity of childlike immediacy and therefore also (given the strong associations of childhood/youth with 'the aesthetic' throughout Kierkegaard's authorship: remember Nero) a kind of repetition of the aesthetic in its primary forms of image and story at the very heart of radical Christian communication.

Yet this simplicity, as we might well expect, is deceptive. Indeed, the whole exercise is itself, in one respect, a deception practised on the child, since the picture of the crucifixion was carefully placed among all the other pictures and yet treated as if it had just happened to be there. Just like the pseudonymous works themselves, the pictures of Napoleon, William Tell and others are used to meet the recipient of the communication where he or she is, but this is only the first step in a process leading to a decisively Christian communication. Yet even when the picture of the crucifixion is discussed there is no *direct* narration of the passion story, no *direct* summons to the reader to take up the cross and follow Christ.

If the ultimate aim of the exposition is indeed to present Christ as pattern in an existentially moving way to the reader, this is not done in a direct way, since there are at least three levels of reflection involved in mediating this message. First, we only 'see' Christ by seeing him 'in' the picture, a picture which, no matter how realistic it is, involves the transposition of actuality into aesthetic form, simply by virtue of its character as a work of art; secondly, we look at Christ *through* the eyes of the child and the child's response to the picture, but we do not immediately identify ourselves with this response since, thirdly, we are throughout seeing the child and the child's response through the eyes of the imaginary adult who is showing the picture to the child. There is thus a complex structure of aesthetic fiction involved in distancing the reader from the reality, a formal structure thoroughly in keeping with the complex reflexivity typical of the 'modern man' of the 'age of reflection'.

But there is a further twist to the tale, since, at the very end of the exposition we are suddenly challenged to change our position from that of spectator (the adult, observing the child's response) to participant. 'Thus *can* the sight of this humiliation move,' Kierkegaard writes, going on to ask, 'can it also move you thus?' (*SV* 16, pp.171f.) This twist evokes the conclusion to the story of the prophet Nathan and King David in II Samuel, Chapters 11 and 12, a story which Kierkegaard commented on extensively in *For Self-Examination*. In it Nathan confronts David with his responsibility for having brought about the death of Bathsheba's husband Uriah by telling a story about a rich man with large flocks who took from a poor man the one little lamb he owned. When David grew angry at the behaviour of the rich man Nathan rebuked him: 'Thou art the man.' In the same way here, the parabolic form of the story creates a distance from the reader which is then suddenly collapsed so that we are confronted all the more forcefully with our own responsibility for responding – not to the story about the child but, like the child, to the reality represented by the picture of the crucified one.

There are still further aspects of the exposition worth commenting on, however. Thus, whatever the artistic merit (or otherwise) of the cheap pictures shown to the child, its response to the pictures of Napoleon and William Tell typifies what Kierkegaard regards as the aesthetic response. In these images the child sees an idealised representation of itself, of its own possibilities and powers – just as it would in the images of the magic theatre. But such imaginary identification proves impossible for the child in the case of the image of the crucifixion. Instead of eliciting identification and admiration *this* picture arouses anxiety and concern, repelling and offending the viewer. Even when the situation is explained to the child it still cannot *immediately* identify itself with the Christ-figure. Instead it wishes to take up his cause, to be a crusader, fighting against those who put him to death – but not to identify with him by suffering with him. Before it can make this response it must become an adult and understand, from an adult perspective, the incompatibility of Christ's death with such retribution.

The child's innocence, its horror at learning what this scene really means, throws into sharp relief the actual horror of the event shown in the picture. It is emphasised that it is beyond the mind of the child to understand how 'the most loving person who ever lived' could deserve such hatred and be the object of such cruelty: and because we are made to see the scene through the child's eyes we too are shocked into recognising again the enormity of the crime committed on Calvary. This shock-element is achieved precisely by the way in which Kierkegaard brings his portrayal of Christ as pattern down to an utterly simple, childlike level. Moreover, this also means that the message comprised in the image is contextualised in the most basic physical, visible and tangible bodily experiences, experiences which are accessible to the somatically dominated life of a child. Thus, dogmatic interpretations are reduced to a minimum: the child, we are told, will not understand what 'Saviour of the world' means – so tell it simply that this was the most loving person who ever lived; it will not think much about such eschatological or theological elements in the story such as the resurrection, ascension and parousia – because it will be too preoccupied with the all-too-human drama of the passion narrative itself. By avoiding theological explanations Kierkegaard allows the actual cruelty of the scene to make its proper impact – and it is in relation to this extratextual actuality that our response must have both the urgency and the character of suffering discipleship.

All this helps to explain the terminological shift from 'guilt' to 'sin' which Kierkegaard makes in moving from a purely immanent type of religiousness to paradox-faith. Guilt has to do primarily with the individual's self-relationship and that aspect of repentance in which we become responsible for our failure to be ourselves. Sin, on the other hand, is not self-related but other-related: guilt is our existence as lack, as nothingness,[23] whilst sin points to our culpability in relation to others. It is therefore the thrust of the passion story to convict us of sin rather than guilt, since this story shows (and shows, as has just been said, in the most fundamental bodily reality of physical suffering) just what the consequences of our failure to be ourselves and to be responsible for ourselves actually are, as and when we are confronted with the pattern of divine love, namely: victimisation, cruelty and murder. Repentance is no less relevant in this context than in the context of the upbuilding discourse or in relation to the task of becoming who we really are, but it now acquires a still further note of seriousness as the work of repentance is extended from that of our reading of our own lives into the sphere of interpersonal relationships.

We are now in a position to see the final thrust of Kierkegaard's critique of the aesthetic. For in relation to the kind of scene shown in the image of the crucified one, the crucified image of God-in-human-form, aesthetic representation itself is judged to be a way of participating in the ongoing cruelty which characterises the human rejection of divine love. And now we discover an extraordinary reversal of one of Kierkegaard's most vivid images. At the beginning of *Either/Or* he had told the story of the tyrant Phalaris who was renowned for roasting his enemies alive in a brazen ox, fashioned in such a way that their screams were turned into sweet music. There, Kierkegaard had spoken of the poet as the victim, the unconscious sacrifice whose suffering was the generative ground of his aesthetic productivity and whose 'holy, radiant images' served to mask (even from himself) the reality of his suffering. Now, however, in the penultimate exposition of *Training in Christianity* Kierkegaard states that the artist who attempts to depict the crucified one is not so much like the victim in this story as like the torturer, the tyrant himself. How, he asks, can the artist sustain the calm, the self-control needed for aesthetic productivity in the face of such a reality? How is it that an artist can go on from painting such a scene to paint a Venus, a goddess of love? For the artist the crucifixion is simply an image, an object of contemplation, of detached appraisal – not the pattern, the lure to cross-bearing discipleship.

When the choice between the aesthetic and the religious is posed with a full consciousness of what is involved it therefore becomes a choice as to whether we are going to take the part of the victim – or of the torturer, of suffering love – or of human cruelty. This choice also comes to coincide with Kierkegaard's critique of modernity. For the modern world, governed as it is by the law of levelling, a law fabricated out of envy and fear, creates a social situation in which violence is endemic. The 'crowd', the archetypal concept of the modern world, is constantly in search of new victims to justify its failure (or the failure of its individual members) to assume decisive personal responsibility. These victims may either be individual scapegoats (something of which Kierkegaard believed himself to have had personal experience in his treatment by the satirical paper *The Corsair*) or else the crowd may look outwards, and vent its incipient violence in war.[24]

For Kierkegaard himself this choice is increasingly couched in the language of other-worldly religiosity as a choice between earth and heaven, between this world and the next, between the totality of humanity's social and bodily life and the purely spiritual, 'angelic' life which God has prepared for those who love him. In this respect it is hard to avoid the conclusion that Kierkegaard resolves the tension of tragic thought into the one-dimensionality of a Manichaean pessimism.[25] And yet this is not the only possible outcome of his writings. Think back to the story of the child and the pictures: there it was precisely by the way in which we were made to *see* the meaning of the crucifixion in its visual representation as a bodily, concrete event, rather than as a theological idea, that Kierkegaard enabled us to discover what it is for Christ to be proclaimed as pattern.

This should not, however, be taken as implying that Christ's suffering is exhausted in his physical suffering; his essential suffering, as Kierkegaard states in a number of places (for example, the discourse on I Corinthians 11:23 'On the night in which he was betrayed'), is the suffering of love which wants nothing but good for those who betray him, deny him and put him to death. Nonetheless, in a manner quite different from that of idealism, which took the physical or bodily image as an external material expression of an inner idea, the suffering body of Christ is the permanent and unsurpassable image of that love of God revealed in the unrecognisability of the servant-form. *This* image reveals both the love of God and the violence of man, and, whereas the temporal compression of the aesthetic image was taken to be indicative of the aesthetic individual's flight from time and mortality, *this* image, this image of the crucified one which is also the crucifixion of the image, is for all time the image of what happens when the tangent of eternity touches the closed world of human temporality, and the God proclaims a Kingdom which is not of this world in the midst of this world. As such it serves to demythologise the psychological and societal whitewashing of cruelty, victimisation and suffering, and, as we have seen, challenges us to choose between the perspectives of the victims and their torturers. Kierkegaard did not at all identify the mystification of this situation with the production and reception of works of art, although he found in 'the aesthetic' a supreme paradigm of such mystification: the Established Church was in this respect no less guilty than the community of artists. Nonetheless, it would seem that as the crucifixion of the image, the image of the crucified one does set a

limit to all art, and offers a revelation of what is deeply amiss in
human life which art, determined by the requirement of formal
harmony and perfection, cannot emulate. Yet though this would
seem to be Kierkegaard's own conclusion, we may well feel that
the situation is more complicated than that. For Hegel, we might
recall, the crucifixion of the image was the sign of the final eclipse
of the Greek religion of art. Yet at the same time the total identification of the divine and the human in that event also opened up to
art a new and effectively unlimited field of artistic practice. For
Hegel the religious requirement is not simply a restriction and
curtailment of the scope of art, but an extension and a deepening
of the possibilities of art.[26] Now may it not be that Kierkegaard's
account of the crucifixion of the image, as we have read it here,
might yield a similar ambiguity? For what if art were to abandon its
consolatory role, to descend from the mountain of transfiguration
(where Romanticism invariably sought it) and to take its place in
complete and concrete solidarity with suffering humanity, among
the victims, outcasts and scapegoats of the world? This is not to call
for an exclusively 'political' or 'socially-committed' art, but simply
to suggest that the ideals of beauty and harmony no longer constrain the work of artists and that, since Kierkegaard's time, art has
become as familiar with the wilderness, Gethsemane and Golgotha
as with Parnassus. Can we go further and say that it has not
infrequently been art, rather than religion, which has given us the
most honest revelations of the terror and the pity of all that man
has made of man since Kierkegaard's time? Perhaps it is from the
remembrance of the crucifixion of the image itself, from the memory of Christ's suffering,[27] that art has been learning over two
millennia not only (as Hegel recognised) that the divine is to be
sought in the heart of subjective human life, but also (and this is
what Kierkegaard saw) that the part we take in history's theatre of
cruelty is decisive as to whether we live 'aesthetically' or 'religiously'.

A REAL PRESENCE?

If Kierkegaard's religious discourses are the 'poor relations' in
terms of the attention they receive in the secondary literature, then
the particular group of discourses written for (and in some cases
actually delivered at) the Friday service of Communion are the

poorest of the poor. Yet they constitute an important pointer to the direction of his understanding of Christian communication. Like the other discourses, they are texts, written to be read, spoken, heard. Whatever they do, they do in language. It is, however, by no means accidental that they are invariably much briefer than the other discourses he wrote, and those which were actually delivered in a liturgical context are the briefest and most succinct of all. This brevity, we might suspect, is a clue to their role. For whereas the reading of the other discourses can itself be interpreted as a way of practising repentance, a spiritual discipline of devotional reading which is an end in itself, the Friday Communion discourses are subordinate and preparatory to another and more direct mode of communication: the Communion itself.

In the Communion of the Lord's Supper we are offered a direct communication of God's love in Christ in such a way that we can speak of a presence of meaning, which, though hidden from the enquiring eye of knowledge and of power, is primitive and irreducible. Thus, Christ

> is himself present; he blesses the bread when it is broken, it is his blessing in the chalice which is held out to you. . . . Only he who instituted this meal, only he can prepare it – for he is the blessing you receive at the altar. See, therefore he stretches out his arms there at the altar, he bows his head towards you – in blessing! Thus is he present at the altar. (*SV* 13, pp.281f.)

The Communion is the preeminent sign of that relationship of forgiveness, blessing and indwelling in which God, in Christ, becomes an actual and creative presence in human life; in which the suffering imaged in the figure of the crucified one is received as love; and in which we are not simply challenged to take up the cross and follow him but accepted and sustained in the way of discipleship. As we approach this presence, the text of the discourse seems to withdraw before it, for this communication is not a communication in words but a communication in physical, material elements, bread and wine. Even more directly than the image of the crucified one (which they also, of course, are) these elements point us into the heart of the corporeal stuff of human carnality, suggesting that the communion of the divine love, the divine, suffering, victimised love, does not occur outside of this. Though the presence of Christ in the Communion in no way undoes the requirement of personal appropriation, though it is a presence only for faith, while the rest of the world can (and does) go its own way as the faithful kneel at the altar, the Communion shows us that neither the limits of language nor the limits of the visual image are the limits of communication and that the sphere of Christian discipleship reaches beyond textuality as it reaches beyond the aesthetic.

Notes

1 Idealism and the Justification of the Image

1. J.G. Fichte, *The Vocation of Man* (New York: Bobbs Merrill, 1956), p.80 (adapted).
2. Idem, *The Science of Knowledge* (New York: Appleton, Century Crofts, 1970), p.188.
3. Fichte (1956), pp.81f.
4. Ibid., pp.98f.
5. Ibid., pp.124f.
6. Ibid., p.147.
7. For example, the so-called 'Atheismusstreit'. See: F. Copleston, *A History of Philosophy, Vol. V, II (Modern Philosophy) Part I: Fichte to Hegel* (New York: Doubleday, 1965), pp.100ff.
8. Friedrich Schlegel, *Kritische Schriften* (München: Carl Hanser, 1956), p.46.
9. Walter Benjamin, *Der Begriff der Kunstkritik in der Deutschen Romantik* in *Gesammelten Schriften* 1:1 (Frankfurt am Main, 1972), p.26.
10. Quoted in Benjamin (1972), p.37.
11. F. Schlegel, *Lucinde* (Stuttgart: Reclam, 1963), p.35.
12. F.J.W. Schelling, *System of Transcendental Idealism* (Charlottesville: University of Viriginia Press, 1978), p.219.
13. Ibid., p.232.
14. Henrik Steffens, *Inledning til Philosophiske Forelasninger i København (1803)* (New edn) København: Gyldendal, 1905), p.21.
15. Ibid., pp.21f.
16. Ibid., p.22.
17. One of the best summaries of Grundtvig's thought in English remains E.L. Allen, *Bishop Grundtvig: A Prophet of the North* (London: James Clarke, 1949). James Clarke have also published (more recently) an anthology of Grundtvig's writings. A sign of increasing Anglo-Saxon awareness of Grundtvig's significance is the recently formed Anglo-Danish conference *Grundtvig and England*.
18. Henning Fenger, *Kierkegaard: The Myths and Their Origins* (Newhaven: Yale University Press, 1980), p.84.
19. F.C. Sibbern, *Om Poesie og Konst* Bd. 1 (Københaven, 1834), p.11.
20. Ibid., p.18.
21. Ibid., p.69. Also note Sibbern's swipe at Heiberg's 'gospel of form': 'There is something which is higher than form and that is: content (*gehalt*).'
22. Ibid., p.220.
23. Ibid., p.255.
24. F.C. Sibbern, *Efterladte Breve af Gabrielis* (København: Gyldendal, 1968), p.111.

25. E.C. Tryde, '*Om Poesie og Konst*' . . . *F.C. Sibbern (rec.)* in *Maanedskrift for Literatur* 13 (1835), pp.191ff.
26. F.C. Sibbern, 'Heiberg's *Perseus*' in *Maanedskrift for Literatur* Vols. 19 and 20 (various issues). See also, N. Thulstrup, *Kierkegaard's Relation to Hegel* (Princeton: Princeton University Press, 1980), pp.150–54, for a summary of Sibbern's monograph.
27. G.W.F. Hegel, *Aesthetics. Lectures on Fine Art* (London: Oxford University Press, 1975), p.38.
28. Ibid., p.361.
29. Ibid., p.433.
30. Carl J. Friedrich (ed.), *The Philosophy of Hegel* (New York: Random House, 1953/4), p.337.
31. G.W.F. Hegel, *The Philosophy of Right* (London: Oxford University Press, 1967), p.13.
32. Idem, *Phenomenology of Spirit* (London: Oxford University Press, pb.1979), p.439.
33. Ibid., pp.440f. (adapted).
34. This is the thrust of Alexandre Kojève's celebrated Hegel-interpretation. See A. Kojève, *Introduction à la Lecture de Hegel* (Paris: Gallimard, 1947).
35. Hegel (1975), p.525.
36. Ibid., p.1037.
37. Ibid., p.89.
38. Ibid., p.101.
39. Ibid., p.103.
40. Ibid., pp.9f.
41. Ibid., p.11.
42. Ibid.
43. Thulstrup, op.cit., p.16. Compare Kierkegaard's satire on Heiberg's 'conversion' in the *Concluding Unscientific Postscript* (*SV* 9, pp.153f.)
44. J.L. Heiberg, *Om Philosophiens Betydning for den Nuvaerende Tid* (København, 1833), p.20.
45. Idem, *Om Vaudeville* (København: Gyldendal, 1968), pp.28f.
46. Ibid., p.36.
47. Ibid., p.43.
48. See my article 'Søren Kierkegaard: A Theatre Critic of the Heiberg School' in *The British Journal of Aesthetics*, Vol. 23, no. 1, Winter 1983; also Chapters 3 and 4, below.
49. Heiberg (1968), p.118.
50. Ibid., p.141.
51. Ibid., p.130.
52. Ibid., p.131.
53. Paul Rubow, *Heiberg og hans Skole i Kritiken* (København: Gyldendal, 1953), p.42.
54. J.L. Heiberg, *Poetiske Skrifter* Bd.2 (København, 1862)
55. H.L. Martensen, 'Betragtninger over Ideen af Faust' in *Perseus: Journal for den Speculative Idee*, June 1837, p.97.
56. Ibid., p.98.
57. Ibid., p.108.

58. Ibid., pp.163f.
59. Idem, *'Fata Morgana' af J.L. Heiberg* in *Maanedskrift for Literatur* (19)1838, p.367.
60. Ibid., pp.367f.
61. Ibid., p.381
62. Ibid., p.388.
63. J.L. Heiberg, *En Sjael Efter Døden* (6th. edn. København: Gyldendal, 1963), p.18.
64. Ibid., p.36.
65. Ibid., p.38.
66. Heiberg (1833), p.41.
67. Heiberg (1963), p.56.
68. Ibid., p.71.
69. H.L. Martensen, *'Nye Digte' af J.L. Heiberg* in *Faedrelandet*, 10.1.1841.
70. E. Tryde, *'Nye Digte' af J.L. Heiberg* in *Tidskrift for Literatur og Kritik*, 1841.
71. From H. Heine, 'Lass die heil'gen Parabolen' in H. Heine, *Sämtliche Werke* (München: Rösl, 1923), Bd. II, p.410.
72. See, for example, D.F. Strauss, *The Life of Jesus Critically Examined* (London: SCM, 1973), p.780.
73. See, Ludwig Feuerbach, *The Essence of Christianity* (New York: Harper Row, 1957). See also my article, 'From Kierkegaard to Cupitt: Subjectivity, the Body and Eternal Life' in *The Heythrop Journal* Vol. XXXI, Number 3 (July 1990), esp. pp.296f.
74. R.M. Summers, *A Study of Kierkegaard's Philosophical Development up to 'Om Begrebet Ironi'* (London University: PhD thesis, 1980), p.56.
75. Poul Martin Møller, 'Om Begrebet Ironi' in *Efterladte Skrifter* (3rd. edn. København: Reitzel, 1856), 3, p.152. For Møller's overall relation to nihilism see Uffe Andreasen, *Poul Møller og Romantismen* (København: Gyldendal, 1973).
76. P.M. Møller, 'Recension af Sibbern's Aesthetik' in *Efterladte Skrifter*, 5, p.213.
77. Idem, 'Strøtanker' I, in *Efterladte Skrifter*, 3, p.3.
78. Ibid., 5, p.67.
79. Ibid., p.66.
80. Ibid., pp.69f.
81. Sibbern, 'Heiberg's Perseus', p.308. See n.26.
82. Møller, *Efterladte Skrifter*, 5, p.41.
83. Ibid., 3, p.160.
84. Ibid., 1, p.122.
85. Ibid., p.134.
86. In Heine, *Sämtliche Werke*, Bd. V. 'Zur Geschichte der Religion und Philosophie in Deutschland'.

2 The Genealogy of Art

1. Uffe Andreasen, *Romantismen* (København: Gyldendal, 1974), pp.11ff.
2. The newspaper articles are not included in the 3rd edition of Kierke-

gaard's Works, which I have used here. They may be found, however, in Teddy Petersen (ed.), *Kierkegaard's Polemiske Debut* (Odense: Odense Universitetsforlag, 1977) and in Vol. I of the Princeton University Press edition of *Kierkegaard's Writings (Early Polemical Writings)*. The text of this address may be found in *JP*,5116/I B 2.

3. Petersen, op.cit., p.112.
4. *Papirer* I B 7.
5. Petersen, op.cit., p.13. Papirer I B 6.
6. III B 1. See also Thulstrup, op.cit., p.211.
7. *JP*,6624/X^{iii} A 99; *SV* 18, p.13.
8. Frithiof Brandt, *Den Unge Søren Kierkegaard* (København: Levin og Munksgaard, 1929), p.126.
9. See Chapter 1, n.48.
10. *SV* 5. Recently published in English, translated with introduction and notes by William D. McDonald, *Prefaces* (Florida State University Press, 1989). To be published in Vol. IX of the Princeton *Kierkegaard's Writings*.
11. A reference to Martensen or Tryde.
12. P.M. Mitchell, *A History of Danish Literature* (København: Gyldendal, 1957), p.135.
13. *Faedrelandet* 7.5.1843, p.9846.
14. The historical section of this work is chiefly concerned with Socrates, but it also contains an important discussion of 'Irony After Fichte'.
15. See Thulstrup op.cit., pp.213ff. Thulstrup believes that 'we cannot imagine that such a shrewd genius as Kierkegaard could possibly have let himself be taken in by Hegel'. This point of view, however, begs a lot of questions with regard both to Hegel and Kierkegaard. See also David J. Gouwens, *Kierkegaard's Dialectic of the Imagination* (New York: Peter Lang, 1989), pp.56f., 79ff.
16. See the Princeton 1959 edition of *Either/Or* I, p.450.
17. The expression comes from Ruskin. See P. Fuller, *Theoria* (London: Chatto and Windus, 1988), pp.113ff.
18. See especially Part II, Chapter 3.
19. See especially his comments on 'The Age of Reflection' in *Two Ages* (*SV* 17)
20. See Chapter 5, below, 'Kierkegaard as Novelist'.
21. See Nietzsche, *The Genealogy of Morals* (New York: Doubleday)
22. See Chapter 3, below, 'Towards a Rhetorical Theology'.
23. See, for example, Nelly Viallaneix, 'Kierkegaard Romantique' in *Romantisme* (8) 1974, p.64.' Søren Holm, 'The Nineteenth Century' in N. and M.M. Thulstrup (eds) *Kierkegaard and Human Values: Biblioteca Kierkegaardiana 7* (København: Reitzel, 1980), p.15.; Gouwens, op.cit., pp.5ff. presents a view closer to my own.
24. Henning Fenger, op.cit.
25. *JP*,1182/II A 29; *JP*,1231/I A 7; *JP*,1302/I A 2; *JP*,5092/I A 72; *JP*,5100/I A 75.
26. See Chapter 1, n.11.
27. 'Do I, then, dream, or is it this fantastic night which dreams of me?'
28. *JP*,1178/I A 104; *JP*,1181/I A 292; *JP*,1183/II A 50; *JP*,1184/II A 56;

JP,5092/I A 72. (Lenau has Faust commit suicide.)

29. The connection between Romanticism and medievalism is well established. See, for a classic statement of the case Heinrich Heine, *Die Romantische Schule* in *Sämtliche Werke* Bd. 5.
30. 'Hero legends are permeated by a very remarkable self-contradiction, an utterly naive lie (which is why these stories are so easily parodied.)' *JP*,5209/II A 36. See also *JP*,5212–4/II A 43–5.
31. *JP*,4066, 5178, 2209, 4067/I A 285–8. It is striking in this respect that Hegel sees both the Catholic Middle Ages and the late Hellenistic world as manifesting 'The Unhappy Consciousness' which is unable to be at one with itself. His remarks in *The Philosophy of History* about the Crusades are very much in the same vein as Kierkegaard's view of the Middle Ages.
32. *JP*,35/II A 383; *JP*,1698/II A 114; *JP*,1978/II A 385; *JP*,2707/II A 468.
33. *JP*,1690/II A 102; *JP*,1711/II A 608.
34. Johann Georg Hamann (1730–88). In his postscript to the Reclam (1968) edition of Hamann's *Sokratische Denkwürdigkeiten und Aesthetica in Nuce* Sven-Aage Jørgensen referred to Kierkegaard as Hamann's sole 'authentic disciple' (p.164). For the differences between the two thinkers see Ronald Gregor Smith, 'Hamann and Kierkegaard' in E. Dinzle (ed.) *Zeit und Geschichte. Dankesgabe an Rudolf Bultmann zu 80. Geburtstag* (Tübingen: J.C.B. Mohr, 1964).
35. The similarities between the philosophy of 'The Rotation Method' and Postmodernism have been pointed out by Poul Lübcke in 'Kierkegaard – Aesthetics and Crises of Metaphysics' in *Kierkegaard, Poet of Existence (Kierkegaard Conferences I)* (København: Reitzel, 1989).
36. *Begrebet Angest* has been variously translated as *The Concept of Dread* and *The Concept of Anxiety*. Since *'angst'* now appears in English dictionaries, however (thanks, ultimately, to Kierkegaard) why not use the closest available word?
37. For the connection between *angst* and nothingness in existentialist philosophy see J.-P. Sartre, *Being and Nothingness* (London: Methuen, 1958) pp.28ff.
38. See also Chapter 6, below, 'Temporality and Figuration in the Religious Discourses'.
39. William Shakespeare, *A Midsummer Night's Dream* Act V, Sc. 1.
40. *SV* 19, pp.215f.
41. In certain respects, of course, Kierkegaard makes a sharp division between the attitude of the poet and the attitude of the bourgeoisie, yet both can be characterised and categorised in terms of immediacy. In *JP*,220/II A 128, for example, the attitude of bourgeois self-complacency is described as 'vegetative' and 'pantheistic' and therefore essentially comparable with the kind of Romantic attitude which Kierkegaard discerned in Schlegel. See Chapter 1, n.11 and *JP*,1019/II A 125. One might observe that the Romantic rebel almost invariably turns out to be the child of a solid bourgeois household and frequently (Rimbaud being a prime example) returns to the bourgeois fold in middle years.
42. See Chapter 3, below, especially the discussion of Kierkegaard's *The Point of View*.

3   The Dialectics of Communication

1. I do not intend to suggest by this that Kierkegaard was mentally unbalanced, although one psychiatric writer has described him as 'the poor, emaciated, thin schizoid' (Rudolf Friedman, *Kierkegaard: The Analysis of the Psychological Personality*, London: Peter Nevill, 1949, p.59) and Josiah Thompson in his *The Lonely Labyrinth* (Carbondale, Illinois: Southern Illinois University Press, 1967) and *Kierkegaard* (London: Victor Gollancz, 1974) has argued a similar case. The point I am making is strictly *conceptual*: that Kierkegaard did not regard the achievement of wholeness as lying within the natural capacities of the human person. That, of course, might be said to represent the orthodox Christian viewpoint; however, in a largely post-Christian age mainstream Christianity itself is widely viewed as pessimistic, and there is some evidence that Kierkegaard's appraisal of the human situation went beyond the mainstream of Christian theology in its judgement on the universality and destructiveness of sin. This comes out, for instance, in his view of sexuality; see my article 'From Kierkegaard to Cupitt: Subjectivity, the Body and Eternal Life' in *The Heythrop Journal* XXXI, 1990, pp.298f.
2. For the Hegelian theory of psychology see Carl Rosenkranz, *Psychologie* (2nd edn 1843). The relationship between psychology and dogmatics is discussed intensively in the *Introduction* to *The Concept of Angst*, Kierkegaard's standpoint being summarised in the following quotation: 'One has called psychology the doctrine of subjective Spirit. If one pursues this more closely, one will see how, when it comes to the problem of sin, it must first be transposed into the doctrine of absolute Spirit. That is where dogmatics holds sway.' (*SV* 6, p.121)
3. Schelling (1978), p.14.
4. Steffens (1905), p.21.
5. The work in question is *Aesthetica in Nuce*. See Chapter 2, n.34.
6. For the 'eternal triangle' constituted by Schlegel, Schleiermacher and Kierkegaard, see my article, 'Friedrich Schlegel's *Lucinde*: A Case Study in the Relation of Religion to Romanticism' in *The Scottish Journal of Theology*, Vol. 38, pp.545–64 (1986).
7. See Chapter 1, n.8. Also *JP*,1455/I C 73.
8. Friedrich Nietzsche, *The Birth of Tragedy and the Genealogy of Morals* (New York: Doubleday), p.88.
9. See Kierkegaard, *Letters and Documents* (Princeton: Princeton University Press, 1978), pp.262f.; *Works of Love* (*SV* 12, pp.127f.) and *JP*,4265/VII[i] A 69.
10. Mynster's comments on *Fear and Trembling* were made in an article (published under his *nom de plume* 'Kts') 'Kirkelig Polemik' in *Intelligensblade* 1844, Nos. 41–2, 1.1.1844.
11. *JP*,648–57/VIII[ii] B 79, 81–9. As these entries are very extensive I shall depart from my normal practice and give references to the Hong and Hong edition by Volume and page number.
12. 'The ethical is as such the universal, and, as the universal, that which is valid for everybody . . .'. (*SV* 5, p.51)

13. See below, Chapter 6, 'The Crucifixion of the Image'.
14. What he particularly objected to was the use by H.L. Martensen of the expression 'witness to the truth' in relation to the late Bishop Mynster. Though Kierkegaard consistently showed considerable respect for Mynster he was also observant of the way in which Mynster's ecclesiastical preferment had brought with it very 'wordly' honours and comforts. One of the best accounts of Mynster and his relation to Kierkegaard is in the unpublished PhD thesis by John Saxbee, *The Place and Significance of Søren Kierkegaard's 'Attack Upon Christendom' in the Development of his Authorship* (University of Durham, 1974).
15. Augustine, *The Greatness of the Soul and The Teacher: Ancient Christian Writers* Vol. IX (Westminster, Maryland: The Newman Press; London: Green and Co., 1950), p.131.
16. Ibid., p.177.
17. Ibid., p.176 and pp.185f.
18. If this sounds like a classic case of institutionalised Christianity suppressing individual enthusiasm, it might be worthwhile to take note of some of Adler's views, such as: 'The world was originally not good', 'The sexual drive is the evil Spirit and comes into the world by means of the evil spirit', or, that witches should be burnt and that a father whose son does not believe in Jesus might justifiably break the son's neck. See S. Kierkegaard (ed. Watkin) *Nutidens Religieuse Forvirring* (København: Reitzel, 1984), pp.13f.
19. See n.18. Further references will be to *BA* in the text ('The Book on Adler' being a common English designation for this work, although my references are to Watkin's edition).
20. Paulo Freire, *The Pedagogy of the Oppressed* (Harmondsworth: Penguin, 1972) pp.45ff.

4 Life in the Magic Theatre

1. Martin Thust, 'Das Marionettentheater Sören Kierkegaards' in *Zeitwende* I (1925), pp.18–38. Also *idem*, Sören Kierkegaard. *Der Dichter des Religiösen* (München: Beck, 1931).
2. See the remarks on language in the uncompleted *Johannes Climacus Or De Omnibus Dubitandum Est* IV B; in Vol. VII of *Kierkegaard's Writings* (Princeton: Princeton University Press, 1985) with *Philosophical Fragments*. An earlier translation with notes by T.H. Croxall was published under the title *Johannes Climacus or De Omnibus Dubitandum Est and A Sermon* (Stanford, California: Stanford University Press, 1958).
3. For the way in which Kierkegaard uses reviews to attune the reader to the 'idea' of the work, see my PhD thesis, *Kierkegaard's Theory and Critique of Art: Its Theological Significance* (University of Durham, 1983).
4. J.L. Heiberg, in *Intelligensblade* 2, No. 24, 1843.
5. IX B 68. An English translation can be found in S. Kierkegaard (tr. S. Crites) *The Crisis and A Crisis in the Life of an Actress* (New York: Harper and Row, 1967).
6. G.E. Lessing, *Hamburgische Dramaturgie* in *Sämtliche Werke* Bd. 6 (Stuttgart: Göschen, 1874), p.90.

7. Ibid., p.112.
8. Ibid., p.403.
9. Ibid., p.409.
10. Ibid., p.419.
11. Michael Kustow, reviewing Peter Brook's *Mahābhārata* in *The Observer*, 3 December 1989, p.41.
12. G. Josipovici, *The Book of God* (Newhaven and London: Yale University Press, 1988) contains an interesting discussion of this in Chapter 12, 'St Paul and Subjectivity' (pp.235ff.).
13. Lessing, op.cit., p.15.
14. Ibid., p.16 Lessing's own drama *Miss Sara Sampson* (recently staged in an English language version as *Sarah* by the 'Cheek by Jowl' Theatre Company, 1990) is an attempt at just such a play, dealing as it does with the key theological issues of grace, forgiveness and reconciliation.
15. This is more in the spirit of Heiberg than of Lessing: Heiberg regarded tragedy as more 'immediate' than comedy and had little respect for Shakespeare. Lessing, as we have seen, saw tragedy and comedy as equally 'ideal'.
16. This point, and its connection with Christianity, is strongly brought out in Josipovici's essay (see n.12).
17. See, for example, Ann Loades 'Simone Weil – Sacrifice: A Problem for Theology' in D. Jasper (ed.) *Images of Belief in Literature* (London: Macmillan, 1984).
18. See Chapter 2, n.3.
19. Kierkegaard's account of 'the aesthetic' as a psychological state seems to me to bear close comparison with the 'existentialist psychiatry' of R.D. Laing's earlier work, as set out in his books *The Divided Self* (Harmondsworth: Penguin, 1965) and *Self and Others* (Harmondsworth: Penguin, 1971).
20. Friedrich Nietzsche, *The Will to Power* (New York: Vintage, 1968) Book One, for example: no. 22, p.17.
21. Hermann Hesse, *Steppenwolf* (Frankfurt an Main: Suhrkamp). Further references are to *S* in the text.
22. Martin Thust, op.cit.
23. The play *Julespøg og Nytaarsløj* can be found in J.L. Heiberg, *Poetiske Skrifter* (København, 1862) Bd.2.
24. *SV* 2: see the editorial note on p.413.
25. Don Cupitt, *The World to Come* (London: SCM, 1982), p.40.

5 Nihilism and the Novel

1. M. Jørgensen, *Kierkegaard Som Kritiker* (København: Gyldendal, 1978).
2. Compare John Hospers: 'formalistically-minded critics would say that literature differs importantly from the other arts, and that the appreciation of literature does involve considerations of correspondence with reality, whereas appreciation of the other arts does not.' In Sidney Hook (ed.), *Art and Philosophy* (New York: New York University Press, 1966, p.129) From a rather different perspective Sartre seems to arrive

at a similar judgement in his *Qu'est-ce Que La Litterature* (Paris: Galli-mard, 1948), pp.26ff. Kierkegaard can, interestingly, be seen as both 'formalistically-minded' and 'existentialist'.

3. Poul Martin Møller, *Efterladte Skrifter*, 5, pp.69f.
4. Mme Gyllembourg is almost completely unknown in the English-speaking world; I suspect, however, that much of what Kierkegaard says about her work could be applied to an English writer who is universally read: I am thinking of Jane Austen, whose work might also be said to contain an implicit and highly ethical theology. Such a view has been recently argued in I. Morris, *Mr Collins Considered* (London and New York: Routledge & Kegan Paul, 1987), pp.162f.
5. If Kierkegaard's judgement on Andersen seems almost brutally harsh, think of the sentimentality and the dependence on circumstance in a story such as 'The Ugly Duckling' or the 'pessimistic' figure of Kay in 'The Snow Queen', who is totally incapable of taking effective action against the emotionally and morally numbing ice-splinter lodged in his heart.
6. Schlegel, *Lucinde*, p.10.
7. For an analysis of the 'shockingness' of Schlegel's book, see Ludwig Marcuse, *Obscene* (London: McGibbon & Kee, 1965), 'Jena 1799'.
8. For the relationship between Møller and the Assessor, see W. Glyn Jones,' Sören Kierkegaard and Poul Martin Møller' in *Modern Language Review* (60) 1965, pp.79ff.
9. This passage, it seems to me, strikingly anticipates the central issue in Ibsen's *The Doll's House*. Although the much-mooted links between Kierkegaard and Ibsen have been questioned, there do appear to be important thematic convergences – however the question of 'influence' may be resolved.
10. F. Billeskov Jansen, *Søren Kierkegaard's Literaere Kunst* (København: Reitzel, 1951).
11. Carl Roos, *Kierkegaard og Goethe* (København: Gad, 1955), p.55.
12. Aage Henriksen, *Kierkegaard's Romaner* (København: Gyldendal, 1954), p.8.
13. Louis Mackey, *Kierkegaard – A Kind of Poet* (Philadelphia: University of Pennsylvania Press, 1971), p.274
14. Henriksen, op.cit.
15. In this context we should take note of the tremendous impact of Shakespeare on German Romanticism.
16. My attention was drawn to the significance of the 'Interlude' in the *Fragments* by an unpublished paper by Marilyn G. Piety, 'A Little Light Music' (delivered at the conference 'Kierkegaard: The Christian in Love with Aesthetics', Durham, April 1990.)
17. This is clear from the evidence of the journals. The two parts were to be called *'Wrong and Right'* and *' "Guilty?" – "Not-Guilty?" '*; the former of these was dropped and the latter, of course, retained.
18. G. Brandes, *Den Romantiske Skole i Tyskland* in *Samlede Skrifter* 4 (København, 1900), p.331. Brandes also wrote one of the first notable mono-graphs on Kierkegaard's life and work (as well, of course, as on Nietzsche).

19. For one example among many, see M. Buning, 'Samuel Beckett's Negative Way: Intimations of the *Via Negativa* in the Late Plays' in D. Jasper and C. Crowder (eds.) *European Literature and Theology in the Twentieth Century* (London: Macmillan, 1990). In a different sphere of artistic practice, one might think of Mark Rothko – see my comments on Rothko in *Art, Modernity and Faith* (London: Macmillan, 1990).
20. Think of the rediscovery of the primitive in the work of Picasso, Stravinsky or (closer to Kierkegaard) in Knut Hamsun's *Growth Of the Soul*. For an analysis of the appeal of the primitive, see C.G. Jung (ed.) *Man and His Symbols* (London: Aldus, 1964).
21. S. Kierkegaard (ed. Hong and Hong) *The Corsair Affair: Kierkegaard's Writings XIII* (Princeton: Princeton University Press, 1982), p.101.

6 Reading, Repentance and the Crucifixion of the Image

1. See especially Part II, Chapter IV, Section II.
2. Although it is clear that certain discourses do have a distinctive Christocentric focus, I believe we should think more in terms of a sliding scale, concentric circles or geological strata than of a sudden, abrupt transition. The significant break in Kierkegaard's thought comes between the aesthetic and the religious rather than between the different forms of the religious. This is indicated by Kierkegaard's own blurring of the edges in the various titles and subtitles of the discourses. Thus, the discourses on the lilies and the birds of 1847 appear in *'Upbuilding' Discourses in Diverse Spirits*, whilst the comparable discourses on the same theme in 1848 appear in the *'Christian' Discourses*; similarly *Works of Love* (1847) is subtitled 'Some *Christian* Reflections in Discourse Form', although they do not contain the kind of *directly* Christological considerations which are found in the 'Christian Expositions' in *Training in Christianity*.
3. A category which Kierkegaard frequently used of his own writing.
4. Anders Kingo, 'Den Opbyggelige Tale' in *Dansk Teologisk Tidskrift* (48) 1985, p.130.
5. Aristotle, *Poetics* and Demetrius, *On Style* (London and New York: Dent–Dutton/Everyman, 1943), p.80.
6. Louis Mackey (1971), p.249.
7. This may be compared with the description of the task of becoming a self given in *The Sickness Unto Death*, where the programme of self-attainment is set out in terms of a sequence of polarised categories.
8. 'The Unchangeableness of God' is the title of a discourse which Kierkegaard delivered in 1851 and published in August 1855, only a few months before his death, in the midst of his final 'Attack upon Christendom' to show that despite the harshness of his polemics against the Church he did not repudiate the spirit of edification which characterised his religious writing.
9. As an example of *that*, one might cite the 'beat-zen' of Alan Watts (in numerous works, for example, *The Wisdom of Uncertainty*).
10. Again *The Sickness Unto Death* provides a complementary, more sys-

tematic exposition of the situation of despair which finds expression in such 'impatience'.

11. In the discourses 'Strength in the Inner Man', 'The Lord Gives, the Lord Takes Away, Blessed be the Name of the Lord' and 'Patience in Expectation'.

12. See, for example, *JP*,5181/I A 382, where Kierkegaard speaks of a 'bankruptcy', a 'mutiny', a 'confusion' in language; or, the critique of the 'Age of Reflection' in *Two Ages*; compare M. Heidegger, *Being and Time* (Oxford: Basil Blackwell, 1962) pp.211ff.

13. The term 'kairos' comes from the gospel logion 'The time is fulfilled, and the Kingdom of God is at hand.' (Mark 1:15) It is also a key term in the existential theology of Paul Tillich.

14. In this connection it may be worth drawing attention to the way in which Kierkegaard also describes silence as a preeminently *womanly* quality. (*SV* 17, pp.88ff.) Note the implication that woman is in a distinctive way a 'natural' phenomenon.

15. One thinks of Luther's *Anfechtungen*, a term which Kierkegaard also appropriated, or (again) of the intensely ambivalent interrelationship between doubt, despair and faith in Tillich.

16. Lucien Goldmann, *The Hidden God* (London: Routledge & Kegan Paul, 1964), pp.22f. See also George Lukàcs, *Soul and Form* (London: Merlin, 1974), p.152. Compare Henry Staten, *Wittgenstein and Derrida* (Oxford: Basil Blackwell, 1984/85) especially Chapter 4, 'Rhetoric, Theater, Death' which discusses the concept of God as spectator/audience of the human situation in relation to Augustine's *Confessions*.

17. Goldmann, op.cit., p.308.

18. Ibid., p.67.

19. Lukàcs, op.cit., pp.113f.

20. See Kierkegaard, *The Corsair Affair* (1982), p.276 (also: *JP*,6348/X^i A 120).

21. Orestes in Sartre's *The Flies*: 'Suddenly, out of the blue, freedom crashed down on me, and swept me off my feet.' J.-P. Sartre, *Altona – The Man Without Shadows – The Flies* (Harmondsworth: Penguin, 1962), p.310.

22. Kierkegaard used the same story, with some variation, in the *Two Minor Ethico-Religious Discourses* ('Has a Man the Right to let himself be put to Death for the Truth', *SV* 15).

23. Compare Heidegger, op.cit., Division Two, Part II, pp.312–48. Heidegger, I believe, is very close to Kierkegaard at this point, however divergent their ultimate aims may be.

24. For instance: 'Schelling is right when he says . . . "When it comes to the point where the majority decides what constitutes truth, it will not be long before they take to deciding it with their fists."' (*JP*,4112/VII^i A 63) And: 'The tragedy at the moment is that the new ministry needs war to survive, needs all the agitation of national feelings possible. Even though we could easily enough have peace – if the ministry is not completely stupid it must see that *it* needs war.' (*JP*,4137/VIII^i A 609).

25. See my 'The Conscious and the Unconscious Sacrifice' in S. Sykes (ed.) *Sacrifice and Redemption* (Cambridge: Cambridge University Press, 1991).
26. See Chapter 1 above, 'Hegelianism'.
27. J.B. Metz, 'The Future *Ex Memoria Passionis*' in E.H. Cousins (ed.), *Hope and the Future of Man* (Philadelphia: Fortress, 1972).

Bibliography

(1) Primary Sources

Danish
Kierkegaard, Søren Aabye, *Samlede Vaerker*, 20 vols (3rd ed. København: Gyldendal 1962).
Idem, *Papirer*, ed. Heiberg, Kuhr and Torsting, 20 vols (København: Gyldendal, 1909–48).
Petersen, T. (ed.), *Kierkegaards Polemiske Debut* (Odense: Odense Universitetsforlag, 1977).

English
Hong, Howard V. (ed.), *Kierkegaard's Writings* 26 vols (Princeton: Princeton University Press, 1978–).
Hong, H.V. and Hong, E.H. (eds), *Søren Kierkegaard's Journals and Papers*, 6 vols with Index (Bloomington: Indiana University Press, 1967–78).

(2) Bibliographies and study aids

Himmelstrup, Jens, *Søren Kierkegaard: International Bibliography* (København: Nyt Nordisk Verlag, 1962).
Jorgensen, Aage, *Søren Kierkegaard-Litteratur*, 1961–70 (Aarhus: Akademisk Boghandel, 1971).
Lapointe, Francois H., *Kierkegaard and his Critics* (Westport: Greenwood, 1980).
Mackinnon, Alastair, *The Kierkegaard Indices* (Leiden: Brill, 1971–3)
    1. *Kierkegaard in Translation* (1970)
    2. *Konkordans til Kierkegaards Samlede Vaerker* (1971)
    3. *Index Verborum til Kierkegaards Samlede Vaerker* (1973)
Perkins, Robert L., *International Kierkegaard Commentary* (Mercer University Press, 1984–): a series of collections of essays by leading scholars, designed to accompany each volume of the Princeton edition of *Kierkegaard's Writings*.
Thulstrup, Niels and Thulstrup M.M. (eds), *Biblioteca Kierkegaardiana* (København: Reitzel, 1978–89): a series of thematic volumes, covering a vast range of topics from Aristotle to Kierkegaard's Copenhagen.

Secondary Literature – A Select List

Adorno, T.W., *Kierkegaard. Konstruktion des Aesthetischen* (Frankfurt am Main: Suhrkamp, 1974).
Andreasen, U., *Poul Møller og Romantismen* (København: Gyldendal, 1973).
Benjamin, W., *Der Begriff der Kunstkritik in der Deutschen Romantik* in *Gesammelte Schriften*, 1:1 (Frankfurt am Main, 1972).

Bertung, B. (ed.) *Kierkegaard – Poet of Existence: Kierkegaard Conferences 1* (København: Reitzel, 1989).

——, *Om Kierkegaard, Kvinder og Kaerlighed* (København: Reitzel, 1987).

Cain, David A., *Reckoning with Kierkegaard: Christian Faith and Dramatic Literature* (PhD thesis: Princeton University, 1976).

Caputo, J.D., *Radical Hermeneutics* (Bloomington: Indiana University Press, 1987).

Dierkes, Hans, 'Friedrich Schlegels Lucinde, Schleiermacher und Kierkegaard' in *Deutsche Vierteljahrschrift für Literatur wissenschaft und Geistesgeschichte* 57/3 (1983), pp.436ff.

Dunning, S.N., 'Rhetoric and Reality in Kierkegaard's Postscript' in *International Journal of the Philosophy of Religion* 15 (1984), pp.125–37.

Elrod, J.W., *Kierkegaard and Christendom* (Princeton: Princeton University Press, 1981).

——, 'Kierkegaard: Poet Penitent' in *Kierkegaardiana* XIII, pp.84–96.

Fenger, H., *Kierkegaard: The Myths and their Origins* (Newhaven, Connecticut: Yale University Press, 1980).

——, *The Heibergs* (New York, 1971).

Fichte, J.G., *Science of Knowledge* (New York: Century Crofts, 1970).

——, *The Vocation of Man* (New York: Bobbs Merrill, 1956).

Gouwens, D.J., *Kierkegaard's Dialectic of the Imagination* (New York: Peter Lang, 1989).

Hegel, G.W.F., *Aesthetics. Lectures on Fine Art* (London: Oxford University Press, 1975).

——, *Phenomenology of Spirit* (London: Oxford University Press, 1979).

——, *Philosophy of Right* (London: Oxford University Press, 1967).

Heiberg, J.L., *En Sjael Efter Døden* (6th. ed. København: Gyldendal, 1963).

——, *Om Philosophiens Betydning for den nuvaerende Tid* (København, 1832).

——, *Om Vaudeville* (København: Gyldendal, 1968).

——, *Poetiske Skrifter* (København: Reitzel, 1862).

Henriksen, A., *Kierkegaards Romaner* (København: Gyldendal, 1954).

——, 'Kierkegaard's Reviews of Literature' in *Orbis Litterarum* (10) 1955, pp.75–83.

Hofe, G. vom, *Die Romantikkritik Sören Kierkegaards* (Frankfurt am Main: Athenaeum, 1972).

Jansen, F.J. Billeskov, *Studier i Søren Kierkegaards Litteraere Kunst* (København: Rosenkilde og Bagger, 1951).

Jones, W. Glyn, 'Sören Kierkegaard and Poul Martin Møller' in *Modern Language Review* (60) 1965, pp.73–82.

Jørgensen, M., *Kierkegaard Som Kritiker* (København: Gyldendal, 1978).

Kingo, A., 'Den Opbyggelige Tale. Om Søren Kierkegaards *Atten Opbyggelige Taler* og deres status i forfatterskabet' in *Dansk Teologisk Tidskrift* (48) 1985, pp.129–40.

Lessing, G.E. *Gesammelte Werke* (Stuttgart: Göschen, 1874).

Lübcke, P., 'Kierkegaard and Indirect Communication' in *History of European Ideas* (Kierkegaard issue) 12/1, 1990, pp.31–40.

McCarthy, V.A., *The Phenomenology of Moods in Kierkegaard* (The Hague: Nijhoff, 1978).

Mackey, L., *Kierkegaard – A Kind of Poet* (Philadelphia: University of Pennsylvania Press, 1971).

Malantschuk, G., 'Søren Kierkegaard og Poul M. Møller' in *Kierkegaardiana* (3) 1959, pp.7–20.

Mitchell, P.M., *A History of Danish Literature* (København: Gyldendal 1957).

Møller, P.M., *Efterladte Skrifter* 6 vols. (3rd ed. København: Reitzel, 1856).

Mullen, J.D., *Kierkegaard's Philosophy – Self-Deception and Cowardice in the Present Age* (New York: Mentor, New American Library, 1981).

Müller, P., *Meddelelsesdialektikken i Søren Kierkegaard's Philosophiske Smuler* (København: Reitzel, 1979).

——, 'Grundprincipperne i Søren Kierkegaards meddelelsesdialektik og deres anvendelse i forfatterskabet' in *Dansk Teologisk Tidskrift* (41) 1978, pp.123–33.

Norris, C., 'Fictions of Authority: Narrative and Viewpoint in Kierkegaard's Writing' in *Criticism*, Vol. XXV, 2, 1983, pp.87–107.

Pattison, G.L., *Kierkegaard's Theory and Critique of Art: Its Theological Significance* (PhD thesis: University of Durham, 1983).

——, 'Kierkegaard As Novelist' in *Literature and Theology*, Vol. 1, no. 2, 1987, pp.210–20.

——, 'Nihilism and the Novel' in *The British Journal of Aesthetics*, Vol. 26, no. 2, 1986, pp.161–71.

——, 'Søren Kierkegaard: A Theatre Critic of the Heiberg School' in *The British Journal of Aesthetics*, Vol. 23, no. 1, 1983, pp.25–33.

Paulsen, A., 'Kierkegaard in seinem Verhältnis zur Deutschen Romantik. Einfluss and Ueberwindung' in *Kierkegaardiana* (3) 1959, pp.38–47.

Roos, C., *Kierkegaard og Goethe* (København: Gad, 1955).

Rubow, Paul V. *Heiberg og hans Skole i Kritiken* (København: Gyldendal, 1953).

——, *Dansk Litteratur Kritik i den 19. Aarhundrede*

Schelling, F.J.W. von, *System of Transcendental Idealism* (Charlottesville: University of Virginia Press, 1978).

Schlegel, F., *Kritische Schriften* (München: Carl Hanser, 1956).

——, *Lucinde* (Stuttgart: Reclam, 1963).

Schleiermacher, F., *Vertraute Briefe Ueber Friedrich Schlegels Lucinde* in *Sämmtliche Werke* III/i (Berlin, 1846).

Schulz, J., 'Om "Poesi" og "Virkelighed" hos Kierkegaard' in *Kierkegaardiana* (6), 1966, pp.7–29.

Sibbern, F.C., *Efterladte Breve af Gabrielis* (new ed., København: Gyldendal, 1968).

——, *Om Poesi og Konst* I. (København, 1834).

Søe, N.H. 'Der Quidam des Experiments als religiöser Typus' in *Orbis Litterarum* (10) 1955, pp.259–67.

Stack, G.J., 'Kierkegaard and Romantic Aestheticism' in *Philosophy Today* (14), 1970, pp.57–74.

Steffens, H., *Inledning til Philosophiske Forelaesninger i København 1803* (new ed., København: Gyldendal, 1905).

Taylor, Mark C., *Kierkegaard's Pseudonymous Authorship: A Study of Time and*

the Self (Princeton: Princeton University Press, 1975).
——, *Journeys to Selfhood: Hegel and Kierkegaard* (Berkeley: University of California Press, 1981).
Thompson, J., *Kierkegaard* (London: Victor Gollancz, 1974).
——, *The Lonely Labyrinth. Kierkegaard's Pseudonymous Works* (Carbondale, Illinois: Southern Illinois University Press, 1967).
Thulstrup, N., *Kierkegaard's Relation to Hegel* (Princeton: Princeton University Press, 1980).
Thust, M., *Søren Kierkegaard. Der Dichter des Religiösen* (München: Beck, 1931).
——, 'Das Marionettentheater Sören Kierkegaards' in *Zeitwende* I (1925), pp.18–38.
Vergotte, H.-B., 'Poul Martin Møller et Soeren Kierkegaard' in *Revue de Metaphysique et de Morale* (75) 1970, pp.452–76.
Viallaneix, N., *Ecoute, Kierkegaard: Essai sur la Communication de la Parole* (Paris: Editions du Cerf, 1979).
——, 'Kierkegaard Romantique' in *Romantisme* (8), 1974.
Wahl, J., 'Kierkegaard et le Romantisme' in *Orbis Litterarum* (10) 1955, pp.297–302.
Walsh, S.I., 'The Subjective Thinker as artist' in *History of European Ideas* (Kierkegaard Issue) 12/1, 1990, pp.19–30.
Zelechow, B., '*Fear and Trembling* and *Joyful Wisdom* – the same book; a look at metaphoric communication' in *History of European Ideas* (Kierkegaard issue) 12/1, 1990, pp.93–104.

Index

Adler, Adolph 79–87, 195
Ahasverus ('The Wandering Jew')
  xxii, 31, 39, 48–9, 54, 55, 96,
  105, 121
Andersen, Hans Christian 25, 36,
  41, 126, 128–9, 132
Andreasen, Uffe 28
angst 51–2, 58–61, 114, 147,
  155 Anna 161
Antigone 105, 113
anxiety, *see* angst
apostle, apostolic
  communication 84–6, 91
Aristotle 65, 81, 103, 107, 108,
  151–2, 158
Arndt, Johann 163, 166, 168
Augustine, St 76–7
Austen, Jane 197

Bakhtin, M. xvii
Beckett, Samuel 198
Benjamin, Walter 3
Bertung, Birgit xi
Bloy, Léon xiii
'blunt reading' xvi
boredom 57–8, 115, 139, 144
Brandes, George 143
Brandt, Frithiof 36–7
Bremer, Frederikke, xxii
Brook, Peter 104
Brorson, Hans Adolf 47
Buber, Martin xx
Buning, Marius 198
Byron, Lord George 27, 98

Calderón de la Barca, Pedro 16,
  18
Carstensen, George 36
Christ/Christology xi–xiii, xvii,
  xix–xx, 12, 13–14, 55, 75, 80, 81,
  87, 87–91, 108, 110, 156, 157,
  164, 167, 174–88
Coleridge, S. T. 5

comedy 13, 16, 18–26, 38–9,
  99–101, 103, 109–10, 152; *see
  also* humour/humorist
Communion xix–xx
conscience 2, 26
Corneille, Pierre 102
crucifixion xi–xiii, 176–8, 179–86
Cupitt, Don 123

Dante, Alighieri 16, 18, 22, 24, 25,
  38
drama 14, 16–26, 38–9, 95–111,
  126, 151
dramatic character 103–5, 111–14,
  120–1
Derrida, Jacques 199
discipleship 89, 180–1
dogmatics 65, 157–8, 170, 174,
  194
Don Giovanni, see Don Juan; *see also*
  Mozart, Wolfgang Amadeus
Don Juan xxii, 48–9, 96, 97–9, 104,
  105, 121
Don Quixote 50
Dostoievski, Fedor 152

Eichendorff, J. von 47
Eliot, T.S. 117
ethics, ethical point of view 2–3,
  74, 107, 113–14, 126, 131–2,
  132–40

Faust xxii, 21–2, 48–9, 67–8, 96,
  105, 121
Fenger, Henning 44
Ferreira, Jamie xxiii
Feuerbach, Ludwig 27–8
Fichte, J.G. 1–3, 7, 28, 29, 33, 41,
  42, 46, 130, 133–4
freedom 2–3, 11, 60–1, 93, 114,
  116, 134
Freire, Paulo 93
Freud, Sigmund 63

Girard, René xii
'gnosis' xvii
God xvii, 9, 22, 24, 26, 66, 80, 81, 84–5, 88, 131, 134, 135, 150, 152–3, 156, 160–1, 163, 165, 169, 171–4, 185 ˋ a g h u n t e r
Goethe, J.W. von 16, 18, 23, 37, 46, 49, 67–8, 140
Goldmann, Lucien xv, 171–2
Gouwens, David xii
Grundtvig, N.F.S. 7, 189
Gutzkow, Karl 129–30
Gyllembourg, Thomasine 127–8, 130–2, 139

Hamann, Johann Georg 54–5, 66–7
Hamsun, Knut 198
Hardenberg, Fr. von, *see* Novalis
Hegel, G.W.F. 9–15, 21, 26, 29, 30, 33, 41–2, 44, 95, 117, 186, 193
Hegelianism in Denmark 15–26
Heiberg, J.L. 16–26, 32, 35, 36–9, 43, 62, 65, 71, 95, 99, 105, 106, 122, 128, 141
Heiberg, Mme Johanne Luise 101–2, 126
Heidegger, Martin xviii, 199
Heine, Heinrich 27
Henriksen, Aage 140
Hesse, Hermann 118–19, 120, 135
Hobbes, Thomas 158
Hoffman, E.T.A. 48, 143
Homer 12, 45
Hood, Robin 113
humour/humorist 25–6, 53–5, 66–7; *see also* comedy

imitation of Christ 177–8
irony 4, 28, 40–1, 50, 53–4, 99–100, 130

Jean Paul 50
Jørgensen, Merete 125–6
Josipovici, Gabriel 196
Jung, C.G. 198

Kant, Immanuel 1–2
Kierkegaard, Søren

(1) Works cited or discussed:
The Book on Adler 79–87, 88
The Concept of Anxiety (Dread) 60, 64–5
Christian Discourses 157, 172–3, 186–8, 198
The Concept of Irony 28, 37, 40, 68, 130, 133
Concluding Unscientific Postscript 42, 64, 73
Either/Or xviii, 37, 39, 40, 56–7, 61, 70, 96–101, 104, 105–6, 115–16, 122–3, 132, 133–40, 140, 141, 142, 146
Fear and Trembling 70, 74
Forewords 38, 192
For Self-Examination 182
Journals and Papers 37–8, 44–56, 64, 107, 114–15, 123, 133
Judge For Yourselves 175–6
Lectures on Communication 73–9, 85
The Lilies and the Birds 166–7, 173–4
From the Papers of One Still Living 41, 126–9
Philosophical Fragments 73, 75, 76, 141
Purity of Heart 161
The Point of View xv, 69–73
Repetition xviii, 38, 111–18, 140
Stages on Life's Way xviii, 107–11, 121, 132, 140–54, 172
Training in Christianity xii, xx, 75, 79, 87–94, 176–86, 198
Three Discourses at the Communion on Friday xvii, xix–xx, 167
Two Ages 128, 130–2
Upbuilding Discourses 70, 156–70
Upbuilding Discourses in Various Spirits 157, 164–5, 198
Works of Love 157, 198

(2) Pseudonyms:
'A' 58–9, 96–7, 115–16
William Afham 142
Hilarius Bookbinder 142
Johannes Climacus 38, 66, 141

Constantin Constantius 111–21, 142

Victor Eremita 71, 78–9, 116, 141, 142

Frater Taciturnus, *see* The Quiet Brother

Quidam 143–54, 155

The Quiet Brother 107–11, 141, 142, 146–54, 172

Johannes the Seducer 58–9, 115–16, 121–2, 142, 146, 155

Assessor William 59, 132–40, 142

Kingo, Anders 157

knowledge xi–xii, 1–3, 15, 29–30, 64, 75, 170, 171

knowledge-communication xi–xii, 74–6, 82, 157–8, 179

Kustow, Michael 104

Laing, R.D. 196

language 97–8, 166–9

Lenau, Nicholas 49

Lessing, G.E. 96, 102–3, 107, 108, 110, 196 Lilies 165/6

Lukács, George 172

Lund, Hednrik xxii

Luther, Martin 22, 177, 199

Mackey, Louis 140, 158

majeutics 68, 76–9

Malik, H.C. xxii

Marcuse, Ludwig 197

Martensen, Hans Lassen 16, 21–3, 25–6, 36, 42, 62, 195

Marx, Karl 27

melancholy 52, 145, 151

Metz, J.B. 200

Middle Ages, the 14 15, 43, 48, 49, 50, 52, 55, 193

modernity 14–15, 23, 30–1, 33–4, 55, 78, 105–6, 106–7, 110, 113–15, 132, 145, 148–50, 152, 179, 184

Molbech, J.C. 52

Molière 98, 152

Møller, P.L. 152

Møller, Poul Martin 28–34, 39–43, 55, 68, 126–7, 139

Morris, Ivor 197

Mozart, Wolfgang Amadeus 49, 96–9, 104–5, 119

Murdoch, Iris xxi

Mynster, J.P. 70, 195

Napoleon 179, 181

Nero 59, 111, 113, 181

Nietzsche, Friedrich 44, 63, 68, 118, 119, 120

nihilism 26–34, 40, 41–2, 56, 57, 70, 72–3, 118, 125–32, 170

nothingness 60–1, 144–5, 168–70, 175–7

Novalis 3, 140, 141

novel, theory of 125–32

Oedipus 11, 105

Oehlenslaeger, Adam 5, 7, 17–18

Ossian 45

paradox 82–7, 89–92, 94, 156, 171

Pascal, Blaise xxii

patience 138, 160–6, 174

Paul, St 84, 164

Phalaris (Ox of) 56, 184

Phister, J.L. 101

Picasso, Pablo 198

Piety, Marilyn G. 197

Plato 68, 114

Poe, Edgar Allen 146 *Prayer* 166

Poole, Roger xvi, xxii

premonition 6, 8, 51–2, 65

Protestantism 15, 22, 49, 77

psychological reduction of art 35, 43–4, 56–2, 63–6, 72

repentance 3, 134, 146–8, 153, 155, 156, 159–74, 183–4

rhetoric xi, 64–6, 107, 157–8, 170, 174

Romanticism 1–9, 28, 40, 43–56, 61, 67, 129–30, 133–4, 139–40, 168, 186

in Denmark 5–9, 10, 17–18, 31

Roos, C. 140

Rothko, Mark 198

Sartre, Jean Paul xv, xviii, 174

Saxbee, John 195

Schelling, F.W.J.   4, 8, 10, 65, 199
Schlegel, Friedrich   3–4, 28, 33, 47, 67, 129–30, 140, 143
   Lucinde   4, 67, 129–30, 140, 143
Schleiermacher, F.D.E.   67, 129
Schopenhauer, Arthur   28, 118, 119, 120, 126, 145
Scribe, Augustin Eugene   96, 99–101
self(hood)   3–4, 28, 47, 57–60, 111–22, 133–40, 159–61, 168–9
Sibbern, F.C.   7–9, 10, 25, 30, 36, 42, 45   Silence 166h
Smith, Ronald Gregor   193
Socrates   68, 76, 85
Staten, Henry   199
Steffens, Henrik   5–7, 8, 51, 65
Strauss, David Friedrich   27–8
Stravinsky, Igor   198
Strawser, Michael   xvi, xviii-xxi, xxiii
Summers, Richard   28
Swedenborg, Emmanuel   25

Ted, William   179, 181
Terence   111, 152

theory of communication   xi–xiii, 17, 69–94, 174
Thust, Martin   95, 120–1
Tillich, Paul   199
time   52–3, 61, 137–9, 158, 159–66, 172–4
tragedy   13, 23, 103, 105–6, 108, 109–10, 152, 171–2
Tryde, E.   9, 26, 36, 39

Unamuno, Miguel   xxi

vaudeville   16, 17, 18, 38
violence   xii, 32–3, 184–6, 199
Voltaire   102

Wackenroder, Wilhelm H.   141
Walsh, Sylvia   xxiii
Wandering Jew, the, *see* Ahasverus
Watkin, Julia   80
Weil, Simone   110
Wittgenstein, Ludwig   199
Wordsworth, William   76
"Woman who was a sinner 167
'Young Germany'   27, 41, 129–30